THE
WHY & WONDER
OF WORSHIP

BOOK TWO · THE FINAL SERIES
REV. J.W. ARNOLD

For distribution, contact and ordering information, please refer to the last page of this book.

© Copyright 2003 by J.W. Arnold
ISBN# 0-9740922-3-1

All rights reserved. No part of this book may be reproduced in any form without written permission from
Rev. J.W. Arnold
Truth Publications
8105 NW 23rd Avenue
Gainesville, FL 32606
(352) 376-6320
www.gainesvilleupc.net

The Why & Wonder Of Worship: Book Two
The Final Series

The contents of chapters within this book
are transcribed from the audio/video series titled:
The Why & Wonder Of Real Worship

Preached by Rev. Jeff Arnold

cover design by Shawna Mansfield

A BookEnds Press Publication
PO Box 14513
Gainesville, FL 32604

WHY & WONDER OF WORSHIP
BOOK TWO · TABLE OF CONTENTS

VOLUME FOUR
CHAPTER ONE

The Priority Is a Person—Not a Place	3
Relationship is Not About Stuff	4
The Proud Never Worship	5
The Religious Never Worship	6
True Worship is Spontaneous	8
You Need Revelation to Worship	8
Revelation and Worship Are Partners	10
You Ascend to Worship—Descend to Serve	11
Worshippers Affect Others	12
The Next Level—To Know Him	14
God Orchestrates Worship	15
Knowing the Glory of God—His Name	17
Revelatory Worship Brings the Miraculous	19
Worship is One on One	20
Worship Will Cost You Something	21
God Fights for the Honest Worshipper	23
The Foolishness of Tolerating Sin	24
Take the Father's Word to Heart	25

CHAPTER TWO

The Past is Not an Issue When God Confronts	29
Our Worship Flows Out of Our Past	30
Learn To Worship Through Practice	31
True Worship is Done in the spirit	32
Our spirit Must be a Sanctuary For God	33
Don't Wait to Understand—Just Do It	34

Beware of Religious Church Folks	34
Beware of Hypocrisy	35
Tradition Sometimes Fights Truth	36
Meditate on What God has Already Shown Us	37
From Confusion to Confidence to Commitment	38
Don't Replace God With What He Uses	38
The Work of Calvary is for ALL	39
True Repentance: The Work of a Moment	39
Repentance Equals a Clean Temple	40
Be There For The New Convert	41
God Will Work With Whom He Fills	41
First The Holy Ghost—Then The Conforming Walk	42
Experiences Can't be Transferred	43
You Must Experience WHO They Experienced	43
A Personal Experience is Needed	43
Our Problem is Lack of Passion	45
Be Passionate For The God of The Doctrine	45
Seek Out What Can Change You	47
We Need God—Not Tradition	47
The Presence of God is Not Always Approval	48
Worship Has a Season—NOW!	48
Our Democracy Concepts Conflict With God's Theocracy	49
God Is Not Desperate	49
Don't Just Sit There: Create An Atmosphere	50
It's God's Initiative That Prompts Us	51
The Prerequisite is Praise and Thanksgiving	51
Worship Has a Time Frame: NOW!	52

CHAPTER THREE

Worship is Part Of the Cosmic Scheme	57
Worship: A Cure For the Ache	58
Worship Harmonizes and Changes	59
Worship is Designed to Change us	60
Worship Transforms the Worshipper	61
We Need to See HIM to Worship	63

Our Problem is Vision—Not Emotion	63
Don't Use Worship to Escape	64
Become Blended Into God's Purpose	65
God's Words Continue On	66
Homogenized to be Used	67
The Process Isn't Painful—It's Powerful	67
The Purpose—So the World Believes	68
God's Desire: That We Be One With Him	68
Worship is God's Gift—Use It	69
Your Vision is Your Victory	69
Worship Requires Action	70
Worship is About Jesus	71
All Things Were Created For Worship	71

CHAPTER FOUR

The Right Approach is Essential	77
Elevate Your Concept of God	79
Worship is a Celebration	80
Worship is About Dignity and Merit	81
Worship is About the One Being Worshipped	82
Only God Can Discern True Worship	83
Anyone Can Worship	83
Worship—More than an Attitude	84
Our Present Actions Flow From Our Past	85
Worship is Lover to Lover Communication	86
Vain Worship—Our Heart is Far From Him	88
Don't Play Games—Come Close	89
So Called Christians—No Desire for God	90
Old Testament Worship—Always Demonstrative	90
Worship—Response to Past, Present or Promised Future Deliverance	92
Great Deliverance Generates Great Response	92
Meditation Brings Flow of Feeling	93
Vain Worship—Action With Wrong Attitude	94

Old Testament Worship—Bow at a Distance	94
New Testament Worship—Up Close Contact	
Two Things Required—Awe and Love Expressed	95
It's Not About US—It's About HIM	96
Worship—His Love to us, Our Response to Him	97
Don't Try to Escape What God Allows to Come to us	98
It's Not Your Situation—It's Your Perspective	99
Worship is About Worthiness of Object Worshipped	99

VOLUME FIVE
CHAPTER FIVE

All Things Come From God	103
We Can Only Give What God Has Given Us	104
We're Made For A Purpose—Worship	105
Revelation & Proper Object Required to Worship	106
Attitude is Extremely Important	107
Service & Belief Can't Replace Worship	107
Study Should Enhance the Majesty of God	108
We Need a Holy—*Huh?*	108
Intimacy & Romance is God's Idea	109
Sacrifice Cannot be Equated With Worship	109
Follow a Worshipping Leader	110
No Exact Way to Worship Keeps it From Being a Ritual	111
God Wants More Than Just What is Prescribed	111
God Wants Our Focus on Him	112
God Wants *You*—Not Just the Sacrifice You Bring	112
Vain Worship—No Focus on HIM	113
Worship is Expressed, But is *Not* the Expression	114
Don't Deceive Yourself	114
Don't Let Worship Become Mechanical	114
Worship Must Flow Out of an Attitude of Adoration	115
Worship is Close Up—Not Long Distance	115
Real Worship is Usually a Deep Response to Him	116
You Can Worship Anywhere	117

Worship Cannot be Taught or Orchestrated	117
You Lean to Worship by Worshipping	117
Everything Should Lead to *Him*	118
Worship is to be a Celebration	118
Worship—A Joyful Response	119
Rejoice—We Have a Better Covenant	120
Emotion is Not Worship—It's the Expression of Worship	120
What You Think of *Him* You Will Express	120
It's All About Restoration to Worship	121
New Jerusalem is All About Worship	121
Become Comfortable in God's Presence	122
Self Worth in God—Important	123
Sacrifice of Praise—The Beginning	123

CHAPTER SIX

A Brief Rehearsal	127
Worship Must Be Demonstrated	128
Worship Is To Be A Celebration	129
God Is Measureless	130
God's Blessings Are Unlimited	131
Worship—Being Comfortable In Expressing Love	131
From Your Heart To Your Mouth—Love Expressed	135
How Do *You* Express Worship?	136
We Must Have Private Worship	137
It's Not How Long But How You Respond To Him	137
How Do You Express Love?	137
Worship Moves God—In Your Direction	138
The Standard For Worship—Mark 12:30	139
Change Your Object Of Worship	140
Be Filled With The Spirit	141
Corporate Worship—Multiple Expressions	141
God Enjoys Diversity	142
Your City Is Affected By Expressed Worship	144
A Mess Before A Miracle—Jesus Deals With The Hypocrite	145
The Kingdom—Jesus Enthroned In Praise & Worship	146

Worship Brings The Supernatural	146
Worship Follows God's Majesty Confronting Us	147
Worship—The Overflow Of A Grateful Heart	148
Worship Should Humble Us	148
The Spirit—Holy Ghost—Comes Down, Flows Through And Back Up To God	149
It's A Spiritual Cycle	150
Pure Worship Has No Petitions	151

CHAPTER SEVEN

God Doesn't Tell Everything He Knows	155
Practice What We Have Heard	155
Self-Worth Must Be Balanced With Truth	156
Self-Improvement—After Self-Crucifixion	156
Let God Kill And Then Raise Up	157
You Can't Have Two Centers In Your Life	158
The Greatest Therapy—Worship	158
Get Back On The Seat	159
True Worship Is The Flow—Not The Form	159
Find *Your* Way To Express Worship	160
The Very Heart Of Worship—Right Attitude	160
Worship Is Focus, Intimacy & Genuineness	161
Doctrines Of Men Bring Vain Worship	161
What Role Does God Have In Your Life?	162
We Must Be Private Worshippers	163
Focus, Focus, Focus—On God	164
You Priests—How Are You Doing?	164
It's The Attitude—Not The Sacrifice—That's Polluted	165
God Is After Us—Not Our Stuff	166
Attitude—Attitude—Attitude	166
What We Offer Is A Reflection Of Our Attitude	167
Our Offering Is An Expression Of Us	169
Our Attitude Will Make Our Offering Contemptible	169
God Is Not Desperate To Accept Any Old Thing	170
Going Beyond Communication To Communion	170

Don't Have A 3:59 Attitude	171
Great Blessings Should Bring Great Worship	172
Public Worship Is Birthed In Private	172
Three Attitudes In True Worship— The Worshipper, Object Of Worship & The Objector	173
We Must Be Broken To Worship	173
A Broken Spirit—Your Sacrifice	174
Brokenness Brings God Close	175
It's Difficult To Get Broken & Honest In Public	175
A Broken And Contrite Heart	176
A Little Talcum For The Hidden Areas	177
Broken—Like The Alabaster Box	177
Uncut Hair—A Sign Of Submission To Authority	178
Worship Makes A Mess Before It Gets Better	178

CHAPTER EIGHT

Worship—The Occupation Of Heaven	183
The Preeminence Of Worship	183
We Are The Replacement Worshippers	184
Another Attitude Of Worship—Humility	185
Real Worship Is Intimate	186
Pride—A Hindrance To Worship	187
Pride Pushes God Away	188
Worship Without Love—Shallow And Pretentious	188
You Can't Remain Silent	189
It's Not About Noise—It's About Expression	190
Where Are The Weepers?	191
Worship Is Attitude Expressed	192
A Love Feast Versus Obligation	192
Don't Appear Before God Empty	193
Worship Requires Sacrifice And Giving	194
There's Always Some To Criticize	196
God Exposes For Us To Conquer	196
Is It God's Church Or Our Club	197
Repent And Get On With It	197

Don't Let The Critical Spirit Defeat You	198
Life Happens!—How Do You React?	199
Non-Worshippers Are Non-Givers & Self-Righteous	200
Non-Worshippers Have Their Own Revelation	201
Concern Yourself With The Object—Not The Critic	201
Attitudes Expressed Bring Attitudes Of Response	203
Real Holiness—Forsake All That Displeases God	203
Don't Criticize—Bless 'Em	204
Receive Faith, Deliverance & Peace Through Worship	206

VOLUME SIX
CHAPTER NINE

God Can Lead You Into Trouble—For A Purpose	209
The Trouble Won't Destroy You	209
The Importance Of Worship	210
Don't Put Traditions Over God's Word	210
Three Want Your Worship—God, The Devil And Self	211
It's Not 'Move Me'—It's 'Move God'	212
Trust Him When You Can't Feel Him	212
God Wants To Take Us Beyond Where We Are	213
Worship Will Cause The Greatest Change In Us	214
Every Thing Is Open Before God	214
Many Times Worship Requires Silence	215
Worship First—And Foremost	215
Separate Yourself From Non-Worshippers	216
It's Progressive	216
You Can't Just Barge In On God	217
You Can't Just 'Believe In Jesus'	217
No Worship Takes Place In Outer Court Or Holy Place	218
Prayer And Praise Is Not Worship	218
But—We Do Need To Pray Better	218
Prayer Is A Warfare	219
Start Prayer With Thanksgiving	220
Wait On God	220

It's Your Attitude In Presenting Worship	221
It's The *Long* Reach Of God	222
Our Priority—To Bless God	223
Thanksgiving And Praise Is A Prelude To Worship	223
Don't Focus On The Judas Spirit	224
You May Have To Worship Alone—In A Crowd	225
Your Focus Must Be On How Great Jesus Is	225
Always Bless God In Spite Of……..	226
Worship Even When God Stays Silent	226
Worship Is Always Primary	227
A Relationship With God Above All	228
Don't Be Lost Because Of Someone Else	229
Beware Of Idols In Your Life	230
Let's Party!	230
You Are The Church	231
Forsake Not Assembling Together	231
Importance Of Worship Is Proven By Scripture	232
It's Progressive—Warrior, Worker, Worshipper	233
Worship Takes Priority Over Work	233

CHAPTER TEN

The Cause Of Worship—God	237
We Must Be Exposed To God	238
God Manifested—Not Just 'In The Midst'	238
Our Comfort Zone—Where We Sit In Church	239
You Cannot Have A High Vision Of God And Live Low	239
Lesser Evils Occur When God's Majesty Is Diminished In Our Eyes	240
We Need A Vision Of God's Greatness	240
God Is A 'Seed' God	242
When God Speaks It—It Exists	242
Our Faith Manifests The Promise 'In Time'	243
Boost Your Faith—Add Up What God Has Done For You	243

The Trial Of Our Faith—Believe For What He's Never Done Before	244
Water Your Seed Of Promise	245
Are You Willing To Look Bad So God Can Look Good	245
We All Need A 'Moriah' Miracle	246
You Have To Go Up Your Mountain Before You Can Come Down With A Miracle	247
You Don't Look Good Going Up The Mountain	248
Our Level Of Worship Depends On Our Concept Of God	248
Praise Is A Must!	248
How Much Do You Pray For Others	249
The Magnitude Of God's Mercy	250
Don't Let The Storm Dim The Promise	252

CHAPTER ELEVEN

Worship—Then Witness	255
All Other Gods Are Idols	256
We Are His Sanctuary	257
Concentrate On 'Him', Not The 'How'	257
God Is Seeking Worshippers	258
Anybody Is Qualified To Worship	258
Non-Worshippers Are On The Devil's Team	259
The Devil's Power Is In His Voice	259
Learn The Voice Of God	259
Worship Flows From, And Back To, God	260
A Holy Ghost Worship Service—Everyone Saying About God What Those In His Presence Are Saying	261
Worship Enthrones God So He Can Loose His Power	261
God Is B-A-D—Terrible	262
God Is Awesome	263
Praise Glorifies God	263
God's Greatness Is Never Diminished	264
We Need Perpendicular Relationship To Deal With The Hell Of The Horizontal	264

Worship Is Our Response To God's Three G's: Greatness-Goodness-Grace	265
Worship Is The Platform For Revelation	265
A Sovereign Call Of God Requires Surrender And Commitment	266
Worship Includes Obedience, Sacrifice And Ascending Higher	267
Want A Deep Move Of Forgiveness—Worship	267
Worship Will Cost What You Are Holding On To	268
Worship Must Be Based On Revelation	269
Worship Must Be Guided By The Word	269
The Word Has Life In It	270
Put Something Worthwhile In Your Spirit	270
But—Put Enough In	271
Sermon Notes—Just Extra Stones	271
Worship Without Revelation Is Ritual	272
Sincere But Vain Worship—Ritual	273
Don't Debate—Respond	273
True Worship Is Always Costly	274
Don't Let Family And Friends Fool You	275
The Best Belongs To The Lord	275
God Functions On Principle—Not Emotion	276
Ask Yourself—Is Tithing A Problem For Me?	276
Beware Of Strange Fire	277
We Must Not Hire It Done	277
The Devil Knows About Worship—That's Why He Fights Us	278
The Cost To Worship Is High	278
Ascend With A Burden—Descend With Joy	279
What Is Worship—Response To Revelation	280

THE WHY & WONDER OF WORSHIP • BOOK TWO

THE WHY & WONDER OF WORSHIP

VOLUME FOUR • CHAPTER ONE

THE WHY & WONDER OF WORSHIP • BOOK TWO

CHAPTER ONE

John Chapter 4 again, we ought to know this by now. Beginning at Verse 19, "The woman saith unto him, Sir, I perceive that thou art a prophet. Our fathers worshipped in this mountain; and ye say, that in Jerusalem is the place where men ought to worship. Jesus saith unto her, Woman, believe me, the hour cometh, when ye shall neither in this mountain, nor yet at Jerusalem, worship the Father. But the hour cometh and now is, when the true worshippers shall worship the Father in spirit and in truth: for the Father seeketh such to worship him."

THE PRIORITY IS A PERSON—NOT A PLACE

Now some people have taken that out of context, I've read the ramblings of mad insane people who sell books, and they have taken this text to say, in defense of their lack of corporate assembling, that Jesus was saying that there was coming a time when you would not worship at Jerusalem, or in this mountain, and that He was saying that you didn't have to go to a certain place. That's not what Jesus was saying. He was saying the place would not be the priority. The priority would be the person. So that's why worship is possible in any locality. If you can get the vision of the person, and the offshoot of that is, if you get a revelation of the person of Jesus and you are a worshipper of Him, why would you not want to join in on corporate praise and thanksgiving and worship? I kind of like to be next to lively stones, instead of some cold turkeys.

"But the hour cometh, and now is, when the true worshippers shall worship the Father in spirit and in truth (apparently the emphasis on true means that there is a false) ...for the Father seeketh such to worship him. God is a Spirit: and they that worship him must worship him in spirit and in truth." God is A Spirit. Correctly, you should be saying God IS Spirit; there are no indefinite articles in the Greek language. It's not God is A Spirit, it's God IS Spirit. They that worship Him must worship Him in spirit and in truth.

I want to rehearse for a few moments just some things that we've learned; in fact, I'm doing it as much for myself as for you. I went back over some of my pages and pages of notes and I thought boy, this is good stuff. In fact, I said today, "I don't remember teaching that, wow!" So just as a refresher course, just for the first eight or nine minutes, what worship really is, because I'm a bit afraid that we're losing the concept of what worship really is.

Worship is to feel in the heart, the blessing of an over whelming awe, an adoration for, it is an inner attitude ex- pressed. To worship is to exalt and bless God for who and what He is; Psalm 150:2. Two aspects; one is praise, one is worship. Praise Him according to His mighty acts; that's praise, according to His excellent greatness; that's worship. We've learned pretty well by now that the difference between praise and worship is that praise pretty much has to do with a performance, worship has to do with the essence of God. We worship God for who He is, we praise God and thank God for what He does.

RELATIONSHIP IS NOT ABOUT STUFF

That's why the scripture says even though God allowed Job to lose all his children and all his stuff he still worshipped God, because his relationship to God was not predicated on his stuff. You have to learn to hold your stuff loose, because in one moment the company you're working for could be sold, the house you hold the mortgage on could increase, a tidal wave could swing by, a disease could be diagnosed in your body, everything that we have is part of a circumstance and it could just go swishhhhhhh. And if our only relationship with God is because He was nice and nifty to us to let us have our trinkets and toys, then when life, or the devil, or God decides to sweep the slate clean you have nothing to express because you've never been a worshipper, you've only been a thanker and a praiser.

That's why I'm having a major problem when I listen to some tapes and read some booklets, and I do read a lot, this check in the mail stuff stinks. This concept that these people are always trying to manipulate God to make Him use His divine spiritual supernatural power to facilitate our natural, carnal, material greed. It's like, if you can get some scriptures and make Him obey you, He'll give you your Mercedes. What an insult, when the whole concept is spiritual, what does it matter whether He gives you a Mercedes or He fixes up your Studebaker? If you love Him and He loves you and you have a relationship with Him. Because we can't take the Mercedes or the Studebaker with us. Naked we came, naked we leave!

So if your worship and my worship is predicated on our stuff, if you're fortunate enough to get to the city, we won't be able to praise and worship Him there because we won't have our stuff! Don't you get it? And I'm not being irreverent to the Lord, but in essence He is supposed to be our stuff, Christ in YOU the hope of glory! You get it? So praise has to do with performance, and worship has to do with who and what God is. We just need to go over this for just a minute. Worship flows out of the wonder of God, it must be done in truth, and it is done in the human spirit. Praise and thanksgiving can be done by intellect, by verbalization; it can be done by hypocrites, by fakers, by plastic people. Even the vilest person can thank God when he gets an answer to something.

I've heard people in hospitals, from people who wouldn't darken a church, when somehow God showed mercy through a surgery or something, or something wasn't diagnosed as disastrous as they thought and they say, "Oh thank God!" I've been to funerals where I've wanted to, but I didn't, because I didn't have the courage, well, maybe I had the courage, but I had the decency not to do it, I wanted to raise my hand and say, "Could I look in that box, because the man you're talking about is not the guy I thought was getting buried." I just want to go up, lift the lid, and say, "man you've got the wrong corpse in here, cuz the guy you were talking about was a dirtbag! He couldn't tell the truth standing on the Bible, and this man is talking like he is the choir director in the New Jerusalem."

THE PROUD NEVER WORSHIP

There's one group of people that will never worship; that is the proud. I'll tell you why, because worship always flows out of revelation. I know that I repeat that a lot, but we need to understand that. The higher your worship will require a higher revelation. As we see Him, behold Him, comprehend, and grasp in a greater measure, it causes a release in us to worship Him, because worship is adoration and awe. Worship requires an object; praise requires a performance.

THE WHY & WONDER OF WORSHIP • BOOK TWO

The problem with the proud is, when you behold God, it creates in you humility. So the proud can't worship because they refuse to become humbled. Those who are proud will not worship, because it indicates to them inferiority and superiority, and they are already superior, why would they worship? That's why 1 Corinthians 1 says, behold not many wise, not many noble, not many very, very smart people, not very many intellectual people.... It didn't say not any; it says not many.

Worship and praise and submission and sacrifice is foolishness, because the self-made man is just that, self-made. I've worked hard, I've studied, I've got my job, I want up the corporate ladder. Who do I want to bow my knee to and why? I've hustled all my life, I've come out of the depression and made a buck; they don't even think that it's God that lets their ticker work. Have no idea.

Believe me folks, I know you hear me say this all the time, but when I woke up this morning my mind was stayed on Jesus. I woke up this morning and when my feet hit the ground, "Thank you Lord." In fact, this morning when I woke up my feet went out kind of slow and I said, "Thaaaaaaaaaank you Lord." I said, "Thank you, I don't appreciate the pain, but ahh, I thank you for the pain, because at least I can feel, and I don't hurt as bad as I have been hurting, and there are people in the hospital this morning who would give their right arm to feel as well as I do. So I don't appreciate this discomfort but considering the other sixty or seventy percent of my body that is working rather well, I thank You!" I appreciate the fact that I have to hobble, I could be like my brother and just sit in a wheelchair somewhere with no legs and he would give his right arm to hobble.

THE RELIGIOUS NEVER WORSHIP

There is another group of people who never worship, and those are the people who think they comprehend things. The intellectual, the fleshly, the religious. For anything that you can comprehend, grasp or explain; why would you ever feel awe or adoration towards it if you could grasp it and comprehend it? Worship is to feel in the heart, awe, adoration, an overwhelming something that wants to express. It causes a humbleness, a feeling of inferiority and superiority. That's why you can't really worship when you're praising, cuz praising is demonstrative,

THE WHY & WONDER OF WORSHIP • BOOK TWO

and it's noisy, and sometimes it's crazy, you take off running and boogalooin', banging into the walls; you're not really worshipping, you're praising God. Nothing wrong with it, you need to have it, because thanksgiving and praise are the prelude for worship. So those of you who never want to clap your hands, and never want to sing or what have you, you'll never reach worship because it's the third station. You enter His gates with thanksgiving, His courts with praise, and then worship is the last station in there. It's that place inside the veil, where you and the raw presence of God deal with each other and you tell Him how great He is.

Anybody ever been close to God? I'm talkin' about just being swept in, not because of yourself but you were either in a prayer meeting, or you were washing dishes or cleaning the house and all of a sudden the Spirit of God comes and tears are running down your face and you feel so overwhelmed. You just start blessing God for how good He is, and how wonderful He is and how great He is, and I'm not thinking about some great thing He did before, I'm taken up with Him. It's almost like He orchestrates this little thing for a few minutes and then boom, it's over and He's gone. It has a way of emptying your spirit out and getting rid of pride and foolishness and being cantankerous and holding a grudge and complaining because God didn't "fix it."

You know it's recorded in Job saying; in essence, you know I've shot my mouth off and talked about stuff I didn't know. It's amazing how honest you get when you get into a dimension of worship where you confess, "You know I didn't really know what I was talking about, it sold a lot of tapes and stuff but now that I'm with You, I'm full of hot air, I really am, and I don't know beans about nothing and if You don't mind I'd like to shut my mouth, and put my hand over it in case my mouth wants to try to say something." The wonderful thing is that the confession that takes place in that dimension of worship...., it did not in any way divorce Job or make him lose the position that God held him in, even though he was wrong, because the very next verse says that God goes and talks to these three characters and says I've got something against you, watch, cuz you have not spoken concerning me correctly, rightly, as my servant Job has, and three times He calls Job, "my servant." Now at that time Job didn't even think he was in the kingdom.

Now you might as well smile, because we've all been there too. Been touched by the Lord when you didn't even know whether you were saved.

TRUE WORSHIP IS SPONTANEOUS

True worship, I'm almost to my Bible study, this is just a rehearsal. True worship can never be manipulated, orchestrated, or engineered. It cannot be. It is spontaneous. Therefore, we are obligated to orchestrate and schedule a period of time where we offer thanksgiving and praise, for it will lead us to that level of worship. Remember I told you that one time, that worship is always followed by praise and thanksgiving and that praise is the prelude, prerequisite, foreplay, warm-up, to worship. It really is. Worship takes you beyond His performance and says if you don't heal me You are still wonderful, and if You don't come through for me like I am hoping and believing and trying to make You do, You are still wonderful, and though He slay me yet will I trust Him. Not only will I trust Him, I'll tell everybody I'm trusting Him. Yea, I will, Oh, Hallelujah, come on, repeat after me, revelation is required for worship. Therefore, if we are bad worshippers, if we are poor worshippers, the only reason is that we have a poor vision.

Where there is no vision, the people perish. What we really need is a vision of the majesty of God. We need a vision of how great He is, and how awesome He is, because as we see Him, as we behold Him, as we grasp Him in a greater way, as we comprehend more, that causes a release, so we can express ourselves. Every time we study these scriptures, you will find people who began to worship God, because of a revelation. You cannot check the book of Luke or Matthew and find the story of the birth of Jesus Christ as a babe where you will locate the wise men worshipping on the journey.

YOU NEED REVELATION TO WORSHIP

Worship requires revelation. "Where is he that is born King of the Jews…. Why? Now watch this..."We've come to worship Him." Now they've got intent to worship, but they can't worship until they get into the presence of the child.

When they got into the house where the child was then they kneeled down and worshipped Him.

Worship is done in the presence of God, praise and thanksgiving can be done long distance. That's why it has to be done in spirit. I'll show you, I'll prove it, in Mark Chapter 5 the mad man of Gadarenes is filled with a legion of devils, correct? It says that when he saw Jesus he ran to Him and worshipped Him saying... He saw, beheld, grasped, comprehended. Now the mystery is; who worshipped? The man or the devils? The devil!

I'll show you. Mark Chapter 5, Verse 4, "Because that he had been often bound with fetters and chains.... And always, night and day, he was in the mountains, and in the tombs, crying, and cutting himself with stones. But when he saw Jesus afar off he ran and worshipped him...." It sounds like the man did it, but watch. Verse 7, "and cried with a loud voice, and said, What have I to do with thee, Jesus, thou Son of the most high God? I adjure thee by God that thou torment me not." Who is talking? The devil. The next verse says that Jesus commanded the spirit to come out, now watch, for He commanded the spirit to come out, and the spirit is talking to Him, and the spirit is showing reverence, homage, awe and honor. Why? He understands the superior. The man is out of his mind, he's insane, he's crazy, he has no revelation of who Jesus is. Worship is done in spirit—these are spirits. Jesus is eternal Spirit in a body; spirits recognize who had thrown them out. Watch what they say, "Have you come to torment us before our time?" You say, "Well, that's worship." Sure, praise is for performance, worship is for who and what. These spirits recognize who they're talking to, they're not playing games with Him like they're pullin' this poor naked Gadarene guy around, the minute they see the man Jesus and realize who He is.... You see, worship isn't always, "I praise you Lord, I love you Lord," worship is always the recognizing of His superiority, "don't torment us, we know who you are."

When He goes to cast a devil out of the man that was in the temple at the synagogue, He told the spirit to be quiet for they knew who He was. They said, "We know who You are, thou art the Holy One of God, torment us not." Don't you know worship is recognizing His superior power to do something with you?

Verse 9, And he asked him, "What is thy name?" Now watch; He shows you who is talking.... "And he answered, saying, my name is Legion: for we are many." There are lots talking in a singular possessive. He said, "my name, we, we are many." He said; well come out, and don't come out one at a time, come out together. And they come out and the demon asks favor.... You see the power of worship in the spirit is you can get God to do stuff for you then. I'm going to tell you something, worship will get close to the heart of God. You don't have to beg God and try to show Him scriptures where He has to obey you. You get to worshipping God, His banner over you becomes love, and He'll pour out His blessings on you. He'll show Himself strong if He has someone who loves Him. Someone who worships Him.... Listen, someone who worships Him out of a fear or a reverence, not even out of a love can get a prayer answered. These guys prayed, I used to teach a sermon on this, when God answered the devils prayer. The Bible says that they prayed Him, that means made request, don't cast us out into the deep, don't make us leave the country, let us go into the pigs, and He being the prayer answering God that He is, He said, "Go!" And those spirits ran into those pigs and those pigs went crazy and ran over the side of the hill and drowned themselves in the river and killed themselves.

And they thought they were getting by. See how inferior these spirits are, they didn't want to leave the land of Gadara because apparently there are certain spots and localities where devils feel that they can work better than other places. They didn't want to leave Gadara, so they think they snow jobbed and fooled God by saying don't cast us out into the deep and don't make us go out of the area here, let us go into the pigs, and they think that they've snookered God and that they've fooled Him. "Oh, at least we're staying in the pigs." The pigs killed themselves, and now they have to leave the area anyway. Isn't it amazing, a pig won't put up with a spirit that some people put up with.

REVELATION AND WORSHIP ARE PARTNERS

Worship is our response to revelation, worship is our response to God's person, worship is our response to His being, not to His doing. The wise men, the Gadarene, the leper of Matthew 8:1-3. The leper broke through the crowd and the Bible says that he worshipped Him saying, "If You will I know You can." What was the worship? Showing His superiority over his disease. But it wasn't predicated on His performance, because he didn't know whether Jesus was going to perform. So he gives Him a demonstration of worship, I know You are able.

When Isaiah saw the Lord high and lifted up in Chapter 6, he worships God. Not for what He did, but for who He was. Listen to me carefully. Revelation and worship are partners. They are two sides of the same coin. The unveiling of Jesus is what moves us to worship. If we are not good worshippers, it's because we don't see Jesus as He really is. That's the purpose of our adversary and that's why the problems of life many times blind us; that we focus on the mess and not on the Master! It's not that we're evil; it's just that we're people.

YOU ASCEND TO WORSHIP—DESCEND TO SERVE

That's why you need time to worship. Look, worship has to be a separated time. Remember when I taught you that one time, you ascend to worship. Moses went up on the mountain to worship. Abram and the boy, we ascend, we go up to worship. Worship is an ascending up; it's not an inferior thing. You descend to serve, you ascend to worship. If you ascend with a right spirit, and you behold Him, when you come down nothing in the valley can devastate you, because of what has happened on the mount.

Genesis 22 Abram goes up with Isaac and he says, "The boy and I go yonder to worship." I didn't mean to teach this now, but I guess I need to. Worship must be done separate spirited. You got to leave friends and neighbors behind to worship. That's why if you worship in a public service, you know what's really happened? You've been able by the kindness and grace of God to insulate and isolate everyone from you and you just penetrate into that veil. That does happen, but it doesn't happen often. There are times when you can just divorce yourself from the days activities and the noise around you in the service and your spirit breaks the barrier and through the obstacles and over the hindrances, because worship is done in spirit, not locality. But worship.... Worship is such a high occupation; it's not easily done with a whole bunch of noise, because your spirit needs to get quiet.

It needs a time to meditate, you need to review, you need to let the parade go by you; let the vision just parade through you, as you have time to get quiet.
Remember the story of the prophet Elijah when he was ticked off at those kings and those false kings of Israel and Judah and he said, "If it wasn't the fact that this king was here I wouldn't even look in your direction." He was so angry with this character that he had to turn around and say, "Bring me a minstrel," because he was agitated. Watch; if you are agitated in a good way or a bad way, you have to get your spirit calmed so your gift can operate. This guy says, "I can't function as a prophet now." Why? "I'm ticked off, I'm angry, I detest this hypocrite here. He's led a whole nation into idolatry, he hates Jehovah, and I despise his ways, and just me standing near him has made me mad and I need a little music." Well, that's quite a confession for a prophet of God to say; I'm upset.

Don't you get the purpose of why we sing, do you think it's just a time filler? Don't you get it, you've worked all day, you've interacted with spirits and attitudes and people and pressures and life and some dreams have been fulfilled and a lot of them have crashed down to the ground and sometimes your body chemistry is different and vitamins aren't working and nutrition isn't working and you've got a headache and you just... it's life; and for you to just kind of bitty bop in here and say, Okay Carrie, we've been dry, come on let's get this thing moving. You know, "usher me in, man, put me on the pancake flopper and just flip me into the presence of God and I'll just boogaloo a while and I'll get out of here with some answers. Come on Arnie, rip and drive baby."

WORSHIPPERS AFFECT OTHERS

Don't you get it? To think that you would travel all the way from your home and not have in your car meditation time, and thanksgiving time, and praise time and just repeat over, "when I think of the goodness of Jesus...," so that when you finally walk in here you brought with you an essence of worship unto God that you could affect someone else. I'm going to tell you something, a worshipper will affect people around them! I don't want to be unkind, because I'm for praise. I'm adamant about praise, but praise, while it may be noisy and it may be appreciated, will never reach the depths of worship.

THE WHY & WONDER OF WORSHIP • BOOK TWO

You need to look around; you think I'm joking when I say, "look around and ask somebody' if you aren't a worshipper, if not, move." Because I'm going to tell you if you try to worship next to someone who is a nincompoop and you've got to drag your spirit and their spirit with you because their spirit don't want to go, because the carnal man doesn't want the things of God. The non-prayerful, the non-intense, the non-desiring, they ain't going. Sit next to some idiot whose writing notes all the time and passing babies and passing out crackers and crayons and ... Jesus help me! Or sitting next to somebody that talks every time I talk. Man, you need to say, "Will you stop it, I'm trying to worship!"

Notice what he said. He said, "We go yonder." I have to separate from you now, and I have to ascend and I go yonder and worship. Worship will cost you something. You can't worship without bringing a sacrifice, Isaac's the sacrifice, worship opens you up to your deepest possible pain. See: praise is always trying to get something. Worship is always trying to give you something. Worship is dangerous. Worship is costly, and you don't worship God with just words, you can worship God with your life. Just by you being a lover, an adorer of God, can alienate you from family, friends and neighbors.

Our worship is a response to the revelation of God; our worship is an expression to exposure to His greatness, His glory, His majesty and His very being. I want to show you all something. Exodus 33:12, "and Moses said unto the Lord, See, thou sayest unto me, bring up this people: and thou hast not let me know whom thou wilt send with me. Yet thou hast said, I know thee by name, and thou hast also found grace in my sight." Now if you got a little room in your Bible just write this word, "level." And just understand that at the end of Verse 12 Moses is declaring that I've reached a level with God, but I don't want to live here. I appreciate the miracles, signs, and wonders, I appreciate the grace of God, and I thank you that you've talked to me and called me by name, but now this level won't get it. Most people would give their right arm to reach that level. Moses says I appreciate that level, but I want to leave this level.

THE NEXT LEVEL—TO KNOW HIM

Verse 13, "Now therefore, I pray thee, if I have found grace in thy sight, shew me now thy way, that I may know thee, that I may find grace in thy sight: and consider that this nation is thy people." See what he's asking for? For more than he's experienced. Show me now thy way, so that I can know you. What do you mean?

Don't you know Him? No, only to that level in Verse 12. Don't you understand? He said there's more to You. I'm hungry for You. I appreciate Your trinkets, but I want You. Show me Your way. I'm not wanting a Mercedes, show me Your way.

That's what Isaiah 55 means. My ways are higher than your ways, My thoughts are different and higher than yours, as the heavens are higher than the earth so are my ways and thoughts than yours. He says; I know that your ways are greater, you got us out of prison over here, and you're going to take us into the promised land, but I'm not ..., he is saying, Lord I appreciate the gift of the promised land, but that's not my bag, I'm really wanting You. Why is he saying that? Because of past experiences and past worship episodes, he has come to realize that God is awesome, and I want more than what I've got. If that desire could be birthed in this church you would have to go to a Florida field to hold church. Exodus 33:14-15, And he said, "My presence shall go with thee, and I will give thee rest. And he said unto him; If thy presence go not with me, carry us not up hence."

Now Moses was saying, "I don't mean to insult you Lord, but that hadn't even crossed my mind. You said, 'My presence is going with you;' I wouldn't have even left Egypt if Your presence wasn't going with us." It's almost like he's saying, "Lord you misunderstood my request. I wasn't talking about your presence, I was talking about Your secret place, I wasn't talking about the cloud that everybody can see. I was talking about the place that everybody can't see, he that dwelleth in the secret place of the Almighty, shall abide under the shadow of His wing. I want to get into that place when it's kind of just, me and thee." You know what he's really saying, "If You don't mind, I'd like to be special."

I'm not claiming superiority, I'm boasting and saying, "You have superiority and I just want to be near You, that's all I want." See, that's what gave Moses such a compassion and an understanding and a kindness to Israel. Even when they were very unkind to him, he was able to be that, because of his constant interacting with the secret place of the Most High.

I'm going to tell you something. If you and I don't learn how to do that periodically, people will tick us off. People will hurt us to the place that we don't want to play no more. People will annoy us until we don't want to be a part of this anymore, because life is just orchestrated that way. It's just against you. You're swimming upstream, you're walking into the wind and the wind is contrary. The only way you can deal with contrary winds is to get up into the presence of Him who controls the wind, take some time with Him, so that when you come down off the mountain, you say, "let the wind blow, I know who controls the wind." Folks, I'm as honest as I can be, sometimes just a few moments in a day, or in a second or third day, is enough strength to help you go through more hell than hell thought you would be able to handle.

GOD ORCHESTRATES WORSHIP

You see, hell orchestrates its attacks and its combat theology on your past performances. How well you did here, how poor you did here, ohhhhhhh you've got a real problem here, you've got a weakness here, that's how he plays your strategy. So when he gets ready to go to combat, he understands it, he has math real good, he has equations laid out, she'll never make it through this, this and this combination.... So God, you know what God does, God is so brilliant, and so smart and so wise, before you end up in the combat, He orchestrates worship. He blows on you, He stirs you, and all of a sudden a wanting to pray, or wanting to worship, and He creates in you a desire that you might worship. He knows that the presence of God will be your power, will give you victory over what the devil is trying to do against you, and He will let you get ushered into just a few moments of worship, and in that He'll just boom, boom, boom and let you drink awhile and then He'll lift up off of you and then say, "okay, give 'em your best shot."

Don't you understand why Job frustrated the devil so much? He figured everything out from a fleshly carnal response. He never took into account that Job was a worshipper. Something mystical, really, it's not magic, takes place in just a few moments when a human spirit touches the eternal spirit. There is given to us some type of armament, some type of ammunition that we may not even sense or feel, but it's invested in us and as we go into the criteria that's given to us to combat and all of a sudden you have an energy. You mean I'm the only one that's been through something that you didn't think you could go through. You've wondered where you got that strength from, and where did that answer come from and how did I get a thought like that and ... it was God.

True worship is actually receiving living waters, living waters rising up in us and then living waters returning to its source. Solomon had the revelation in Ecclesiastes 1:7. He didn't fully understand it, but he said that all the rivers they flow into the sea, but it's not full, it returned to whatsoever they came. Where did they come from? The heavens, the condensation that comes down in rains and causes the rivers. It goes up and the sun goes over the ocean and vaporizes the water and brings it back up, puts it through clouds and it comes down. It's a full cycle. That's why anytime you sense a pricking in your spirit, a moving in your heart, worship Me now. It is God coming down to settle on you silently, and unnoticed by many, it happens during the night. He comes and He refreshes you, and then goes back up.... And what do you do? The dew goes back up, right? The sun draws.... The same thing happens as you begin to bless Him and exalt Him. The very worship that He orchestrated and initiated in you comes through, goes back up as praise and worship and thanksgiving and makes this cycle. For it's God that worketh in you both to will and to do of His good pleasure.

Exodus 33:16, "For wherein shall it be known here that I and thy people have found grace in thy sight? Is it not in that thou goest with us?" Okay, now watch this, I'm going to tell you somethin'. The Christian world doesn't want this scripture. They say it's the law, but it ain't the law! This is all about grace, Chapter 33. But this is the key to grace. He said, "How is the world going to know that we're your people unless you're manifested presence shows up and because of Your presence we separate ourselves and are different? 'So shall we be

THE WHY & WONDER OF WORSHIP • BOOK TWO

separated, I and thy people, from all the people that are upon the face of the earth."

Verse 17 "And the Lord said unto Moses, I will do this thing also that thou hast spoken." That says to me that God is open to suggestions. It was Moses that came up with the idea that I want more than the level that I am at. God turned around and said, I like the request, you got it!

KNOWING THE GLORY OF GOD—HIS NAME

Verse 18 "And he said, I beseech thee, shew me thy glory". Show me thy glory! Now wait a minute, now he's wanting another level! First he's happy with the level he's at, then he's not happy, he says now I want beyond this level, show me Your way. So then God turns around and says I'll do this for you, and Moses figures man, I'm hittin' it pretty good and then asks to see God's glory. As long as You're in a giving mood and we got a rapport here.

Verse 19 "And he said, I will make all my goodness pass before thee." No, No! I didn't ask for your goodness, I want Your glory; I want to see Your glory. And God turns around and says, My goodness is My glory. "And I will proclaim the name of the Lord before thee." Do you want to know the glory of God? All you got to do is find His name. The glory of God is the goodness of God, and the name of God manifested. 2 Corinthians 4 says that the glory of God is manifested in the face of Jesus. That's why when Jesus prayed He said, "Father glorify thy name," He said, "I have glorified it, and I will glorify it again. ... and will be gracious to whom I will be gracious, and will shew mercy on whom I will shew mercy."

Verse 20, "And he said, Thou canst not see my face: for there shall no man see me, and live." You can't see His face, because He is pure light, if you looked at Him in pure light you'd burn completely up; you can't see His face. The glory of God is seen in the face of Jesus. Jesus becomes the filter of the glory that Moses was not allowed to see, but we can see. Wow! "And the Lord said, Behold, there is a place by Me in the rock, and I'll put a cleft in the rock and you can get in the rock, I'll put you in the rock, and I'll let my glory pass by and I'll pull My hand away and you'll be able to see my hinder parts." If you read in the original, it says you'll be able to see My afterglow.

Verse 5 of Chapter 34, "And the Lord descended in the cloud, and stood with him there, and proclaimed the name of the Lord." The Lord proclaimed the name of the Lord. The Lord descended, and the Lord proclaimed the name of the Lord. Verse 6, "And the Lord passed by before him, and proclaimed, The Lord, the Lord God, merciful and gracious, longsuffering, and abundant in goodness and truth, Keeping mercy for thousands, forgiving iniquity and transgression and sin, and that will by no means clear the guilty; visiting the iniquity of the fathers upon the children, and upon the children's children, unto the third and to the fourth generation." You need to write yourself a note saying, Verses 6 and 7 is the glory of God. It is the revelation of His name and the revelation of His nature. For His nature is longsuffering and kind and good and merciful. Wait a minute; and He is full of holiness and justice.

Verse 8, "And Moses made haste, and bowed his head toward the earth, and worshipped." What did I tell you 20 minutes ago? The prerequisite to worship is revelation. God just gave Moses a revelation of His glory, His nature and His name. Now what did it do to Moses? He worshipped. Don't you get it? Worship has to do with the object. Not any kind of performance. He is blown away by what he has just been exposed to; the essence of God's being. You can tell people who have been into a little presence of the Lord, they want to go out and tell everybody what they've just heard. You get anybody who has been in a worship sequence, they don't want to tell anybody nothing, they just want to stay awhile.

Out of revelation came worship. Now watch; Moses made haste and he worshipped. Exodus 34:9-10, "And he said, If now I have found grace in they sight, O Lord, let my Lord, I pray thee, go among us; for it's a stiff-necked people; and pardon our iniquity and our sin, and take us for thine inheritance. And he said, Behold, I make a covenant: before all thy people I will do marvels, such as have not been done in all the earth."

THE WHY & WONDER OF WORSHIP • BOOK TWO

Now hear what just happened, I want you to get the sequence. He's at a level, he wants to go to another level, 'show me Your way.' God says I'll do it for you, while He's in a good mood he says okay I'm going to bring My glory down, but I'll have to just filter it for you because I'll burn you up if you see it all. Then he comes down and He gives him a revelation of His glory, His nature and His name. It provokes and prompts Moses to fall down, because part of Moses is prostrate, adoration and awe and humility. He falls down and begins to bless God, not asking Him for nothing, blessing Him for what's just been revealed to him. Now watch what happens, on the heels of real revelatory worship, God will give that person, church, congregation, city, nation, a promise of the miraculous.

REVELATORY WORSHIP BRINGS THE MIRACULOUS

For on the heels of his worship God turns around and says, because you worshipped Me of the revelation I gave you, I'll tell you what I'm going to do for you; I'm going to do wonders among you. Cuz' I can trust people who are worshippers to do wonders. We've got a society who wants God to show His stuff, but they don't want to worship. Notice this, one guy worshipped God, and God gave a covenant to a whole nation. Come on and say, God I hope there is a worshipper on this row. If there is a worshipper on this row, man, their very worship and their stepping into the secret place of God, might bless this whole pew.

You think I'm kidding. You have no idea how powerful one worshipper is on one pew. You think I'm in a comic book, did I read this right? Read Verse 10. You think I'm in a different Bible. "And he said, Behold, I make a covenant: before all thy people I will do marvels, such as have not been done in all the earth." Wow! Out of worship will come wonders never seen before! "nor in any nation: and all the people among which thou art shall see the work of the Lord." Everybody else is going to be blessed because you decided to be a worshipper. "for it is a terrible thing that I will do with thee." Now that word "terrible" doesn't mean, terrible, terrible. It means, "awesome, magnificent." It's a terrible thing that I will do. Notice what He said, "for it is a terrible thing that I will do with thee."

WORSHIP IS ONE ON ONE

Whoa, whoa, whoa, whoa, whoa, whoa, "It's a magnificent thing that I will do with you Moe!" They're going to get blessed, I'm going to show signs and wonders among them, but I'm going to do some heavy stuff with you. He didn't say I'm going to do the heavy stuff with them, He said I'm going to do it with thee. Why? Because worship is one on one; which tells me that I don't care if you live with a bunch of carnal idiots, or a bunch of wackos, you can step out of the parade and you can move into a realm with God and God will let you come back from the mountain and live with a bunch of hell on this planet and be a witness for Him. That's why we're crazy when we say we're going to get all our strength from a Wednesday night service, and a Sunday. That's silly; that puts undue pressure on the singers, and the musicians and the preachers, that's not the way it should be. This ought to be a conclave of a weeks worth of worshippers who just come walkin' in here sayin', "Been with Him." Instead of walkin' in and saying, "boy, I hope it's a good one today. I'm ticked, I'm tired, I could have been fishin', I could have been somewhere." Jesus have mercy!

Do you realize how awesome it could be, most of our visitors are here on Sunday morning and Sunday night. Do you realize how overwhelming it could be if half the church decided to be a worshipper. While the sinner sits next to you and doesn't know beans about what's goin' on, can't understand. I'm going to tell you something; the human intellect doesn't need to understand anything, the human spirit can respond very, very quickly. That's why God said that you worship in spirit. Because when you worship spirit to Spirit, you can bypass understanding, and you can bypass the mind, and you can bypass the intellect, and people can respond to God.

That's why most people want intellectual churches, so that they don't have to worship. That's why they hire choir directors, and music directors, and worship directors. That's why they hire their preacher while they have a liturgy and have all this craziness. They sit on their duff and think that somehow that someone can produce worship in a can for an hour and a half and give it to them. It don't happen that way! In fact we can't do it in this church that way either. Worship is a one on one episode, and the wonderful thing about worship is that I'm invited, and you're invited.

The Bible says that God seeketh such to worship Him. God's looking for anybody, it doesn't matter if you've got anything right in your life, it doesn't matter if you got everything fixed or not. He's looking for somebody who will worship Him in spirit and, here it is, and in truth. What does that mean? It doesn't mean that you have everything together. What it means is that you're honest and that you'll worship, and you're saying that you messed up over here, and I didn't do good over here, and I promised to do this, all He wants, oh yes, is somebody that's honest and open and transparent that He can just deal with.

WORSHIP WILL COST YOU SOMETHING

I don't know why we have such a hard time being honest with Him folks. He's so smart we can't snow job Him anyway. Everything is naked and open before Him with whom we have to deal with. I may not be able to read your mail but He knows your mail. He knows our thoughts are far off. He knows our schemes and our finagling. He knows every nickel and every dime. He knows every wasted moment. ….someone who puts up this charade, praaaaaaaise Jesus, praaaaaaaaaise Jesus, He just kind of goes …yuck! You get frustrated when you go to praise God and nothing happens, cuz' He ain't lookin' for praisers, He's lookin' for worshippers. It'll cost you something to worship God.

You get to worshipping God; He'll get to rearranging your whole criteria and your schedule. He'll mess up your life, He'll mess with your finance, He'll go in your clothes closet, He'll go in your video library, He'll go in your tape room, He'll check your magazines. Oh, you're going to be a worshipper, look out Jack. If He's going to show His glory, and His nature and His name to you, you got to be willing to let Him walk in every locked room in your mind. Why? Because worshipping is like intimate lovers; no secrets. I don't want to be rated R, it's kind of like two adults naked. They're in romance, they're in love with each other, they have a right to, they have an intimacy, they have a relationship, there's nothing phony, there's nothing hidden.

Here I am, wrinkles and all. I know you wanted to marry the Olympian ideal but I missed it. I realize you wanted a 29 inch waist but my waist is hanging somewhere down around my navel and a few inches past, this is it babe. Yeah, yeah.... Do all you want to during courtship, just put on your corset and suck it in until your waist is about that big, but after you get married, you just let it all hang out there, Jack. Everybody is just open and naked with..., but before, uh huh. You're lookin' mighty fine and smelling good until you get married and all of a sudden he's got to look at the stretch marks. He thought those were a different kind of stockings, them are varicose veins, Jack!

Embarrassing when you get married and she says, boy I just love the way you smile and he says, well, here, do you want to look at them? (Meaning his teeth) Some of these people getting kind of undressed to go to take a bath, it's kind of like an erector set; there's more parts than there's things. That's why we all like big robes and loose pajamas. Comfort the feeble minded among us, hallelujah.

Anybody ever, besides me, ever get in front of the mirror and just kind of suck it in. Then when you can't hold your breath anymore you just kind of ahhhhhh-hmmmmmm. You say, "Let's get some peanut butter balls and get some serious stuff going on around here!" Go through all the clothes on the rack you don't know why you keep them; you haven't been in them for four years. But you live in a fantasy world, "I'm coming back!" Then you see those little britches and those little skirts goin', "not in a hundred years you won't pass by here, that's for sure." You pass by since I knew you when? We lie to each other, we lie to ourselves. The neat thing about it is that the Lord, before we kind of took all the facade off, He knew where all the boils and the calluses and the warts were! He knew about the veins and the wrinkles and the ripples. He knew about the hang-ups and the messes and the childish things and the foolish things, and the hiding, and looked at us and before He ever stripped us down and tried to remake us, He said I just love you, I just love you, warts and all I love you. That's why I don't understand why we have such a hard time being honest. That's what worship is all about, being honest.

GOD FIGHTS FOR THE HONEST WORSHIPPER

Exodus 34:11, "Observe thou that which I command thee this day: behold, I drive out before thee the Amorite, and the Canaanite, and the Hittite, and the Perizzite, and the Hivite, and the Jebusite." Please hear me, if you want God to fight against the things that are resisting and fighting you, you need to become an honest and transparent worshipper. God said, "I will go to battle for you and drive out things that are trying to hinder you." All of this flowing out of the fact that one man slipped on the side of a mountain and said I'll worship You, I want You. Maybe this nation wants Your stuff and wants honey and stuff. But me, I'd just like to have You. And because he wanted God, God said; "well then, I want you, and I'll show you My stuff, and I'll do things for you that I won't do for other people." You say, "Well, God's not a respecter of persons." No, He's not, but He is a responder to people. He's not a respecter of persons. What He's saying is that anybody that wants to, you want to pay the price for worship—you can come on up!

Exodus 34:12, "Take heed to thyself, lest thou make a covenant with the inhabitants of the land whither thou goest." Now notice what He's saying. He said, watch, out of worship comes the promise of wonders. Out of the promise of wonders comes the God of battles, who's going to battle things for you. But He says, listen to me, if I'm going to battle things for you then I require from you responsible action. Don't get into covenant with people that hate Me lest it be for a snare in the midst of thee. Verse 13, " But ye shall destroy their altars, break their images, and cut down their groves" Verse 14, "For thou shalt worship no other god: for the Lord, whose name is Jealous, is a jealous God."

So is God a respecter of other religions? No! Why? Because false worship is an insult. Worship, to be right, has to have the correct object. God was adamant about it and there're people sitting here tonight that you still think that this is a hard-nosed way to go, that God is still adamant about you not going into covenant with people that have false doctrine for idols. You need to be careful who you run with, lest they be a snare unto us. That doesn't mean we need to be unkind to people, but there is a line, I'll go this far and no farther, and I'll not embrace your doctrine and I'll not play games with them, lest they be a snare unto me and I give away what God gave to me.

THE FOOLISHNESS OF TOLERATING SIN

I'm telling you we're living in a generation of homogenization of Christianity, and this tolerance foolishness, it's crazy! It is a snare on our society trying to make anybody who is adamant, or intense about what they believe to be guilty of hate crime! But God turned around and said I don't want you to cut them no slack, I want you to break down their images, I want you to destroy their altars. I want to burn them down; I don't want you to save it for later. In one scripture He says, "Lest you desire and love the silver of the idol."

I'm going to tell you something, jealousy is a terrible trait in the human specie. It is an awesome and majestic trait in God, because our jealousy is an inferior jealousy born out of ignorance, but when God says that He is jealous you must understand that everything that God does is holy, righteous, just, and true so when God is jealous over something He is jealous from a standpoint from a perfect knowledge. Jealousy is a product of love, not envy; sometimes we misunderstand the difference between jealousy and envy. The Lord said that "I'm jealous." Why? "Because I love you. But you have to understand something, I'm not loving you like a husband sometimes or a wife or relative sometimes tries to possess something." No, No. He said, "I love you with a perfect love, and I know tomorrow, and I know the idiosyncrasies of the human race and I know all the spasms that your spirit goes up and down. I love you with a perfect, righteous love therefore I have a right to be jealous over you, because I love you unconditionally, and I know everything that can hurt you and hinder you. So when I say, don't play with this, don't let some guy come and tell you, don't let your wife tell you, your brother, your daughter, your sister, your uncle... don't let them tell you, oh your just too biased and narrow minded and bigoted."

Boy I'm strikin' fire with this assembly, you still don't believe it. You're going to live to regret not believing this, you're going to live to regret it, because all of this toleration stuff. You can see a tremendous example in the wisest man that ever

Believe
in
miracles.

WBR513N
© HMK. CDS.

lived outside of Jesus of Nazareth was Solomon, but when he got old, he got tolerant, and he put his heart in his hand and handed it to these gals and these gals lingered around every tree, and he built altars and he made idols and he became a heathen at heart. He even had a supernatural visitation of God where God stood by his bed and asked, what do you want? Solomon said give me an understanding and wise heart, and God said I'll give it to you, and I'll give you what you didn't ask for. As long as Solomon walked with God with intensity ... but then he had this thing about you know... don't be so negative, you know you're not the only guy that knows and 'ahhhh' how come you're so narrow minded.

TAKE THE FATHER'S WORD TO HEART

God is so smart, when He says make it narrow, make is straight, don't cut any tolerance for certain things, He knows what He's talking about. He knows where the quicksand is and where the swamp is. He knows the propensity of the human spirit to get sucked into something, because He said; "they shall be unto you a snare that they will turn you from Me." Oh, I can see all these people saying, "not meeee, not after all that God has done for meeee." Well, let me tell you; almost everybody I've ever known that's ever backslid from this church has backslid having said, "Not meeee, God's done too much for meeee." I could go down and remember asking them not to do this, or go here, and I told you to be careful about this, and watch that, and after a while you start getting like, well, you know, we can think for ourselves, we don't need no dumb preacher to tell us nothing. Fine; then don't take a preacher's word for it, take the preacher's Father's word for it.

THE WHY & WONDER OF WORSHIP

VOLUME FOUR · CHAPTER TWO

CHAPTER TWO

Two portions of scripture; one in the book of Ecclesiastes 3:1, "To every thing there is a season, and a time to every purpose under the heaven:" 3:17, "I said in mine heart, God shall judge the righteous and the wicked: for there is a time there for every purpose and for every work." John 4:19-24, "The woman saith unto him, Sir, I perceive that thou art a prophet. Our fathers worshipped in this mountain; and ye say, that in Jerusalem is the place where men ought to worship. Jesus saith unto her, Woman, believe me, the hour cometh, when ye shall neither in this mountain, nor yet at Jerusalem, worship the Father. Ye worship ye know not what; we know what we worship: for salvation is of the Jews. But the hour cometh, and now is, when the true worshippers shall worship the Father in spirit and in truth: for the Father seeketh such to worship him. God is Spirit: and they that worship him must worship him in spirit and in truth."

THE PAST IS NOT AN ISSUE WHEN GOD CONFRONTS

We are learning John Chapter 4 quite well. I am continuing our theme in worship... I have taught two or three lessons on confrontation, that it usually brings confusion. I said in those lessons that confusion isn't always the work of the devil, sometimes it is the work of divine confrontation as truth clashes with our concepts and God is the revealer of our confusion rather than the cause of our confusion. If you want to stay safe and be unconfused, keep your distance from deity and you'll be safe in your little ritual. Any time God steps up into your face, I don't care how wonderful you've been and how religious, and how saved and how experienced you and I may be in the rich things of God, any time God steps into your face I can guarantee you, you are challenged what you are, or what you believe and what you've become.

It is a neat thing to me that when God steps into your face He never brings up your past—we do. He is too great to pick up yesterday. He looks at you and me and says, "I have such a future for you, I can't let you drag this baggage from yesterday; I won't even bring it up." But usually we bring it up. Ever got into the presence of somebody that you said something about or had hard feelings about, or thought that they had feelings toward you, or just that there was miscommunication or whatever and there was just bad vibes, and they walked up into your presence and without them saying anything: your past showed up? Ever been guilty of something or went to talk to someone and they never brought it up, but you brought it up, even if you brought it up just in your mind?

Well, I'm going to wait on everybody to join the class. See, the problem with God is that He is so wonderful and we are not. He is so pure and we are not. He is so grand and we are not...that it gets very awkward in His presence. All our polished theologies, philosophies and theories just kind of crumble when you meet the real McCoy. I've often thought and have asked the Lord for mercy that I won't have to be confronted with some of the stuff I've preached over these years. Especially when you say, "You know, the Lord showed me." Then He just brings it up and says, "What exactly did I show you now?" There is a place in faith where you can absolutely say the Lord showed me, then there are other times when you're not quite sure and you say, "I think the Lord showed me." Nothing wrong with leaving yourself an out if you're not sure. If you're sure, you don't need an out.

OUR WORSHIP FLOWS OUT OF OUR PAST

We have been studying for a number of weeks about the woman at the well and just as a refresher for a few moments, she was a worshipper. Remember that? It wasn't that she wasn't a worshipper, she was a worshipper, but she was worshipping ignorantly. She didn't know what she was worshipping. Her confusion came from the fact that, now get this, because I'm going to mess with us tonight, her concepts of worship, like our concepts of worship, always flow from the previous generation--from our past and our founders. Her concepts of worship were not present-day revelations, she referred to, "our fathers taught us...," she could not say to Jesus, "now I know different." She said, no I just picked it up and thought it was the truth. You see, the battle is always how much truth do we lose when we marry ourselves to tradition.

I don't think the Bible is against tradition as long as tradition doesn't violate truth. And there's always that danger that tradition has the subtle ability to replace, very minutely, aspects of truth over generations until finally, when the generation is handed the next baton they think that everything they just got is pure. That's why God calls every one of us daily to know Him, and to become intimate with Him, so that we can decipher and discern and disregard stuff that will hinder us. Turn to someone and look and say, "What in the world is he talking about, we're the people of the truth we couldn't possibly be wrong."

LEARN TO WORSHIP THROUGH PRACTICE

Worship is always best learned by trying it. You can learn a lot from seminars and tapes, but nothing like being in the presence of God; you'll find out what works and what doesn't work. That's why sometimes when there's a very strong move of God and I notice a certain clientele that's here, they never worship. I can tell why. Their theories are being crushed. You don't ever worship if you are uncomfortable. In Psalm 137, Israel's problem was that they couldn't worship God, because they were locked into locality. If you read Psalm 137, they talk about that they hung their harps on the willows and they were in captivity in Babylon and they were asked to sing a song of the Lord and they said, "How can we sing the Lord's song in the land of captivity?" That's the best place to sing it! Aren't you getting tired of singing to each other? Don't you ever get tired of telling each other what you believe? I thought the Bible says iron sharpeneth iron.

You can't sharpen an axe head with butter, there has to be resistance, there has to be grinding. Truth is best proved in the laboratory of life, not in the laboratory. People want to make their experiments all the time under governed conditions, but God doesn't like it that way. He says; No, get out in the middle of the refuse and see if it will work. That makes all of us nervous, that's why my phone rings. "What exactly do we believe about…baptism for the dead?" I just talked to someone about that and said, "Well, what do YOU believe?" They said, "I've never been asked that, I don't know what I believe." Well, then, tell them you don't know what you believe.

What's so bad about saying; I don't know? That's like saying; how much does the moon weigh? Who cares? How many eyeballs does the Praying Mantis have? How do I know? You don't know? There's a world you're living in that will try to make you look like a fool, because you don't have an answer to their stupid questions. You don't have to be expert in everything; you need to be an expert about salvation. You need to be expert about what you know about God, and about what God has done for you. You don't have to be expert in discerning every word that is in this book. You need to know, well, I'll tell you, well, I don't know about that, but I can tell you what I used to be and where I came from and where I am now. I can tell you how good God's been to me; I can tell you how He forgives sin, and how I was baptized and how He gave me the Holy Ghost. You don't have to be an expert about all that foolishness.

TRUE WORSHIP IS DONE IN THE SPIRIT

True worship, according to Jesus in John 4, true worship must be done in spirit. Notice that the writer has put spirit with a small "s." I just read a fabulous dissertation on worship, a hundred and some odd years old, and the man gave 9 pages to stupidity. This guy is famous for his knowledge, and he says, the bible says John 4:23-24, that you have to worship in spirit and truth and he says that's the Holy Spirit. I wrote in the book, you are so stupid! The listing in the Greek and the English translation is small "s," the Holy Spirit, is capital "S." If it's the Holy Spirit then nobody can worship God without the Holy Spirit, but that ain't so, cuz lots of folks worship God without the Holy Spirit.

Come to think of it there's a whole bunch of us did it before we got the Holy Ghost. Be kind of ticked off if somebody said; you know, those 28 years you were a Baptist, a Methodist, Presbyterian, Charismatic, Episcopalian; that you weren't worshipping. Of course you were worshipping, because it's a small "s," it is the human spirit. God is giving us a revelation that the human spirit is the sanctuary of God; it is the human spirit that the Holy Spirit regenerates. It is the human spirit whereby the Holy Spirit comes in and gives the human spirit another nature.

That's why you have two natures in you. A human fallen spirit and a Holy Spirit. You got two natures, I don't care what anybody teaches you; you got two natures in you. The Bible says that all things have passed away, that's right, that means their control has passed away. Don't ever think your old spirit left. Don't pray for 48 hours and see if your old spirit doesn't say, "Hey, how are you doin'?" You think I'm kiddin' you? You don't pray for 2 weeks and let's see how spiritual you stay! That old man will climb back up on the throne and drive you crazy. It will! Yeah, he will!

OUR SPIRIT MUST BE A SANCTUARY FOR GOD

So what He's talking about is that we ought to worship God in our spirit. Therefore, our spirit must become a sanctuary for God; it must become a temple for truth. It must become a place of praise, a dwelling for the divine. That's why it is imperative that you have a clean spirit. That's why we Pentecostals preach so much against certain things. It's not even so much I am convinced that those things will take you to hell, as so much as they will help you go to hell. They will fight the thing that God wants working in your life. These various things, places, people, will cause us to have a war that's unnecessary in us. We've got a war already without helping the enemy fight us anymore. There's no sense reading girly magazines and snortin' cocaine, and drinking Jack Daniels and honky tonkin' all weekend and then comin' to church like a drunken sot and say, "Okay Jesus, dry me out." Let me tell you something; God ain't desperate. He let a whole world be lost for eight people to go into a boat. He ain't desperate, He can start all over.

It ought to scare the fire out of us that God has a replacement standing by for every one of us. For every one of us that decides that God has too high of a price tag, He's got somebody sleeping under a bridge just waiting to get in the choir. You don't believe me, but I'm going to tell you; ain't none of us worthy of God. When God found us, every one of us was lost and undone. We might have been moral, we might have been honest, we might have been raised in a kind, godly family, but I'm going to tell you; we were lost and undone without God, none of us were acceptable to Him, nobody could reach His criteria, or match His standard.

He had to reach down and pull us up and pull us out, and right now He's still working to pull us through!

DON'T WAIT TO UNDERSTAND—JUST DO IT

Our problem is sometimes we are waiting until we understand everything about something before we do it. The best way to do it is to spend time with God and you will by association be impacted with assimilation. The more Moses stayed on the mountain, the more He glowed. You get people who stay in the presence of God, they get different.

BEWARE OF RELIGIOUS CHURCH FOLKS

Watch: you get people who just go to church, they're different too. That's why the world doesn't like church people; I don't care for them myself. Church people are a pain in the neck; they're a righteous bunch of bigots. Bunch of self-righteous jerks that don't know beans, they have five little pet scriptures and made a few adjustments in their life and all of a sudden they're God's guru to the spirit realm. That's so ignorant. That's why I don't like going in a bible bookstore; all them dumb church people are in there. I pick up on their spirits, I don't like 'em. You think I'm wicked, but I don't like 'em. Let me tell you something, my father didn't like 'em either, and I'm not talking about George, I'm talking about Jesus. He didn't like 'em either. Come to think of it, it was the religious ones that always hunted Him down. It was the religious folks that were always fussin' with dottin' the I and crossin' the T. It was the religious folks that took Him to the cops; come to think of it, it was the religious folks that got Him crucified.

Jesus never had confrontation with bold brazen sinners. He had nothin' but compassion and pity and kindness for people who were snared in their sin, but He absolutely went volcanic, read Matthew 23, when He got to talkin' to the religious scum. Hypocrites, whited sepulchres full of dead man's bones. Looked good on the outside...stink with putrification on the outside. Make clean the platter, but inside was filth and looked like sheep, but inside...ravening wolves. He didn't cut 'em any slack, because let me tell you something; God would rather have you been an open blazing sinner, than a religious hypocrite! You know why? Because a sinner knows he is a sinner, but a hypocrite is playing a role. God can deal with people who are mistaken a lot easier than with folks who are playing. When you are sitting in a church building and you are playing, and the preacher comes and the sword of the Spirit comes, and the Holy Spirit comes, and you're playing, you say, "I wonder who he's talkin' to?

BEWARE OF HYPOCRISY

When the Lord began to deal, in Acts Chapter 10, with Cornelius, who was a righteous man, a God fearing man, a man who gave much alms of fasting and praying often, who was kind to people, who had a tremendous experience. We know it, Acts 10:1-6, where an angel flew into his living room and said, "Your prayers and alms have come up as a memorial before God, now send to Joppa for one Simon Peter who dwelleth with Simon the tanner by the seaside...." Now this is a very humorous thing, because in the story Peter is aghast at going to deal with a Gentile. Now he is already in total violation of Jewish law, because no Jew was allowed to fraternize or fellowship with a tanner. He was never allowed to deal with anybody who dealt with dead skins or dead animals. That's what a tanner does. He said Simon Peter is playing a church game; he's down with Simon the tanner, he don't know I know he's there.

Now watch Peter play the church game. When I tell him to go talk to a Gentile, he's going to say, nothing common or unclean has ever been in my mouth. It's almost like God is saying, well, now, whose house are you in? See it's funny how we'll allow certain things in our private life, then we want to get real righteous and religious in our public life. Well, that didn't go over very well. Cornelius is confronted by an angel to experience more than he already has. The hardest thing for anybody religious to do is to go beyond what they've experienced. Come on, all you religious folks. Yea, we all have a form of some type of religion.

It's very hard for us Pentecostals to go beyond anything than what we have learned through truth and tradition and the tunnel of time. Usually when I say that stuff, I have a feeling you're saying, "Boy, that's right about them!" Brand X.

THE WHY & WONDER OF WORSHIP • BOOK TWO

It's us! I am firmly convinced, it's not I think so; I am firmly convinced that God has got us on His Holy Ghost hit list to change us. He's forcing it, whether you like it or not. He's causing us to embrace new truth. There's no new salvation truth. You've only got one gospel. How we live and how we apply and how we work with it, we need some expansion. And anytime the Lord deals with people who pray and then tells them something that they're not familiar with, it messes with them.

Now thank God Cornelius wasn't as religious as Peter, because God only had to talk to him once and then Cornelius did it. God gives Peter a vision three times and almost threatened to kill him. He argued with Him. God said, "Arise, kill and eat Peter." Not so! Have you ever looked at that? I've never heard anybody preach on that. Was the man crazy? God said, "Arise, kill and eat," and Peter said, "No!" That's scary. What's fabulous is God's grace turns around and says, "I said, arise, kill and eat," but Peter says, "No, nothing unclean or common has ever been in my mouth." God says, "what the Lord has cleansed call not common or unclean," and the mystery little napkin just kind of folds back up, lifts all the animals back up into the sky.

TRADITION SOMETIMES FIGHTS TRUTH

Now watch, God is going to give Peter an experience beyond an angel. He's going to give him an experience beyond what he has already, the man has something wonderful from God, he is known in the heavens, he loves God, he may be limited in light, but he loves God. God wants to take him beyond where he is. Simon Peter loves God, he has more light than Cornelius, he has the Holy Ghost that Cornelius never heard about, Simon Peter is baptized in Jesus name and has the keys of the kingdom; God wants to take him beyond where he is and he don't want to go. The only reason he don't want to go is because his tradition is fighting this truth.

Acts 10:15, "And the voice spake unto him again the second time, What God hath cleansed, that call not thou common. (16) This was done thrice: and the vessel was received up again into heaven." Now watch; here's where I am and I think where some of you are. (17) "Now while Peter doubted in himself what this vision which he had seen should mean..." It is possible to receive an experience that you don't deserve and you didn't earn. It wasn't because he was a great man of prayer; he fell into a trance, because his belly was growlin'. The man was up on the roof hungry, waiting for them to make dinner, and he got hunger pains and fell into a trance. It says he was hungry and he was waiting for them to fix dinner, and he went upstairs; God gave him the vision. He didn't earn the vision, it just came to him. God is Sovereign, it just came to him and he sees this blanket let down with unclean four-footed and creeping things...see; isn't it funny how God, as brilliant and spiritual and as deep as we are, he's got to give us pictures. Isn't that neat how God will just acquiesce to this silly level that we live at, give us little pictures, here's a little tiger and here's a cat, ...instead of writing a big sign: "Gentiles."

Now watch; when Peter doubts in himself what the vision means... (17) "...behold, the men which were sent from Cornelius had made enquiry for Simon's house, and stood before the gate, (18) And called, and asked whether Simon, which was surnamed Peter, were lodged there." And here's the key. (19) "While Peter thought on the vision ..."

MEDITATE ON WHAT GOD HAS ALREADY SHOWN US

There's the key to where we're going next. If we could start in our personal lives, meditating on the things that God has been telling us, and showing us, and talking to us personally, even though we don't have an understanding about it. The Bible says, "While he thought on the experience the Spirit spoke." Had Peter thought what his brethren would say, the Spirit wouldn't have spoke." You've got to get in on what God is saying and doing. And as you begin to think...and God is not insulted when you and I say, "I don't understand it," and you rehearse it again in your mind and spirit, in that avenue of rehearsal it gives a leeway for the Spirit to say, "I'll take a look at this." I think we miss a lot of second moves in the Spirit because we turn around and ask our brethren, "What do you think this means?" Or we debate it with our tradition, or we debate it with our own little bifocals, and what we think is right and wrong, and the Spirit is never allowed to talk to us, because it's going to have to go through all that garbage. If we could just somehow say; now God, if you could just talk to me, I don't fully understand what you are saying, but I want you to help me.

Peter was rehearsing over and over in his spirit and his mind what God had showed him. He didn't have understanding, but he was rehearsing the experience, and God took that as a platform to walk right out and speak. The Spirit spoke and said, (20) "Arise therefore, and get thee down, and go with them, doubting nothing: for I have sent them." And then the Spirit acquiesced to Peter's own level and said, "I have sent them." If we could just hear God sometimes say, "Ah, I did that." Boy would it free us. If we could just hear Him say, "I let that happen, I caused that."

FROM CONFUSION TO CONFIDENCE TO COMMITMENT

As soon as he heard the Spirit say, "I sent them;" Peter jumped down and said; what do you guys want? Talk about going from being stupid to being, oh, yes, I be Superman, what do you want? It's amazing how you can go from confusion to confidence when you hear the Spirit of God say, "I sent them." When you are sure that God is in it, you're confusion gives way to confidence, and confidence will allow you to reach commitment. Even then, he still didn't understand what it was all about. He just said the Lord told me he sent you, what do you want? Then they give him the story about Cornelius praying and an angel flying in his living room telling him to go send for some guy named Simon Peter who lives with Simon the tanner and here we are and so he starts giving this little thing, you know, well, you know it ain't right for me to among you Gentiles, he starts in again…tradition, tradition, tradition. He's doin' this crawfish thing, in my mind I see Peter talkin' to these guys like, now look, you know I'm a Jew and this guys a Gentile…

DON'T REPLACE GOD WITH WHAT HE USES

Peter goes to the house and Cornelius falls down at Peter's feet to worship him. He's a worshipper; he's just got the wrong object. I wish the TV preachers would read that scripture, because it is possible that the medium God uses can replace God. Cornelius is thinking, God told me to send for you, you must be some mighty one and he falls down at his feet to worship him, Peter yanks him up and says, "Get up on your feet, I'm a man like you are!"

THE WORK OF CALVARY IS FOR ALL

Cornelius starts to tell Peter what happened; I saw this angel, and he said that you should come, now what's the deal? So then Peter gives this big discourse about, you know I'm a Jew and you're a Gentile and you're not supposed to be with me and I'm not supposed to be with you, and I hope the general board doesn't hear about this cuz they'll pull my license and I'll be in a lot of trouble, and yet God has told me that from now on I'm not supposed to call you unclean or common.

Apparently, Calvary's work is for you too, I thought it was just for the Jews. Through seeing animals on the little napkin, I've learned that apparently you Gentiles have been allowed to come in. And so he starts talking to him, telling him that God is no respecter of persons, and Peter was getting bolder and bolder and bolder and while he was preaching Jesus Christ to him, the Holy Ghost falls on them and they all get the Holy Ghost just like they did at Pentecost; cuz that's the only way you get it---I don't care what anybody says. Peter said, "They have received the Holy Ghost, as well as we, can any man forbid water that they should not be baptized who just got the Holy Ghost just like us; we heard them speaking in tongues." That's why God sent those men with Peter, because if Peter had gone by himself the board would have beat his brains in, the board would have said, "They didn't get the real Holy Ghost. They got some jibberish, hicka, ma-hoky stuff."

TRUE REPENTANCE—THE WORK OF A MOMENT

"They didn't really repent; it took me fifteen months to repent." You mean God's going to give it to that dumb Gentile in five minutes? Well, maybe you were a stubborn idiot and that's why you needed fifteen months, you wouldn't let go of some stuff. I'm going to mess with you now; we've been taught for years that however we repented that's how everybody else ought to repent. That's not necessarily so. Repentance means to change your mind, you can change your mind, sittin' right there, if you admit and confess your sin. I know we were taught to innumerate everything. My Lord, it took me fifteen months to remember it all!

Right now in this church we don't believe an ole brazen sinner can walk in here and say; oh God, I'm sorry for..., and we stand back and say; boy, I hope he starts really repenting soon. Let me tell you, he can do one big sweep and God can just wash everything out of that man's soul. I've heard it in this church; "Oh, he needs to get some real repentance." Well, what is fake repentance? What you're really saying is, "I'm ticked off because I had to do that and they ain't got to do it. Made me stand in the altar all those weeks and all those months, now they're getting this easy..." Oh, I'm messin' with you now. Now I'm for repentance, but I'm going to tell you something, say what you want to; God won't give nobody the Holy Ghost that hasn't repented. Say anything you want to, and there's no scripture in here that says that He called Cornelius to repent, he didn't have to repent, he was already repented then.

REPENTANCE EQUALS A CLEAN TEMPLE

God won't give people the Holy Ghost that won't repent. Wait a minute; He will give people the Holy Ghost that repent and smoke and whore around and honky-tonk and live stupid and live immoral, yes He will. Our tradition will say; oh no, they have to get all that crud straightened up, God ain't going to dwell in an unclean temple. Let me tell you something honey, the minute you repent the temple's clean! Let's be honest. Let's forget brand X, let's talk about us. How many of us, after we've reeeeeeeally repented, and God gave us the Holy Ghost, that the Holy Ghost found some crud in you that needed fixin'. Now did He move into an unclean temple, or did He just move into a temple that just kind of needed some more work?

Come to think of it; I've been in this twenty some years and, my Lord, He's still beaten on shingles and puttin' on roofing and still working on me and finding little cabinets in my soul that need fixin', and attitudes that need straightening out.

I've got stuff that I'm still trying to take out and I think I'm doing okay and as soon as I get to the next level God says; now let's deal with this. It's so easy to damn and condemn brand X. Let's just kill a few holy cows and have some hamburgers tonight, what do you say? Why don't we just deal with it? Can God give people the Holy Ghost and then they go out and vilely sin? Now before all you traditionalists say no; ask yourself, how did you do? And some of us who have had the Holy Ghost for a number of years, and then pulled off some stupid things and sin; did the Holy Ghost just step outside and wait on the corner while we pulled off our shenanigans and then came back? And the Holy Ghost stepped back in and said; whew, glad you got that out of your system. I don't want to live in a dirty house.

BE THERE FOR THE NEW CONVERT

I don't know of anybody in this place that wants to be more pure and godly and transparent than I do. I want this church to live pure and godly and above-board and righteous and transparent; but what are we going to do for a church until you decide to get there? Have you ever said that someone got the Holy Ghost in one of the services or whatever, and all of a sudden they did something, or wore something, or whatever, and then say; I thought you had the Holy Ghost! I guess they didn't get a real good dose. A dose of what? A dose of the Holy Ghost or a dose of your concept? What didn't they get? Well, when I got the Holy Ghost they made me spit right, walk right, live right.... Great; They need help. Now that you are at that high plateau, why don't you rush over to 'em and help 'em.

GOD WILL WORK WITH WHOM HE FILLS

I got thrown out of one of the districts of this whole movement, over preaching a message just like this to four thousand people. When I sat on the stage and just let my legs hang over, just whistled a while and took the microphone and said, "Wellll, we had two people Sunday got the Holy Ghost and both of them had packs of cigarettes in their pockets and they talked in tongues for twenty five minutes and I baptized them and they went outside and lit up." And I know what you nincompoops say; "they didn't get the Holy Ghost." I said, "Don't tell God that, cuz He's the one that gave it". It could be that they're not aware that there are some things that they're better off not doing. Now listen to me, some of us get the Holy Ghost and there comes with it a deeper sensitivity than others get.

See now, what's scary is that this makes room for all kinds of crud and garbage. What's our church going to become? All kinds of people doin' all kinds of things. What about our image? Well, maybe God wants to kill our image. Well, maybe we ought to just get rid of our image.

FIRST THE HOLY GHOST—THEN THE CONFORMING WALK

I can remember when I was so desperate and hungry for God; I was on the verge of divorce, I was sick of livin' like I was. If God would have asked me to walk naked and upside down and backwards to Belgian Congo on broken glass, it would have been fine with me. But there are some people that they have not gotten that tired and disgusted with sin and they get into a service and the Holy Ghost just puts them under conviction and they begin repenting and God fills them with the Holy Ghost; but these other areas of their life are so deeply entrenched they need to be taught. It's such an insult to tell people; "You didn't get it."

Let me tell you something, I smoked three packs a day and fifty cigars every two weeks and God in His kindness took the desire away from me; probably ten months before I ever got the Holy Ghost and I walked out and put my cigarette out and never smoked again. It's been twenty some odd years, and I've seen people get the Holy Ghost that keep smokin' and fussin' and arguin' and just fighting that stinkin' habit and they're ashamed by it and they're beat up by it and I've looked back over my shoulder and say; "I don't get it." Cuz I smoked two to three packs a day and fifty cigars every two weeks and when Patty Arnold said, "Pentecostals don't smoke;" I just put the cigarette out, and took the cigarettes and beer back and that was the end of that. I had no problem with it.

For many years of evangelism I had held people who had problems with it in utter contempt—"You didn't get what I got!" Now I look back, I didn't get anything. God just kindly and sovereignly reached into my life and just took it out. I can't say I prayed and fasted until I broke that devil's back. No, I didn't. I was just standing there looking stupid and God just said; he's too stupid to work with, I'll just take it away from him. You know, God in His kindness probably looked at us and said; you know you'll never be able to beat that, I better just beat it for you.

EXPERIENCES CAN'T BE TRANSFERRED

Let me try it again, most of our concepts of worship come to us from our forefathers. Now listen carefully. From our founders, from our past, if you will study past revivals that have been recorded; in every past powerful revival that has been recorded that swept nations, their times of worship always involved singing, shouting, dancing, weeping, brokenness, long prayer, and fasting. And in everyone recorded, from Martin Luther to John Wesley to the Welsh revival; Glossalalia, talking in tongues. The problem is; experiences cannot be transmitted. Nor can they be transferred to the next generation that believes it.

YOU MUST EXPERIENCE *WHO* THEY EXPERIENCED

Luther had a powerful experience with God. He was listed in religious history as a reformer, a talker of tongues and worker of miracles. John and Charles Wesley were tongue talkers, avid sanctification people, morality, methods of living. What happens is; when an experience becomes codified, you cannot experience the experience, you experience the code. To be what Luther was, to be what John Wesley was, to be what the Welsh revival was,(that's where the Apostolic's draw their roots from—the Welsh revival) you must experience WHO they experienced. If you just codify it and label it, it will be lost from word to mouth.

A PERSONAL EXPERIENCE IS NEEDED

It takes a personal encounter and experience. Ask Abraham. Abraham was given a great experience, a trans-forming experience. Jacob believes in it, but Jacob is not like Abe. It isn't until Jacob has his experience in Genesis 28, when he first talks to God with the ladder in Bethel, and then Genesis 32 when God finally breaks him, that now he becomes like Abe, and he is aligned with Abraham's experience; because he's had it. Watch what happened to the Jews; Abraham's our father. Yeah, but have you had Abraham's experience. Have you wrestled with Abraham's God? Have you dealt with Jacob's wrestling partner? Or have you codified their experiences and put it in a box and then called it religion? So that I'm a Lutheran, or I'm a Baptist, I'm a Presbyterian, I'm a Pentecostal, I'm an Apostolic, I'm an Episcopalian.

Fine, whatever you are, but you must understand that if you are going to bear proper fruit you need to have the same thing the root has. And to say that your founder had an awesome experience with God and wrote it down and told you and then you try to duplicate it by mechanics. Say what you want to, but Moses isn't anything without the bush. The reason why Israel could never really embrace Moses' passion is because they never had a bush experience. They had a deliverance experience and a liberation, but they didn't meet the life giver until the life giver shook Mount Sinai, and when he shook Mt. Sinai then the Jews, who were the disciples of Moses said; we don't want that! You tell us what to do; we'd rather have a code than an experience.

Job believes God. Job is honored by God. God says that he's the most honorable man in the east; he's his man, he's his picture, he's his puzzle to the devil. And yet it's not till' Job goes through all that hell and all that chaos and all that loss and all that pain and all that problem that God shows up in his front yard in that whirlwind.

And when God reaches out of that whirlwind and grabs a hold of Job and says, "who's this that darkeneth counsel without any wisdom, stand up, gird your loins like a man I'm going to make you talk to me seein' that you're full of hot air and you know everything. Here I am, let's talk." When those four chapters are finished, you ain't got the same Job in Chapter 41 and 42 that you had in the previous forty chapters; because he has now had an experience with God. When he has his experience with God, He gives him double than what he used to have and that doesn't just mean material possession; it means revelation, it means power in the Spirit, it means understanding.

OUR PROBLEM IS LACK OF PASSION

What makes Paul so powerful? Why is he so different than the early church? Everybody has the same Holy Ghost. He's got experiences with God that transcends the average churchgoer. Now I know that God is Sovereign and God sovereignly chose Paul to do a work that He didn't choose anybody else for. Fine, that's his work, but I'm going to tell you something; everybody in the kingdom can have experiences beyond what they have if they went after God. They may not have the sovereign one that God gave to Paul, but they can have more than they're enjoying. That's exactly what my next note is; our problem is lack of passion. It's the argument between, I'd like to be—I'd rather know Him. If I know Him, being saved is incidental.

Here's what I'm trying to tell you. What is passed on from our founders is really not their experience, it's the history, and the telling of their experience; but it's not their experience. What is usually passed on is doctrine. Thus, we are given a man or woman that has an awesome experience with God. They try to relate it, we codify it, we write it, we solidify it and what we receive out of that is a doctrine and a story of an experience that hopefully can be duplicated. But when it's not duplicated, what we do is we then inherit from them forms and ceremonies that are embraced, that have no life vitality in them; but we say they do because they flowed out of one who did have life.

BE PASSIONATE FOR THE GOD OF THE DOCTRINE

Paul said it this way in 2 Timothy Chapter 3:1-5 and when you reach Verse 5 it says, "beware in the last days perilous times shall come, men shall be lovers of themselves, boastful, proud ... lovers of pleasure more than lovers of God, then he says, having a form of godliness but denying the power thereof." They have a form. The form is right, the form is true, but it's empty, it's void; so that when Jesus meets the Jews who are the One God people, they're nothing like what took place with Moses at Sinai. That's why He's angry with them, because there's no reason for that to be that way. That's why God goes on record and says, "I'm sick of your offerings and your sacrifice, I'm sick of the stench of the burning flesh; I don't want to drink the blood of animals." Don't you understand? "I only gave you a sacrificial, ceremonial system to make you understand how holy I am and how unholy you are, and you cannot approach me just like you want to. I had to educate you; you've been slaves for four hundred years."

Don't you get it? If you liberate a man or a woman who's been a slave for X number of years all you have is liberated ignorance. You have lust that's unbridled, you have passion that has no direction, you have a man that can't spell, can't write his name, doesn't know how to hold a job, doesn't know how to keep a bank book. He's a slave, he may be free, but in his heart he's not free; he's a liability. That's why when God brought them out of Egypt He didn't take them to the Promised Land, He took them to Himself. He said, you won't make it over there if you don't know Me. That's why He said," make the tabernacle and let Me be in the midst of the people." Why? So that they can interact with Me, not interact with my laws. But Israel started enjoying the form. Now you smile and say, yeah, that's them Jews. Let's look at us. We too have form, and we have received traditions, and I thank God for some and I'm glad others are going away. I thank God for truth that has come, and for life that has come; but we need to reevaluate where are we in all of this.

Just because a previous generation believes something that doesn't mean that's Jesus. Well, they were godly men. Well, there were godly men and women before the last generation; there's always been godly men and women. Do you know that some of the most godly men and women were screwballs at times? Have you ever looked at God's hero list? You wouldn't ask them to be on your church board. Thomas always doubted, Judas sold his master, John and James always calling fire down from heaven, Peter fussin' and cussin', cuttin' people's ears off; you don't want none of them on your board. Those one God Jews, thirty two thousand people with Gideon, anybody afraid to go home? Twenty two thousand men beat you to death with road dust.

SEEK OUT WHAT CAN CHANGE YOU

See; you can have a crowd, but you may not have a church. You can have a building full, but you may only have a handful of people that are ready for the coming of the Lord. If the truth or tradition that we receive is no more than ceremony and ritual then it lacks the vitality that is there to change your life and my life. Then we need to get away from it and find out what CAN change us. The only thing I know is personal encounters with God and His word. There's nothing else that can do it. Ceremony and ritual won't do it. If John Wesley, if Martin Luther were resurrected from the dead and walked in to their churches they would have a heart attack. It wouldn't be anything like what they had.

Now you're smilin'. But wait a minute; if God would raise the Apostolic church up from the grave and walk in here, they'd have a heart attack. The first thing they'd say is how come these people always have to be entertained? How come so much of your service has nothing to do with Jesus? How come worship is something you try to get out of the way? How come you've given such a priority to preaching and so little to worship and thanksgiving and praise of the One? Why is the sermon an hour, and the singing fifteen minutes? Why is our prayer service five minutes, and the preaching sixty? You're saying, Bro. Arnold, you're going to put yourself out of a job. Good, then I'll just be a little shepherd boy and feed you when I can.

WE NEED GOD—NOT TRADITION

I know that preaching is the priority, I know that preaching is what we consider preeminence, but I'm going to tell you somethin'; Jesus Christ is the star and if you think that you can get what you need from preaching and teaching better than what
you can get from one on one worship confrontation, you're nutty as a bessy bug. I'll go hundreds of miles to hear the best preachers in Pentecost. I love to hear preaching, but if you were to tell me Jesus is out here and He said I'll give you a fifteen minute interview; if you think I'm goin' two hundred miles and listen to some guy scream his vocal cords out and I can go fifteen minutes in the raw

presence of God, you can just go buy me a tape. Are you hearing me? This is about worship, this is about Him, this is about intimacy, this is about interacting with Him, it's all about....

THE PRESENCE OF GOD IS NOT ALWAYS APPROVAL

Matthew 15:6, "And honour not his father nor his mother, he shall be free. Thus have ye made the commandment of God of none effect by your tradition." So you've lost the power, cuz' the commandment of God has got life in it. But if you null and void it, then all you've got is your tradition, and you can use your tradition to replace the truth, and if you do it little by little, over generations, after a while what you think is truth can be just total tradition, and then we go back to fussin' and cussin' "well we've always done it this way." Then we can say, well, we must be right, God shows up. Wait a minute! Aren't we the people that damn and condemn all those people that don't live right and dress right and God shows up in their meetings, and we say, that couldn't be God, look at the way they're dressed, look at the way they live, look at the what they do. So then apparently, the presence of God isn't proof of approval.

WORSHIP HAS A SEASON—NOW!

Does worship have a time frame? For everything there is a season. Apparently worship has got a season. It has a time frame. Worship is actually an attitude expressed in action; it is the motion of emotion. Worship is communicated affection and adoration between God and man; it cannot take place if God is absent. Worship always flows from the concept of God, that's why most churches are full of workers and lousy worshippers; because if your concept of God is low, your level of worship is also low.

It is impossible to approach God with a bad attitude. Thus, I defend the music, musicians, worship leader and all our praise singers that they are doing exactly what God wants done; because we come out of a day's activity and we must have a prelude to worship. You cannot approach God with a bad attitude; He won't give you an appointment. That's why you have to enter into His gates with thanksgiving and into His courts with praise. Be thankful and bless His name. You cannot bless God's name with your lips shut. We, according to Hebrews 13, are to offer up the calves of our lip, the sacrifice of praise; the fruit of our lips. But the Greek says, the "calves" of our lips. In other words, it's the sacrifice of praise. You can't sit there and say nothing. What you're doing is sentencing yourself to the inability to worship. You see, we western type people, we don't know beans about protocol; we think Christianity is American.

OUR DEMOCRACY CONCEPTS CONFLICT WITH GOD'S THEOCRACY

You got to get this. We're in a democracy that messes up our spiritual concepts, cuz' everybody has got rights and we vote on stuff, and who we don't like we throw them bums out. You won't do that with God; He's a ruling monarch. He is the universe's good dictator. Oh yes He is. He is the absolute ruler. He has absolute authority and absolute power. You do not go in the eastern countries, barge in and say, I need to see the king! Not hardly Jack, they'll cut your head off and mail it home. You don't barge in on those people; they have learned that there is a way to approach regality. There is a way to approach royalty! You don't just storm in and say, "Hey, my toilet is running and my roof is leaking, hey, fix it!" Yet we come to church sometimes with all kinds of attitudes and problems, I'm not talking about a bad attitude, I'm talkin' about just an attitude. We come with our family squabbles and kids dirty diapers, car ain't runnin' right, bank accounts runnin' low, got all these crazy attitudes; and we walk in like God is going to accept that puke because He's desperate.

GOD IS NOT DESPERATE

He's not desperate; He's got billions of angels right now worshipping Him around the clock. He's not hard up for praise and worship. You come in and don't get involved in song service, don't get involved with clapping, raising our hands, open our mouths, and have the audacity to say, well, I'm a word person. You're a nincompoop is what you are. You're not a word person, because the word won't find a place in our hearts unless there's some worship along with it. Unless there's some praise along with it.

We do have a scriptural commandment to enter His gates with thanksgiving and praise. You can't be thankful and keep an attitude. You may come with an attitude. I have come to church lots of times with attitudes, but if God would help me to get through some thanksgiving and praise, I finally get into a position where I can bless God! Sometimes you and I have to rise above all the crud and the garbage and it will not go away during an hour of service; but that doesn't matter. It doesn't have to go away; we just need to get close to Him, because He's the focus of our faith. He's the answer to our dilemma, He's the solution to our situation, He's what we need; but you can't just barge in on Him. That's why clapping and singing and praising God is imperative to the quality of our life and the quality of the service.

DON'T JUST SIT THERE—CREATE AN ATMOSPHERE

I guess what I am trying to say is, can you be saved from your praise and antics at this service? If this is your last service, how did you do? How would you rate it? Did you clap? Did you say hallelujah? Did you ask God for help? Did you repent? Could you go to hell or heaven from this service? It's important! Did you take advantage of the last service? Did the choir have to move you? Did the preacher have to ring the bell? I know you're tired, I know you're in pain; I'm tired, I'm in pain! But He's worthy! He's been good to us, He gave us a chance. We have a chance to make things right tonight! We got a chance to bless the Lord. You got your mind on tomorrow. What happens if you have an aneurism at eleven o clock tonight; you haven't got a tomorrow.

I'm trying to help you! Sit there with folded hands, crossed legs, nothing going on. Well, why don't you create something; you are a sanctuary! If He inhabits the praises of His people, why don't you praise! Why must you always be provoked! Why don't you provoke yourself? Why don't you stir up the gift that's in you now? Why must the choir move you? Why must the music and worship leader move you? Why must the preacher move you? Come to think of it, why does the Holy Ghost have to move us? Don't we have enough knowledge? Don't we have enough past experience? What's the matter with us? How did I do last Sunday?

Did I do okay...? See, we keep waiting for some magic something to make us become something. We're going to chase that rainbow until we're out of time.

IT'S GOD'S INITIATIVE THAT PROMPTS US

Don't you get it? When you and I come near God, if we have a desire, it is an indication that God has already given us that desire, cuz' we can't create that desire. It's what Psalm 42 says, deep calleth unto deep. What He's actually saying, is that the deep of God calls unto the deep of man, and causes the deep of man to respond back to the deep of God. So, unless God orchestrates it, and originates it, it can't happen. That means that if you have any kind of desire for the things of God, it shows you that God is working in your life. Everything in your life might not be right, but God is working! If you have any desire to be better than you are, closer to God than you are; God is working in you. Don't you get it? Jesus said, in John 15, "you didn't call Me, I called YOU, you didn't choose Me, I chose YOU!" Don't you get what He's saying? If you have any desire to worship, what He's actually saying, I've given you an invitation to come. Cuz' unless He invites, you can't come. Why? He's King! You can't barge in on Him. You only come by invite. That's why Esther was afraid to go in, I ain't been invited. Don't you get it?

THE PREREQUISITE IS PRAISE AND THANKSGIVING

Praise and thanksgiving is the prerequisite to get us into the presence of God. Now watch; worship is what we do once we are in His presence. You give thanks and you offer praise to get there, worship is your antics once you're there. Worship is my release and your release of our spirits to God. It is an exchange of an emotions experience. God does have emotion; He's on record about it. He loves, He cares, He groans, He grieves; He has emotion! When you worship God, when you're intimate with God when you're close to Him, He moves with His emotion towards you, and your emotion moves towards Him. It's intimacy, it's one on one!

Suppose there are two people that are in love with each other and they are, because of their job, or they are separated for whatever reason, you are absent from each other. Now watch; in the absence of each other's physical, visual presence, the love's not diminished, but the expressions are different. So in the absence, the fellow writes letters, sends roses, buys cards, sends a telegram, makes a call; they are expressions of love, but it is done in absence. When he lands and she's at the airport and he gets off the plane and he comes down the runway and he comes through the concourse and there is his baby. Now watch; he and she are embraced, they are hugged, hopefully, smooch. Okay? Wait a minute. Now, love is flowing, love is expressed in person; transcending cards, roses, candy, letters, telegrams, phone calls. They were all required, they were all preliminary; but now here is the real deal! When we give thanks and we offer praise, it's preliminary, and when He shows up and steps into this place, then the embrace! Then it's the kiss and the hug and I love you, and I missed you, and I need you, and you're precious, you're so sweet....

WORSHIP HAS A TIME FRAME: NOW!

Good intentions are poor substitutes for godly worship. It's like a promise that's never performed. My bible study was; does worship have a time factor. I gave you the answer when we read the scripture. Jesus said, John 23, the hour cometh, here it is, and NOW is the time to worship. Does worship have a time factor? Yes. When is it? NOW! Not when you FEEL like it. Not when you are in a better mood. He said, NOW! Worship is NOW. It's not later, it's NOW. Old time Pentecostals, we sang in the Swinford's church, "When we all get to heaven, what a day that will be." Remember that song? That's the problem. We got people sittin' on their pews, that that's their worship concept; they're saving it for when we all get to heaven.

I read a little line in a guys book I thought was just right; "to praise above, with the saints we love, oh what glory that will be, but to praise below with the saints we know, now that's another story." What a tragic thing we live in a generation that longs for the pearly gates, longs for the walls of jasper, longs for the streets of gold, longs for joining the saints there, the throng around God's throne; but while

THE WHY & WONDER OF WORSHIP • BOOK TWO

they're here, they're non-worshippers, and non-participators, and live in the folly and the dismal foolish counterfeit concept that for some reason when they get raptured, they're going to automatically become worshippers. If you don't worship here, you will NEVER worship there! If you are not excited here, you will never be excited there! If we are not in love with Jesus here, you will never be in love with Jesus there. You know what you are saying if you believe that, my worship is predicated on a good atmosphere. My bible tells me, NOW is the time of worship. That means, I can worship, anywhere, anytime, anyplace. I don't need this building, I don't need this music, I don't need a bugle, a trumpet or a tambourine. I can worship God in my mind, in my spirit, in my car, in my home; because He inhabits everything!

David said, "I'll bless the Lord at all times, His praises shall be continually be in my mouth." He said, "Oh magnify the Lord with me, and let us exalt His name together." There is a blessing in corporate worship, but when you went to work this morning and I was privileged to be home for a little while in the morning and I was praying; I didn't need you. I love you, I like worshipping with you, but I didn't need you. When I prayed tonight for the service; I worshipped. When I go to bed; worship. When I drive my car, I'll worship.

What a sad thing that we become Pentecostal procrastinators. I'm going to worship someday, I'm going to get with it someday. Like people who say, "I'm going to get saved; someday. Going to get the Holy Ghost; someday! I'm going to get my tithing record straightened out; someday. I'm going to get my morals fixed up; someday." What a terrible thing to say; I'm going to be a worshipper someday. Someday? Jesus, said, NOW, not someday. NOW!

Don't you get it? It's not the place. Jesus told the woman it's not the place, and it's not your past, it's Jesus as the object of our praise and thanksgiving. For everything there is a season and a purpose to every time under the heaven.

THE WHY & WONDER OF WORSHIP

VOLUME FOUR · CHAPTER THREE

THE WHY & WONDER OF WORSHIP • BOOK TWO

CHAPTER THREE

WORSHIP IS PART OF THE COSMIC SCHEME

Psalm 86:5-13, "For Thou, Lord, art good, and ready to forgive; and plenteous in mercy unto all them that call upon Thee. Give ear, O Lord, unto my prayer; and attend to the voice of my supplications. In the day of my trouble, I will call upon thee; for thou wilt answer me. Among the gods, there's none like unto thee, O Lord; neither are there any works like unto thy works. All nations whom thou hast made shall come and worship before thee, O Lord; and shall glorify thy name. For thou art great, and doest wondrous things: thou art God alone. Teach me thy way, O Lord; I will walk in thy truth: unite my heart to fear thy name. I will praise thee, O Lord, my God, with all my heart; and I will glorify thy name for evermore. For great is thy mercy toward me: and thou hast delivered my soul from the lowest hell."

Daniel 4:34, "And at the end of the days I Nebuchadnezzar lifted up mine eyes unto heaven, and mine understanding returned unto me, and I blessed the most High, and I praised and hounored Him that liveth forever, whose dominion is an everlasting dominion, and His kingdom is from generation to generation: and all the inhabitants of the earth are reputed as nothing: and He doeth according to His will in the army of heaven, and among the inhabitants of the earth: and none can stay His hand, or say unto him, What doest thou?"

One thing we need to understand is that worship is involved in the total cosmic scheme. There is a scheme in the universe, in the cosmic order of things, and worship plays an integral part. It has much more to do with it than you and I going "Hallelujah." Worship involves the entire cosmic scheme, and the reason why God is so adamant about us learning how to worship Him, is that when we worship truly, as John says in John 4:22-24, that "God is Spirit, and they that worship Him must worship Him in spirit and truth, for the Father seeketh such to worship Him." The one thing God is looking for is a worshipper who will worship with his human spirit, (which is the sanctuary of God), and "in truth", which means you cannot worship God with a bad attitude, or duplicity of agenda.

Because man fell, man has a depraved nature, and though he's depraved, he still reaches for the Eternal, for the unchanging, for the solid, for the perfect, for the Everlasting, and he doesn't know how to find it. So, God, in His kindness, according to Psalm 42:7, David says, "deep calleth unto deep at the noise of thy waterspouts." What he's actually saying is, the deep of God calls to the deep of man, so we can understand that worship originates with God, and it moves to us, and touches us in the deepest part of our fiber, regenerates us, creates desire in us, and then we respond to Him. It's like a full cycle. Worship is God's idea, because prior to chaos, prior to rebellion, and usurping of Lucifer, the entire universe lived in harmony. God is a God of balance, and order and harmony. Everything is synchronized; everything is in its place, and everything has its place. Nothing is out of kilter; nothing is out of order. God is a God of balance, because God is total perfection. There aren't any areas of God, or His creation, that don't work.

You have to understand that the universe is smaller than God. Come on, just think for a minute; all these science things you see in the National Geographic, and all this star stuff, and these galaxies, and these billions of stars that they find in this little hole here, God extends past that because the universe is contained in Him.

WORSHIP: A CURE FOR THE ACHE

If a certain factor in your body, or my body, starts to misbehave, it really messes with us. From an ingrown toenail, to a scab on your elbow; to a toothache, a backache, a leg ache the ache will get your attention. You will not say to it, "I will not let you bother me, tooth", and go on your way. You're crazy! Now what you can do is, maybe, numb it. You'll either take medicine or booze, and just try to numb it. That's why beer saloons, that's why honkey tonks try to numb it. Numb what? The ache! You reach for the wrong stuff: drugs, immorality, entertainment, whatever, when you don't know where the ache is, or what's causing it. You just know there's an ache! That's why man is always reaching, 'cause he knows something is wrong, but he doesn't understand what is wrong. Now you have enough sense to understand when there's something wrong in your very physical frame, or nothing is wrong in your physical frame, but something is out of kilter in your emotional make up. You can be perfectly physically fit, and be going through an emotional trauma, a pressure cooker. The kids could be in trouble; your loved ones are going through a divorce situation, or there's been a baby lost or a loved one; or whatever pressure it is. I don't care how healthy your physical frame is, you are not just physical. We are emotional, we are spiritual; we have a soulish realm. And so what we do is we become acutely aware of the disparity here.

Well, God, who created the universe, so that He contains the universe, ended up with an insurrection, (with the rebellion by Lucifer), now inside of Him, something ain't working right. Every time His heart beats, this thing says "wrong, wrong; insult to Your majesty." Problem, deteriorating, 'cause nothing of God deteriorates, but now, something is deteriorating. Nothing of God dies, but something is dying. Nothing of God disobeys, but something is acting in rebellion. It causes His attention and focus. So, God offers to the human species the gift of worship, because worship is one of the keys that God gives to us to get us back in sync with the cosmic order. So that we, on earth, start saying the stuff they say in heaven: "Holy, Holy, Holy is the Lord God Almighty. The earth is full of His glory." We begin to say what the writer of Psalms said, "Thou art great, and there's none like You", and "nothing is impossible to You", and "You are my God, and I am Your servant", and I'll put You in Your roll, and I'll stay in my roll, and when that happens, there is harmony, even if you're forced to go through hell!

WORSHIP HARMONIZES AND CHANGES

So, point number one: worship harmonizes the creature with the cosmic scheme of things. Worship is an imperative to our life because it puts God at the center, and us next. It proclaims, as the writer of Psalm 86, that the Lord is the Creator and Sustainer of all things. Thus, by our worship, we allow a Creator/creature harmony. So I don't have to be taken out of things. I don't have to live my life trying to escape problems. If I am in harmony with God, what can harm me? Worship is the part of the Divine plan that allows us into His process...of what? Change. Now this is interesting: prior chaos, worship was for the magnifying and exalting of God, not for change, because the angels were perfect, and so was their object. The atmosphere was perfect. Nothing was deteriorating. Nothing could get better. When you are in God, you can't get better! Now wait a minute. I'm talking "pre- chaos", but when chaos came, God let worship come down to the fallen race, not just to magnify Him like "pre-chaos", but now He allows worship to be the key element in the process of change for the worshipper.

Sin and God are incompatible, and we got a problem, because God swears, by Himself, I can't change. Well, guess whose going to change! And you can't, and I can't just change because we "gots" to, and we "s'pose to", and we "wants to". Something has got to be provided for us beyond the mess that we're in from another arena, to step down into our chaos, and let us step into a process whereby we can contact another Energy Source that will let us be in a change mode. Don't you get it? Worship is the key that God gives to us so we can change, that we might be harmonious with the cosmic order. What am I saying? So that we say what heaven says about God. What kind of city would you live in if 100,000 people in Gainesville all said "Holy, Holy, Holy is the Lord. The Lord is Righteous and worthy of all praise, and He's my God, and I'm His servant, and I won't do anything against Him nor His kids." Look out! Don't you get it? It's the wonder of worship, that worship is one of God's tools to change me.

WORSHIP IS DESIGNED TO CHANGE US

I'm not trying to be unkind; I'm trying to be honest because there's a lot of people, I'm sure, preaching on TV or radio who are honest people. I'm not smacking at that. I'm smacking at the charlatans, at the jokers; at the people who play the "name it and claim it" and "grab it and blab it" game. Those people who are trying to let their praise twist God's arm to make Him obey their sensual desires: "Give me my VW with a new Mercedes engine in it"; "Give me my castle on the side of a hill"; "I've got some scriptures here, now You obey me." What an insult! What a tragedy! Because worship was never designed to get God to work for me. Worship was designed to get me to become like Him, and that way, He can work through me. He don't have to work for me, He can work through me. Worship works for me. Worship helps me step into the process of change so I start becoming like the One I worship. According to Paul's writing in the epistle of

2 Corinthians Chapter 3, we are changed into that image as "from glory to glory". As what? "...As we behold" the One that we worship. You become what you behold! That's why watching TV a lot is dangerous. That's why listening to crazy stuff is dangerous. That's why sitting next to a critic is crazy. Don't sit in a church service next to a critic, or someone who talks all the time while the service is going on. Be polite, and say, "Shut your nasty mouth" and then move! Say, "God's fixing to kill you and probably everyone on this row. I'm going on the next row." You think I'm kidding you, but God don't mess with people who are critics, and disinterested people in a service.

WORSHIP TRANSFORMS THE WORSHIPPER

Worship has one great factor to it. You've got to get this: Worship always is creative. That's the key to all worship. Worship is designed by God, 'cause He invented worship. Angels didn't invent worship, God invented worship. He let them play. Worship has, at its heart, one aim: creative. Creative what? Transform the worshipper. Don't you get it? The purpose of worship is the transformation and the transfiguration of the creature. How many people want to get like God? Learn to worship! You'll never get like God just by studying the book and quoting the scripture. You get like God when you get into His Presence, and you behold how awesome He is, and how needless we are, and how great His Grace is that He lets us approach, and as we behold Him, we become like Him. It really happens! In worship, something in me dies, and something of Him is born. There's an impartation in worship. He deposits in me another part of His Essence, and subtracts from me another part of mine. It's the great exchange. That's why the devil fights worship.

When we worship, what we actually do is we elevate God to His rightful place, and we put us in our rightful place...submission. Mark 5: 5-7, "and always, night and day, he was in the mountains, and in the tombs..." (talking about the mad man of Gadara, the demon possessed man with a legion of devils, wears no clothes; the original streaker, living in a cemetery), crying, and cutting himself with stones." Now when you don't have worship, you're in self-annihilation. You may not be cutting yourself with stones, but you're cutting yourself. And you're wailing during the night, and you're unfulfilled. And when you're unfulfilled, you fill your life, and I fill my life, with substitutes that will stick for the moment, but you wake up in the morning like the hungry dreamer of Isaiah 29:8, who said, "I still hunger and I still thirst."

Oh yeah, we might as well be honest. Did you ever get a craving, and you know what you do? You take a trip. " I'm going to Epcot, I'm going to Disney World, I'm going skiing, I'm going scuba diving, I'm going..." whatever! Fine! That's okay. There's nothing wrong with trying to enjoy yourself and having a little bit of fun, but you come back, you're still searching. Sometimes, that craving was a call from God to come near. In order to come near, you got to lay stuff down; you got to interrupt your schedule; you got to change; you got to make priority changes, and you got to give Him pre-eminence, and that old stinking flesh says, "naw...just get in the car and go for a ride." You don't have a virgin voice here. I'm talking as one who knows! I've made that mistake so many times. Years ago, when I had more money, I'd get an itch in my spirit, I'd buy something. Either it would be a trick, or a puppet, or I'd buy an old car. I'd just buy something. And I'd polish that "dude" until I finally realized it was still itching! Then I'd sell that "dude".

Mark 5:6, "But when he saw Jesus afar off, he ran and worshipped Him". How many times has the church heard me say this statement, "your vision is your victory"? When he saw Jesus, he stopped doing what he was doing, and ran towards Him, because he perceived that there was some help there. Isn't it amazing, a demon possessed man, with a legion of devils, could run to Jesus, and there's people here that don't have devils that can't move! Now something's crazy! I think that guy was desperate, and we're not! I think he was weary of living the way he was, but we've gotten used to living the way we are. We can do that even "being saved". We can live at a level of Salvation, we go no further. Comfortable right here! I still think God is always saying, "Come on, come on, come on, come on". Get it with me...cosmic order. Restoration of cosmic order. Symmetry, balance; equal balance. So God says, "The only thing they need is not their sins being removed, it's worship.

WE NEED TO SEE HIM TO WORSHIP

They'll never worship if they don't see Me. They'll only make noise if they have religion. Now, if they see Me, give them room. They won't need the ukulele, and they won't need the saxophone, and they won't need the choir and they won't need Brother Arnold, and they won't need nothing, if they see Me. Now if they don't see Me, we need to use these other things to try to help them where they can get to see Me." Everything in this service ought to be directed towards us getting to see Him somehow in our minds. You may not see Jesus with your natural eyes, and you may. I read lots of books where I personally think they're "nin-com-poops." They say nobody ever sees Jesus anymore. I don't know whatever gave them the right to say that. They're speaking for God, and God is good enough to speak for Himself. I read a book the other day that says nobody ever has these miracles anymore. That's so stupid! Don't read those kinds of books. Let me read them, because I write in those books "this man needs to be shot"; "this man needs to cut his arm off, rip his tongue out, and he's so stupid. Somebody needs to break his fingers; he's writing poison to all kinds of crazy people." You know why he's saying that? You can't have what I haven't got. Now if God would fill him with the Holy Ghost, talking in tongues, and the fire of God and the Baptism that God talked about, he'd jump up and down and say "you know, this stuff is real!" But being that he ain't got it; he graduated from some "cemetery" somewhere, he turns around and tells everybody else, "you can't have it 'cause". Cause what? "Well, because I ain't got it". That's like walking up to someone who got healed by the miraculous power of God that you usually can't explain how it happened...God just did it...and then try to tell him, "you know, God doesn't heal." Well, you've come too late to tell me. I was already sick, and the Lord healed me! That's like people telling you can't get the Holy Ghost. You've come too late to tell me. What do you want me to do, give it back? I already got it!

OUR PROBLEM IS VISION—NOT EMOTION

Mark 5:7, "And cried with a loud voice, and said, What have I to do with thee, Jesus, thou Son of the most high God?" Now the Gadarene is using his vocal chords, but it's not him speaking. It's the spirits in him speaking. Now watch this...even though they are fallen, evil anti-God spirits, even they worship when they get in His presence! Isn't that funny? A devil, who is God's enemy, is so awed by how awesome and great God is; even he will take a role of submission and worship. So then, apparently, our problem with worship is not emotion, its vision.

Vs: 5, "always, night and day, he was in the mountains, and in the tombs, crying, and cutting himself with stones. (6) But when he saw Jesus from afar off, he ran and worshipped him." He ran and worshipped him. You know what he just did? He said "I know I'm out of "sync" with the cosmic order, but I know how powerful you are and I'm willing to get back in order.

DON'T USE WORSHIP TO ESCAPE

Let me try it again: pre-chaos...worship is for the magnifying and exaltation of God only. After chaos, worship is two-fold. 1) to bring the creature back into relationship with God; to bring harmony to the chaotic cosmic order. 2) devils use worship in a fear mode to keep from being punished. They have no intention on serving the One they're worshipping. They're only using their worship to escape. Sounds like TV...sounds like modern Christianity, using thanks and praise and worship to escape from a situation, rather than subject myself in a role of submission to His perfect will. These devils worshipped God, but they worshipped for an inferior reason: don't torment us. I'll worship You if You let me off the hook. Now let's see if we're worshipping to restore the cosmic order, or do we worship so that God will get us out of our fix and off the hook. Because, if we're doing that, our partners are devils! The end of this thing is when these devils finished giving their plea; worship will move God to move. Watch! Even if it's for the wrong reason. That's why there are lots of people under the banner of so-called Christianity that are having a move of God, and a demonstration of God, but it's under the banner of the wrong reason. And they're reading into that move as approval. It's actually Divine deception! We've always been taught that if you don't have your criteria right and your attitude right that God isn't going to hear you. I think not! The only thing we have is in Psalms, where David said, "If

I consider iniquity in my heart, the Lord will not hear me". If I'm going to practice lawlessness, and ungodliness, in my approach, then God won't hear me.

But I can come to God with an honest effort that I want escape, and I want out, I want blessings, and I don't intend on doing the other stuff. God will say, "I'll deal with this aspect right here, because I'll respond to worship, even if your attitude is going to use My power for the wrong thing." That answers, at least to me, the dilemma of how can God move in these auditoriums and coliseums with tens of thousands of people, and these dirt-bags have the morals of a roach, and couldn't tell the truth standing on a bible, looking at Jesus. How does God show up? He's the Responder of worship! The scary part is you need to know what is the criteria of your worship. What is the aim of your worship? Is it to bring you back into harmony with God? God can't be fooled. He looks in your heart and my heart and says, "if your only reason is to get Me to move, fine! I'm so good I'll move for you, but you're going to be deceived, and you're going to read into that My approval. And it ain't My approval! I'm just good!" (I've opened a can of worms here now, haven't I? Good stuff to use for fishing).

BECOME BLENDED INTO GOD'S PURPOSE

Has anybody ever heard of the word "homogenized?" They used to teach us those words as kids; homogenized...pasteurized. I got to looking up the words "homogenized" and "homogenization". I realize this may not sound spiritual, but it really is. "Homogenized," or "homogenization," is the process whereby the manufacturer makes every particle the same size, so that it blends together smoothly. Three or four examples that they gave was cosmetics, baby food, peanut butter or milk. I want you to get this because this is neat...homogenization is the process whereby all the particles are reduced or increased to the same particular size so it flows smoothly, blending. Now watch. As we worship God, we are homogenized into God's whole purpose, so that we are reduced or enlarged to meet the blending need of His program. We become uniform with God's purpose, thus through worship, there comes a blending of heavenly things with earthly things, so we see the same thing, speak the same thing and live the same way.

GOD'S WORDS CONTINUE ON

John 17:20-23, "Neither pray I for these alone, but for them also which shall believe on Me through their word." How in the world could you be lost? Jesus prayed for you! And If I understand that Jesus was God incarnate, then His prayer cannot die, His words never cease. They keep going and continuing...abiding word, so His word is still speaking. Your words and my words go phfftt-its over! Why? 'Cause they have human origin. He's got Divine origin. "I speak, speak, speak, speak..." It just keeps going out there. That's why the universe right now, according to scientists and brilliant minds now in 1996 have gone on record in saying "we just discovered something. The universe is still expanding" No kidding!! How did that happen? "Well, we found a book that said in the beginning, God said." And when God spoke and said, "Let there be light," it just keeps going. This whole thing is expanding.

See, it's hard for us to grasp, because we are creatures of time and matter and we have beginning and end. You deal with God, unfortunately for us, or fortunately, however you see it, He has no beginning and has no end, so when He speaks, it just keeps going. His words just keep moving through the whole universe. You say, awh come on, it's got to stop somewhere. No it don't. The only way it stops is when He says, "Come back". Don't you get it...when God speaks, He's creative energy, and when He speaks, wherever His energy finds something that's anti His energy, it bows, and His energy keeps moving! That's hard for our little minds to comprehend, but I can believe things I can't comprehend.

Too many of you folks are saying, "manna". You know what "manna" is? Israel said "manna"..."what is it?" Well, I ain't going to stop eating 'cause I can't figure out what it is! Pick up the bread, put some jelly on it and let's hoof it! What are you eating? "Manna" what is it? "I don't know...tastes good. Let's keep going." There's a whole bunch of things in life you can't explain, especially spiritual things. Man, I'm going to eat the bread; I'm going to drink the water; I'm going to enjoy the presence of God. I can't explain a lot of stuff. Let God be God and every man a liar!

HOMOGENIZED TO BE USED

Vs 21, "That they all may be one as thou. Father, art in me and I in thee" That was Jesus' prayer, that we might be (here it is) homogenized! One! Not big lump, little lump. All the same lumps. Homogenized, processed, until there is a blending into the purpose. What made Jesus so powerful? It wasn't just because He was God in the flesh. He had a human will. He bent and subjected His human will to the Divine will of the Father, so that He was a moving homogenization process...." I do always those things that please My Father." "I don't speak what I want to speak. The words I speak are the words I heard My Father tell me, and what He told Me, I speak. What I've seen in the Spirit, I act out in the flesh. We're one, and I pray for my church, My believers to be the same way." Homogenized...reduced or expanded to the same level in the process. Conversion; momentary. Process; lifelong.

THE PROCESS ISN'T PAINFUL—IT'S POWERFUL

Vs 21, "that they all may be one as thou, Father, art in me, and I in thee". Now He told you how He wants the oneness. He said, "Here's how I want them to be homogenized. Just like we are. I am in You, and You are in Me. I want them to be the same way. I want them to be the same way. I want the Divine to inhabit them, and I want humanity to lay hold of Divinity, the same way." He prayed all night; we pray 15 minutes. Lumpy! Chunky! Big curds! Prayer ain't working for me. If you stay at it long enough, it will! You say, "Well, I've prayed 20 or 30 minutes." Great! Maybe you need to pray another 30 minutes. Maybe a couple of hours, maybe all night. What does it matter what it costs you if you break through and all of a sudden you get into the process? He said, over in the book of Hebrews, when He was coming in incarnation, He said "I come to do Thy will, O God", then in one place He said, "I delight to do Thy will". The process isn't painful to me, because I'm involved in the cosmic order, therefore I submit to the process, and the process now is powerful to me, rather than painful to me. I don't have to meet this particular need that I never met before and have to go into some deep moaning and groaning prayer meeting. I'm in the process all the time, so it doesn't matter whether I need a great thing or a little thing; I'm able to deal with it.

THE PURPOSE—SO THE WORLD BELIEVES

"That they also may be one in us: that the world may believe that Thou hast sent Me." There's the purpose of homogenization. Not so that we have a great church; so that the world will believe that Jesus has come in the flesh, and we've submitted our lives to His Lordship. That's what the bottom line is. We're wanting the Holy Ghost to blow over the whole world, and God is not going to do that. He has chosen to work through His body. We're wanting God to do stuff for us, and God has told us, "I hold you responsible. You do it." Isn't it funny that the Lord, in all His miracles, signs and wonders, He never prayed for the sick. Can't find one instance where He ever prayed for the sick. He just spoke to it, because He was in the process. We are one. What I say, you say. What you say, I say. That's why we're not even supposed to pray about a lot of things. We're supposed to speak to them. We're supposed to command them. The reason why our commands are kind of shaky is because our homogenization is kind of lumpy! I didn't say "you," I said "we."

GOD'S DESIRE: THAT WE BE ONE WITH HIM

Vs 22, "And the glory which Thou gavest Me I have given them; that they may be one, even as we are one." There you go. That's the desire of God that we could be one. Why? If God had total control of my life, no area out of order, God could go "Yeh"..., and I'd say "yes," and I think that that's really in all of our hearts. We really want to be religious robots for Jesus. Just put it in there. I've prayed for years, "God, just override my bad circuitry," and God says, "Naw, I don't work with no taped ends. I ain't going to go in and solder you." You know why? 'Cause the Lord knows if He uses us, and we have all this crud, lumps and garbage and stuff in us, we don't think we will, but after a while, we'll pose for our picture. Come and hear the Jeff Arnold ministry.

THE WHY & WONDER OF WORSHIP • BOOK TWO

WORSHIP IS GOD'S GIFT—USE IT

Worship is God's gift to us to create in you and me a desire to want to please God. We often refer to David as the man after God's own heart, and yet, I don't know if we understand the fullness of what David said when he said, "thy statutes have become my songs in the days of my pilgrimage." He actually said, "Thy mandates are my music." I tune my life to Your tune, and every time I'm homogenized, power flows. In worship, we are given the privilege to blend, and to conform and to unite with God's nature. In worship, we become one with God, in Spirit, in purpose, in will, in works. Are you understanding what I'm saying? Worship is the universal work. Everything in the universe worships God. According to Job 38:4-7, when the sons of God saw the tremendous demonstration and majesty of God, the Bible said that they expressed joy and worshipped God for His tremendous demonstration of His holiness and His righteousness and His creative power.

Isaiah 6:1-6, the year Kind Uzziah died, Isaiah was caught up and saw the Lord high and lifted up, and was overwhelmed, and just kind of blown away with the majesty of God and the great worship service going on there. That's a powerful sermon. You can affect people around you who are not right if you'll get up to worshipping God for yourself. That worship service put him under conviction. It brought him to a place of confession. It brought him to a place of cleansing, and it took him to a place of Divine commission. All from a worship service. Why? Because everything around the throne was homogenized with the Power and Presence on the throne...the Lord is great...the Lord is holy...the Lord is wonderful...the Lord is awesome...the Lord is full of majesty. You get every one around agreeing with everything that's on the throne, and the sinner ain't going to sit there and go "nice service." They're either going to get in or out. They won't stay neutral.

YOUR VISION IS YOUR VICTORY

In Chapters 4 and 5 of the book of Revelations, the Bible tells us the 24 elders fell down and worshipped God, and the 5 living creatures fall down and worship God.

Revelation 5:9, "and they sung a new song saying, Thou art worthy to take the book, and to open the seals thereof; for thou wast slain, and hast redeemed us to God by thy blood out of every kindred, and tongue, and people and nation; and hast made us unto our God kings and priests; and we shall reign on the earth. And I beheld, and I heard the voice of many angels round about the throne..." now, notice what you got here. You got the redeemed worshipping, now you got angels joining in, "...and the beasts and the elders...," now you got the elders, and you got the 4 beasts. 24 elders and 4 beasts, and they catch onto it. "...and the number of them was ten thousand times ten thousand, and thousands of thousands." That's a hundred million. See, when you start doing this, Hallelujah, you join that crew, 'cause they rest day nor night. That's been going on ever since creation. See, we start a worship service. They don't ever stop a worship service. You know why? Because they keep having a vision of the majesty of God and the greatness of God and they're in the presence of God constantly, and they can't do nothing except boast on Him and bless Him and eulogize Him, exalt Him and magnify Him. Your vision is your victory. That's why life tries to get you looking at everything else. You're here and you got cancer, TB, you get this, incurable, can't operate. Whose report will you believe?

WORSHIP REQUIRES ACTION

Vs 12, "Saying with a loud voice"...worship is noisy. Now wait a minute. It doesn't mean worship cannot be in silence, because you worship from your spirit. But worship is noisy; worship is physical; worship is demonstrative; worship is emotional. Watch! Here's what we are: We're a tri-part being. We're not a trinity, there's no such thing. We are body, soul, spirit. The spirit of man is the place of the sanctuary. It is the place that God redeems and regenerates. He doesn't redeem your body; He doesn't redeem your soul; He redeems your spirit. He regenerates your spirit. Now watch! It's the deepest part of your being. You worship God, according to John 4 in spirit...small "s"...that's human spirit. That's not Holy Spirit...small "s"...human spirit. In order to worship God in the human spirit, for it to come out, it must pass through 2 factors: soul, body. If anything explodes in your spirit, it's going to affect your soul. Your soul is your emotional realm. Usually, if your emotional realm gets activated, the physical realm will act up. Now you may not "boogaloo" or do the "watusi" down the hallway, but you may cry; your lip may quiver; you may say "amen, hallelujah," you may shake your hair, but you will do something! One of the words given in Greek for worship is to bow forward and kiss the hand. It's an act of awe, surprise and adoration. It's an affection toward majesty and greatness.

WORSHIP IS ABOUT JESUS!

Rev 5:12, "Saying with a loud voice, worthy is the Lamb that was slain to receive power..." see, worship ain't about us. Worship has to do with the proper object. Worship is about Jesus! It's bragging on Jesus! It's blessing Jesus! It's magnifying Jesus! "...riches, and wisdom, and strength and honour, and glory, and blessing. And every creature which is in heaven, and on the earth..." did he say every? "...and under the earth." There's only 3 spheres in the entire universe that we know about. In the heavens, in the earth and under the earth. "...and such as are in the sea..." and in the sea! "...and all that are in them heard I saying..." wait a minute! I heard everything in the heavens, in the earth, under the earth, and in the sea. I heard them. Now, how can you worship silent? Blessing and honour, and glory and power, be unto him that sitteth upon the throne, and "...unto the Lamb forever and ever."

Don't you get it? Worship is the restoration of the cosmic order. You don't worship good here, you'll be very uncomfortable there. In fact, you probably won't even be there! Because that whole place is taken up with worship. Not ball games; not old cars; not taken up with antiques, it's not taken up with CD's; it's not taken up with your other suit; it's not taken up with your favorite team. It's taken up with HIM. You say, "ain't you going to' get tired of that?" Have you ever been tired of the presence of God? I've never been tired of the presence of God! I get tired of me and my stupidity, but I don't get tired of God!

ALL THINGS WERE CREATED FOR WORSHIP

Now I'm going to step out where I've never seen anybody step. I'm going to prove to you, by the next 4 scriptures, that even inanimate objects offer a form of worship to their Creator. Inanimate objects applaud the Almighty in their own way. According to 1 Chronicles 16:31, "Let the heavens be glad..." Inanimate object! Atmosphere! Let an inanimate object, called the heavens, show emotion. "...and let the earth rejoice...." The earth? It's dirt! It's gas...it's chemicals...it's oxygen...it's iron ore. It's inanimate. It rejoiced. The word "rejoice" means to jump or leap up and down. Act crazy! A whole lot of shaking going on. "...and let men say among the nations the LORD reigneth." Then let the MAN say something. Now we can respond to that one...oh yeah, that's us. Uh Uh, we're the only creatures that worship by choice. The others worship because they understand how great God is. "...let the sea roar..." wait a minute! The sea? Seems inanimate to me. It ain't like us. The fields rejoice.... Yet, apparently, when it roars, it's saying, "You're alright!" "...and the fullness thereof." Let the grass? The pastures? The weeds? The flowers? The roses? Let all of nature just act up and say, "Great job?"

"...and all that is therein. Then shall the trees of the woods sing out..." Trees singing? You've never heard a weeping willow? You never had a pine praise? They even give wave offerings! Did you ever see how a pine gives a wave offering? When the wind blows. We got wind. Come on wind...blow on me a little bit. I need to give You a wave offering. Vs 33, "then shall the trees of the woods sing out at the presence of the LORD, because He cometh to judge the earth." Now notice how it happens, and what I've taught you all these weeks. Worship has to be with the presence of God, and even nature, itself, can't fulfill what it's supposed to do until the presence of God shows up.

Psalm 165:13, "The fields rejoice, the trees sing, the pastures and the valleys shout for joy."
Psalm 98:8, "Let the floods clap their hands and let the hills be joyful unto the Lord."
Psalm 69:34, "Let the heavens and the earth and the sea and everything thereof bless God."

Nature, in its own wonderful way, glorifies and applauds its Creator. It honors God with its worship. According to Jesus, in Luke 19, if you don't praise God, the stones will. Now, people have thought that was stupid. Not according to all these scriptures. Apparently, nature can respond to God if the highest creation won't.

THE WHY & WONDER OF WORSHIP • BOOK TWO

THE WHY & WONDER OF WORSHIP

VOLUME FOUR • CHAPTER FOUR

THE WHY & WONDER OF WORSHIP · BOOK TWO

CHAPTER FOUR

Matthew 15: Verse 7, "Ye Hypocrites." Was it something I said? That's what the book says. "Ye Hypocrites, well did Esaias prophesy of you saying, this people draweth nigh unto me with their mouth, honoureth me with their lips; but their heart is far from me." Lots of talk, no walk. "But in vain they do worship me." They do worship me, but in vain. They worship, and they do have the proper object. I am the proper object. So apparently, there is more involved than worship and the proper object. There must be a proper attitude of the worshipper.

THE RIGHT APPROACH IS ESSENTIAL

Contrary to popular opinion, and a lack of protocol in the American concept, we think we can barge in on anybody we want. "Hey you, I want to talk to you." Not so with God. You will approach God properly or He will lock you out. Believe me. As much as God is love, He will not have some smart aleck just run in and say "Hey you." Not hardly. He's the King and Monarch of the universe. There is a way to approach God properly. And it transcends wordeology. It has to do with attitude and what you plan on doing after you've worshipped.

He said, "For in vain they do worship me" and here's where their vanity came from: "teaching for doctrines the commandments of men." They have traded the truths of God to be one of the boys. They have lost the Savior trying to slide into the system.

I've never heard this taught before and it's impacted my life. I just feel like we are going in the right direction and that we can, if we can reach this place of worship, it will handle so many problems. It will take care of so many things. It will not be this cheap, TV, Charismatic cowboy fix, where you name it and claim it and you blab it and grab it, and somehow God is on the throne to fix your crud. That is an insult. That is not what worship is all about. Worship is a surrendering and giving of myself to Him, and to His design, and His purpose, and His desire. It has nothing to do with petitioning.

Verse 6 of Hosea, Chapter 4: "My people are destroyed for the lack of knowledge." Proverbs 29 says, "Where there is no vision, the people perish."

Luke 19 Verse 35-40, "And they brought him to Jesus..." this is the donkey, "...and they cast their garments upon the colt, and they set Jesus thereon. And as he went, they spread their clothes in the way. And when he was come nigh, even now at the decent of the mount of Olives, the whole multitude of the disciples began to rejoice and praise God with a loud voice for all the mighty works that they had seen; Saying, Blessed be the King who cometh in the name of the Lord: peace in heaven, and glory in the highest. And some of the Pharisees from among the multitude." There's always somebody among you not interested in the program. You can't let the nincompoops stop you. You got to understand something. They had God incarnate coming down the hill on a donkey and they were unmoved to worship. How much less, when we don't have God incarnate per se, coming down on a donkey. And we try to exalt God and magnify God cause' we've become the house of God. If there's lots of people around you who say I'm not into worship, don't get insulted. Don't get stymied and stopped because somebody on you pew is clipping their fingernails. Their relatives are in the Bible.

"And some of the Pharisees from among the multitude said unto him, Master, rebuke thy disciples..." tell them to cut it out, "...And he answered and said unto them, I tell you, that if they should hold their peace, the stones would immediately cry out."

The last chapter, I was handling the subject of worship, as far as worship helps us harmonize with the cosmic order. Because the order of the cosmos is the worship of God, and the adoration of the Lord. And I believe that the last point I made was about homogenizing. The process whereby all parts kinda become similar in size so it can be taken care of, and there's a blending. When we worship there is a blending of heavenly things with earthly things.

I finished with different scriptures showing you that the heavens are glad and the forest rejoices and the floods clap their hands. And the heavens and the earth rejoice. And everything that hath breath praise God so that even nature itself, in its own way, is a worshipper and a blesser of God.

ELEVATE YOUR CONCEPT OF GOD

What I am trying to help you and I with, is to elevate our concept of God. That's all I'm trying to do. And, all the rest of this stuff is superfluous if you do not grasp a fresh vision and an awesome splendor and wonder of how great God is. It is God's greatness that will move you to be a worshipper.

It is God's majesty and God's greatness that will help you and I try to live godly. You cannot legislate holiness. Now I can legislate dress codes, and standards, and behavior patterns; but I can't enforce them. And if you and I need enforcing it is because we have yet to be illuminated with how awesome He is. Because when you get a glimpse of Him, you realize that He doesn't need you, that He is self-sufficient. He is the self-proclaimed I AM. He literally is the Jehovah, the one who is always becoming.

I like that statement when Moses wanted to know who should I tell Pharaoh. You know what it's like? You know what God said? "If I took time to tell you who I am you'd never finish telling him. You'd run out of commentaries. Let me simplify it for you Mo; just tell them I AM THAT I AM. Cuz if I go into detail about what I am, the universe can't hold it." And our problem is because we have small thinking. We put God in this cubical and just say well God, He's there for Sunday, and He's there for when I have a funeral, and He's there for a wedding, and for my birthday, and when I'm in trouble or I got cancer or a sick headache.

But if we could understand that, we are already in God. That God fills the entire universe. He may not be manifesting Himself where you're sitting but you are in Him. For the Bible says in Him we live and move and have our being. That's why the sinner can't hide. Because by the time you get to your destination God's been putting nickels in the meter, waiting for you to park you carcass. When they landed on the moon and said, "Here we are," He says 'been waiting for you." If they ever get on the other side of a black hole, God will be standing there going

"What took you so long?" See, God doesn't have to go anywhere; He is everywhere.

And so we have to lift our sights and behold how majestic God really is, how awesome God is. And so that God doesn't become a sugar daddy and a fix it man for us. And that's what I think is a great danger that I see happening across the canvas of Christianity; God is somehow now been painted on the canvas of peoples' minds as Jesus the fix it guy. That you just name some scriptures and you put God in a hammerlock, and you make Him obey. And He just has got to do it because "I believe." And there's a scripture here and I'll just nail myself to it.

Well, that's nice, but we do look through a glass darkly. And even as we walk with God, we start to elevate our concept as God illuminates us. We begin to look back over our shoulder and say "Boy I thought I knew something then." Scripture didn't change and God didn't change, we changed because light expanded.

WORSHIP IS A CELEBRATION

Worship. Worship is the celebration of God. It is the ovation of the supreme object. Being that God is the paragon of excellence and wonder (Psalm 95:3), that He is totally great, that He is unique and separate and above all others. He is the source, and the substance, and sustainer of all things. He is the epitome of all goodness and virtue. He is perfect in every way. He is powerful to the point of being measureless in His power. He knows everything. He is changeless. He is always at His best, totally glorious, always gracious, superbly excellent.

The more we study and learn about God, the more overwhelmed we become. The more overwhelmed we become, the more we will act up. Exposure to the Eternal will always cause an expression. You cannot be exposed to God in His majesty, and grace, and love, and kindness, and mercy, and forgiveness, and stay expressionless.

There's something that happens when you and I all of a sudden behold Him. I'm not talking about with your natural eye. I mean with your mind, with the eye of faith, with your emotions, with your heart, with your feelings. Something happens because there's something within you that desires to be expressed outside you. I'm not trying to make everybody Pentecostal clones. I'm not trying to make everybody boogaloo, and shout, and jamboree, and run the aisles like everybody does. That would be phony. But what I am saying is, there is a place for that in the body. And that if you do not express your wonder towards God, there is one of two things wrong. You have no wonder, or you have wonder, but you're full of peer fear.

WORSHIP IS ABOUT DIGNITY AND MERIT

I'm teaching the words involved with worship. And I'm only going to deal with two of them. Worship is concerned with the dignity & merit, and the worth of the person or thing worshipped. I feel like the devil has beat a lot of us up, life has beat a lot of us up, our past has held us hostage, as we somehow get ready to magnify God, and our lack of self-worth stops us. Well I'm going to ask for a witness here. Ever had a real bad day and found it hard to worship God? Wonder why? God didn't change, neither did His worth diminish. That's why the Bible says in Psalm 150, Verse 2, "Praise him…" what? "…according to his mighty acts, according to his excellent greatness." So one time you bless and exalt him because of what He does, and then you bless Him because of what He is. Well sometimes He's not doing anything, but He's always being something.

God always is. He's always great. So when you're having a bad day, He can't have a bad day. So when you and I feel unworthy cause we stuck both our feet in our mouth, and we didn't handle the situation well, and we fell off the wagon into a mud hole, God is still altogether glorious and magnificent and awesome. And He's full of wonder and amazement and He's waiting for you to open your trap. And sometimes we keep our trap shut because "I feel bad cause I said something bad, watched something bad, read something bad, did something bad," and God looks down over the balcony of glory and says, "I ain't done nothing bad."

THE WHY & WONDER OF WORSHIP • BOOK TWO

WORSHIP IS ABOUT THE ONE BEING WORSHIPPED

Worship has got nothing to do with the worthiness of the worshipper. That is one of the most painful statements I have ever made from any pulpit. It has taken nerve to build up to that, to say that tonight. Cause I have had a major problem with people who worship, that couldn't tell the truth standing on a Bible looking at Jesus. I have had a major problem with people who shout and boogaloo, and carry on, and they're unfaithful in their tithing, unfaithful in their living, sometimes immoral.

I have sat here with a question mark for a brain saying, "how can these things be." And here comes this person that I just know, they got the morals of a roach and a tongue of a snake, and they're down here just dancing. And God, He makes me so annoyed sometimes. He's enjoying it. And I'm so ticked off, I can't see straight.

And I lose my chance to bless God because I happen to know about her. Never thinking God is saying, "So do I. But she's telling me I'm wonderful, and she's already repented, and she's ashamed of what she did. And you might as well stop holding her hostage, and you can't do anything about it. And I can do everything about it. And she's blowing Me kisses and she's telling Me I'm wonderful and lovely. Why don't you just stop it and bless Me awhile. Cause you're missing the chance of My presence coming by and helping you."

Am I talking to the United Pentecostal Church of Gainesville? Now let's look. Come on let's be honest. Class is in. Come on. Help me out a little bit. Am I alone in what I just said or felt? Turn to someone and say, "You know I've felt that way so many times." In fact, come on let's go a little further. "Sometimes I've been even wondering about Brother Arnold, why he doesn't sit her down. I just wonder why Brother Arnold just kinda even lets her sing, lets him play. You know he used to be strong." Remember there's a word that goes with strong, and sometimes he's been wrong.

ONLY GOD CAN DISCERN TRUE WORSHIP

You're going to understand me when I get half way through my notes. I'm going to show you where we've had a problem. Now God is the only one that can discern true and vain worship. But somehow in my spirit I say, "You want to bet. I can tell if it's honest and sincere." Why? "Cause I know some stuff."

It's like the elder brother sitting on the back end of the plow seeing his kid brother come home and hug his dad and kiss him and bless him. And the elder brother says, "I know that stuff's fake cause I know what the boy's done." But the father says, "I know it's real. Just come on and kiss me some more." They go to the party. The elder brother sucks his thumb on the back porch, never does eat any of the cake. What kept him out? His knowledge of his brother's failures. If he had heard a good report about his brother investing and making some money in CDs and bought half of the interest in Amway and come back and was a success, he'd a went to the party and have two beers with him. But he knew his brother had been a failure.

There's a difference between preaching a visiting sermon and trying to build a church. I'm trying to get you people ready for the coming of the Lord! I got to higher responsibility! I've got to present you and myself as a chaste virgin unto the Lord! That's scary business!

ANYONE CAN WORSHIP

Worship. Worship is concerned with the dignity, the merit, and the worth of the person being worshipped. As a noun, the word we translate into English refers to the dignity of his worship. As a verb (cause we know verbs are active), it has to do with paying homage, respect, reverential devotion, service, and honor to a person or being.

Thus, worship becomes our response (watch) to God's worthiness, not my lousy day, not my 126 failures. I'm going to take your excuse away for not worshipping. Worship has nothing to do with the worthiness of the worshipper. How worthy is a stone? And God turned around and said, "You shut your mouth, you watch them stones cry out." Now God is so yearning and desirous of real worship, He'll let nature replace you.

I'm going to show you something. I read this. This is so neat. I wish I'd a thought of this, but I didn't. But I read this little story, and in this story it kinda made a reference to what I wanted to talk about tonight. And it said it was a unique picture for the queen of England with all her regalia and all her adornment, and all her jewelry, and her finery, and all her attendants riding down downtown England in her gorgeous coach with her horsemen. And it said it was a mind-boggling event to watch the queen come by in that carriage. And there lining the streets were thieves, prostitutes, skid row bums, all bowing and curtseying to the queen. And the queen accepting their homage. For worship has nothing to do with the worth of the worshipper. In Luke 19, when Jesus come riding in on that donkey, the Pharisees were upset at two things. That Jesus was the object of worship, and the status of the worshippers. Outcasts, publicans, sinners, harlots, tax collectors, boozers—worshipping. And so they measured the thing by who they saw doing it. They said, "That couldn't be good. God couldn't accept that. Look at the condition of the worshipper."

But you can never tell the condition of the worshipper at the moment of worship. You may be able to tell their condition up to that moment; but you can change your mind in a moment. You can repent in a moment. You can be overwhelmed by your own shamefulness and guilt and repent and be overwhelmed by the majesty of God in a moment and you can be an absolute acceptable worshipper in that moment.

WORSHIP—MORE THAN AN ATTITUDE

Worship is more than an attitude. In Luke 15, they accuse Jesus because he started teaching. Luke 15 starts with then, which means it's a continuation of the previous verses. Because they didn't believe that God was interested in Pharisees and Sadducees, or in publicans, and in low-lifes, and harlots, and immoral people.

And so after they did all that and Jesus gave his teaching, it starts with "Then drew near unto him all the publicans and sinners for to hear him. And the Pharisees and scribes murmured, saying, This man receiveth sinners, and eateth with them." And then comes the threefold story of the lost lamb, the lost coin, and the lost boy. And Jesus takes a few moments in his parable teaching to show them the heartbeat of God and how precious in the sight of God is every human being. And that's why he gives them the story of the lost sheep, the lost coin, and the lost boy. Because their concept of God was incorrect. And they got annoyed because of the riffraff that gathered around him.

Worship is more than an attitude. Now it is an attitude. They worship in vain. You cannot have an impure attitude and have acceptable worship. You can have failure in your life, but if your attitude is wanting to please God, it will be accepted. You can have everything right to the crossing the T and dotting the I, but if your attitude isn't to magnify, and exalt, and adore God, and to draw closer in your spirit to Him, it's vain worship, sounding brass, tinkling cymbal.

I'm going to help all you people that never like to make noise. The depth and the intensity of your expression in worship, varies with people. Some people find it very easy to say "Praise God!" And another man or woman loves God just as fine as you do could never bring their lips in a public meeting to say "Amen." Must be careful to look at them and say, "You don't love God." They may very well love God more than you, but just don't have a freedom of expression because of their upbringing, because of their make-up.

OUR PRESENT ACTIONS FLOW FROM OUR PAST

Boy, I am crossing some lines here. Because the depth and the intensity of our expression in worship flows out of our previous experiences, our knowledge of God. Our personality also affects our action. Some people can almost get saved thinking about a parade coming by. Other people, the president of the United States is going to sleep at their house and say, "Well don't make a mess in the back bedroom." Their personality is not given to explosiveness. Wait a minute. Doesn't mean they don't love God.

Now I'm going to cut you the other way. While I've cut you a little slack for your non-expressiveness because of your personality, or because of your upbringing, or your experiences. Let me add a little P.S., a little post-script on there. One problem is that a lukewarm heart can never perform boiling hot worship.

All the years I dated as a young kid I never liked to kiss a cold mouth. Now you don't know what I'm talking about, cause you came out of your mother's womb with your girlfriend. You've only had one girlfriend. Fine. But some of us have had a few. And it was always a bummer and a waste of time and money to go out with a girl who kissed like a piece of wallpaper. No electricity. You want me to get plainer? You don't even have to kiss. There are some fellows and gals that you've interacted with over the years that there was an electricity just being with them. I had enjoyment holding a hand and going for a walk.

Oh, going to be rated X here in a minute. I'm talking some serious stuff. I can't believe you can walk through life holding God's hand and you act like you got a salamander by the tail. You act like you got a dead mackerel by the hand.

You're talking about the lover of your soul. You're talking about someone who knows everything about you and loves you anyway, and will never turn His back on you no matter how many times you make a mistake. I can't believe you cannot be excited to some emotional expression that God is your boyfriend.

WORSHIP IS LOVER TO LOVER COMMUNICATION

Have you never been in a service when the presence of God just went whoosh, came by you and your hair stood up and your goose bumps ran around? And you went "Whew!" And but it just stayed a while and all of a sudden there was a warm glow inside of you. And you weren't sad and tears rushed down your eyes. And you were like "Ho!" Like you were just enveloped with the kiss of God, and there was just something saying, "I know I haven't made everything go away yet honey, but it's all right, I got you covered baby. I got you in my hand and nothing's going to separate you from the love of God."

And there's something happens to you and if you don't go "Hallelujah," at least you lift your heart to Him and you lift your voice to Him in some way. And you tell Him how much you love Him and how much you appreciate Him, because worship has to involve some type of human expression. Because worship at its purest level is no more or less than love responding to love. How can you respond to love like a dead salamander? God who loves you and I unconditionally, though he knows everything about us; that we don't want to respond to Him. We want to give Him a handshake. "Oh praise the Lord. How are you?" You ever shake hands with people, some of the people in this church? You want to sing that song "Pray for the dead and the dead will pray for you." You just shake hands with them and you just go "Hey how you doing? Ah, been suffering long with this disease? Are you palsied in all parts of your body or just that one hand?"

I like to make eye contact with people when I come in. "How you doing?" You got people right here in this church sitting here right now, never want look at you. "Hey, how you doing?" "Hey, nice." Now I worry about people who don't want to make eye contact cause that's the first sign. Listen to me and I'm not trying to be unkind. I realize that might be your personality. But those of us who have dealt with devils and casting out devils, that's how you find out peoples' got devils. Devils don't like making eye contact with Holy Ghost filled people. People who got a bad attitude don't like making eye contact with Holy Ghost filled people. People who have a dishonest agenda on the calendar don't like to make eye contact with you. I'm not telling you to go around here all night and just stare at everybody. "You got a devil?" That's not what I'm talking about.

Am I the only person that has a personal hang up, a human, fleshly hang up, that I don't like talking to people who don't look at me? "How are you?" "Oh just fine Brother Arnold." "Is there something on the tile here?" "Would you talk to me when I?" "Oh I just can't, you make me nervous." "I make you nervous. Are you lying? Are you immoral? Are you dishonest?" "No." "Then you got nothing to be nervous about."

Is it hard to carry on a conversation with someone who just, "Hi how are you doing?" "Yes well, you know how...." When I was a kid and you did that, your mother bopped you upside your head. Your mother go to talk to you and you turned around and looked out the window. Boy she'd yank a knot in your head, man, and put three vertebras out in your neck. Bring you back and say, "Look at me when I'm talking to you!"

I don't know why mothers always think you hear better watching. I told you this, but it's worth repeating. Worst beating I ever got was when my mother said that to me one time. I said, "Mom, I see with my eyes. I hear with my ears." She said, "And you speak fresh with your mouth!" Whack! Then she took a bar of lava soap and washed my mouth out. Like a bubble bath with gravel. "Don't talk to me." "What?" "I'll beat you upside the head." Chase you down the hall with a belt.

Now I know what brutality was, when I was a kid. My mother hit me with old wooden coat hangers if she couldn't find a hairbrush. Hit you with a hairbrush and broke the hairbrush, and then beat you with something she could find because you broke her hairbrush.

See, now you understand. I ought to have money coming from the government because I was brutalized as a child. I come from a dysfunctional family. My father thought I had to do what he said. How dare him. My mom didn't buy me PF flyers when I was a kid; I ought to burn the house down. If I did that today, the government would give me a grant to go to college. It's expressing art. I'm into fire. We're living in a sick world, man.

VAIN WORSHIP—OUR HEART IS FAR FROM HIM

A lukewarm heart cannot perform boiling hot worship, nor can a rebellious life bless God with any depth of sincerity. "In vain they do worship Me." They worship and they got Me as the object, but it's vain. Why? He said, "For their heart is far from Me." They have the ritual. They have the ceremony. They have the form. They have the priests. They have the benediction, the doxology. They got it all; but their heart's in Chicago. Their heart's in Wisconsin, in South Africa, in Nova Scotia, traveling everywhere.

"Their heart's far from Me, because I don't really want your words. I want you, because there is more to you than words and performance. I made you. I know what you are." You think you know what you are, but God looks at you and says, "I know the potential that I laid in you before you was ever formed." You got to hear me.

DON'T PLAY GAMES—COME CLOSE

God put treasures in you and I before we were ever formed. In the mind of God He laid up things for us before we ever manifested in time; and it takes God to touch the potentials in us to bring them to fruition. That's why it is so silly for us to play church games and not want to walk with Him, not want Him to touch us, not want Him to sit down in the pew or wash the dishes with you ladies, or clean the house, or go into the job, or a ride in the car. Talk to me Jesus!

Maybe I'm just a sick puppy, but every morning I'm up and I'm seeking God. Every day "God let the words of my mouth and the meditations of my heart be acceptable in Your sight. Help me to touch somebody. Help me to hear Your voice, to feel a quickening of the Holy Ghost. Lead me today Lord. Help me stop chasing this magic rainbow of tomorrow." "This is the day that the Lord has made. I will rejoice and be glad in it." "O come magnify the Lord with me. Let us exalt his name together."

Look at this day as you ain't got tomorrow. This is it. I got a chance for God to touch me, God to talk to me, God to release me, God to reveal something to me. Don't you realize that most of us in this house, we do love God, but we're chasing a magic tomorrow and a rainbow with a pot of gold. And we keep thinking someday, someday, someday. Do you realize you might die before someday gets here? That you got to do something right now while you have this moment? And this moment could become a miracle. It could become majestic to you. It could become powerful. It could be life changing—this moment. No wonder the Lord said "blessed are they that hunger and thirst after righteousness." They're going to be filled but you got to hunger, you got to thirst, you got to desire. Didn't I tell you, you can't do anything without desire? And the worst curse anybody could ever have is blasé, mediocrity, apathy, no desire.

SO CALLED CHRISTIANS—NO DESIRE FOR GOD

The curse of "so called" Christianity is "so called" Christians that I meet. And I say, "So called" and you think I'm unkind. Well then I'm just unkind, "so called." People who say they are Christians and they have no desire to pray, no desire to talk to God, no desire to read the Book, no desire to be in His presence, no desire to get broken, to weep, to hold onto God. What kinda Christians are you people? That's like a man saying "I love my wife so much in about five years, I'm going to write her a letter." "You know she keeps cleaning this house so good, two weeks I'm going to give her a kiss." Two weeks you're going to be in a divorce court, you idiot. How can you say you love somebody and not express it? It's like these dopes that come home and beat their wives up and then turn around and say, "I didn't mean it." What in the name of? What are you? What do you mean you didn't mean it? "I really do love you."

My wife and I have had a wonderful marriage. Yeah we have. Had a lot of fun. She's been a ball. But we had a common understanding when we got married; and it was a simple thing. We had an understanding. "Jeffrey, if you ever slap me or beat me, just remember you'll have to sleep sometime." Now she said that before she had the Holy Ghost. She's still looking at me saying "Still holds, buddy." In fact, now she's saying, "If you got the Holy Ghost and whip me, I'll break both your legs while you're sleeping." Yeah, yeah, yeah. I know. I know. I know. I'm sorry. I didn't mean to get into all this marital stuff.

OLD TESTAMENT WORSHIP—ALWAYS DEMONSTRATIVE

Okay, I'm trying to talk about the words in worship. Two words I want you to understand, okay. Two words for worship. There are about 12 or 15 I have, but I want to use two of them. One is the Hebrew word. The word is S-h-a-c-h-a-h. Shachah! It is translated in the Old Testament 172 times for the word worship. It means to do obeisance—to bow, to fall down, to prostrate oneself, to stoop, to beseech humbly. It is the word translated when Abraham had the three angelic visitors come. The Bible says, "He bowed and prostrated himself before the LORD." Shachah!

It is the same word translated in Genesis 24:52 when Eliezer is looking for a bride for the son Isaac and he finds Rebekah at the well. And when he finds it's Rebekah, the Bible says, "He bowed his head and worshipped God." Now watch, cause the Hebrews are very, very emotional people and very, very expressive. Very, very demonstrative. Very, very emotional. Wait a minute. And very, very God's people.

They didn't learn that worship from nobody else. They got it direct from Yahweh. He taught them how to do this; and Christianity came out of Judaism. But somewhere along this filter system we got real polished. And so if anybody boogaloos, or shakes, or bounces, or lays down, there's something wrong with them cats. So we've traded the substance of the savior hood of God for just statue impersonation. Isn't it amazing that you'll have a worship service and nobody worships.

In Exodus 4:31, the Bible says that Moses comes to the slaves of Israel and tells them of the I AM's impending plan of liberating all those Jews from the Egyptian bondage of over 400 years. And the scripture says all the elders of Israel and the people with them fell on their face prostrate and Shachah—worshipped God.

So 172 times it's recorded for the word worship. One hundred seventy two times it shows that they did something as a verb. Every time, they did something. They bowed. They kneeled. They prostrated. They reached forward. They gestured. They expressed physically what they felt emotionally. That doesn't make you an imbalanced kook. It makes you a worshipper.

THE WHY & WONDER OF WORSHIP • BOOK TWO

WORSHIP—RESPONSE TO PAST, PRESENT OR PROMISED FUTURE DELIVERANCE

Worship should be our response to the promised deliverances of God. Or, worship should be our actions for past deliverances. Psalm 126, Verses 1-3, "When the LORD turned our captivity, then we were like them that dream. Then was our mouth filled with laughter, our voices filled with singing. Then we did rejoice before the LORD." It means to leap in a circle. Apparently, the only people that are loosed are the leapers.

Have you ever noticed a former drug addict, or a real former drunk, or a former cult person, or some type of addict, when they are delivered, how uninhibited and full of thanks they are? Anybody ever been delivered from drugs or drinking, or been delivered from immorality, or lying, or cheating, or dishonesty? Couldn't help yourself with certain habits but God stepped in and broke the shackles and spoke a word of deliverance. And when you get to thinking about the goodness of Jesus and all He's done for you, you don't need any music. You don't need a cheerleader. You're so thankful that God did it. Even right now, to think that God's kept you out of the bar and kept your mind straight, paid your bills, gave you a measure of health and strength, gave you a family.

GREAT DELIVERANCE GENERATES GREAT RESPONSE

A hundred and seventy-two times they responded in an action verb. Listen carefully. For great deliverances often generate great thanks, great praise, great worship. Now, I'm not saying this is true. I'm asking a question. Could it be that the reason why some have a diminished expression is either they are personally inhibited, or they are non-emotional people, or there hasn't been much deliverance? Or there's been great deliverance but it was a long time ago and the story has gotten old.

I didn't say it was. I asked a question. I think one of the problems that we have, and I'm saying that from the personal reference point of myself, that I love God but I get frustrated with the lack of the feeling of my love for God. I do love God but I get so frustrated that I don't feel the depth that I want to feel so that I could express it freer.

And I ask God constantly, "What is wrong with me? When I think of what I could have been and where I might be right now and if You hadn't stepped in my and Patty's life. And if You hadn't orchestrated things for me, I might be in a devil's hell. I might be a crazy criminal, or locked up in jail, or shot somewhere, or paralyzed. God, why is it that I can't seem to generate that emotional explosion and expression more often?"

MEDITATION BRINGS FLOW OF FEELING

And it was almost like I got an answer. He says, "That constant flow of the feeling will come more often if you will meditate more frequently." See, when I start boogalooing around here, and juking, and start telling you how good God's been and how great—something just grabs you. And you go "Woo, hey, that's right!" You know what you're doing? It's flashed into your mind and you're meditating on some things that God's helped you with and all of a sudden that feeling comes. But then it goes quickly.

That's why the scripture's always teaching, in the Old Testament especially; meditate on the things of God. Constantly think on the goodness of God. You don't need a church service. You can drive down in your car and begin the think about how good and kind God has been. I promise you the Spirit of God will come right near you and you'll have a tear run down your eye, or goose bumps run up your neck. And God will step right in that car. You know why? Because meditation will bring a release for the Master to come close and you'll sense that flow, that fulfillment that you want.

Every use of the word, (I better say it, s-h-a-c-h-a-h. Shachah! I'll just translate it, worship) indicates an action, an expression of inner feeling, emotion, and desire through the body. An inner attitude and feeling of thankfulness. See the thankfulness is your attitude. Your expression is your action.

VAIN WORSHIP—ACTION WITH WRONG ATTITUDE

Now watch. God said their worship was vain. Why? Because they had the action, but the attitude was not pure because their heart was away from Him. So when you have the action, but you don't have the corresponding attitude, it's vain worship. It's rejected by God. That's why attitude is so important, that we have clean attitudes. That's why a person with unforgiveness or bitterness, or anger, or frustration, or unwillingness to change has a hard time worshipping, because God checks the attitude and not just the action.

In the Old Testament, when a worshipper came and offered the sacrifice, God wasn't just tied into the animal that was sacrificed. He watched the sacrificer. God's problem really wasn't just with Cain's offering of vegetables and fruit; it was with Cain. For the Lord told him "If you do right, shalt thou not be accepted?"

Did not Jehovah complain to Israel "I'm full of your oblations and your feasts and your new moons. I've seen rivers of blood. My nostrils are full of smoking animals. I don't want that. I want you."

Now we go to the New Testament. I can say this word. It's Greek. Proskuneo. It is translated in the New Testament "worship" 59 times. Proskuneo. Comes from two Greek words "pros" which means toward, "kuneo" which means to kiss. Now watch. When it is translated historically, proskuneo was the gesture of kissing the hand of a bishop or a dignitary, or a worthy person. Or if you were in subjection or humility, it was to kiss the feet of one. It was what Mary did to Jesus. Proskuneo.

OLD TESTAMENT WORSHIP—BOW AT A DISTANCE
NEW TESTAMENT WORSHIP—UP CLOSE CONTACT

But I got something better for you. Song of Solomon Chapter 1 Verse 2, he says "Let the lover of my soul kiss me with the kiss of his lips." Watch. You can bow at a distance, Old Testament. But if you're going to step into the New Testament, to kiss, you have to make contact. To kiss you have to come close. You can't kiss long distance. Don't you understand the magnitude of the insult and the hurt that Jesus felt when Judas got close enough to kiss Him. A gesture that should have been one reserved for a worshipper of one that adored the object.

No wonder the writer says in Ephesians 2:13 we need to thank God for the blood of Jesus Christ, for the blood has made us nigh. In other words, the blood has reconciled and brought us close enough to kiss the lover of our soul. Why would you want long distance salvation when the blood said, "come close?" Well I've been a liar, and a cheat, and no good. Doesn't matter. The blood forgives all.

In the Old Testament saints bowed before, they gestured towards. But in the New Testament, we have a greater covenant with a greater high priest, a greater sacrifice, and greater promises. Therefore, we are privileged to get close enough to embrace, to kiss, to pour out intimate affection and adoration.

In John Chapter 4, Jesus talking to the woman of Samaria, all about worship and Samaria, and the hills, and Mount Gerizim, and this, this, that, and the other. When Jesus talked to her in John Chapter 4, 10 times the word worship (now you go home and count it cause I counted it), 10 times the word worship shows up in His conversation with the woman. And 10 times the word is proskuneo. So what He was saying to the woman was, the worship that God's after ain't long distance honey.

The worship God wants is close enough to embrace, hug, and kiss. It will involve your emotion and your affection. It is the interplay between two parties possessing a deep love for each other, a commitment to each other, and having loving feelings toward each other.

TWO THINGS REQUIRED—AWE AND LOVE EXPRESSED

There are two things that are required. Worship's words reveal two things: an element of awe, reverence, and respect; and an inner attitude of affection that must be expressed. If you and I are poor worshippers, maybe we need to re-examine, and stop kinda blaming the fact that "Well we were raised different."

Maybe we're not really seeing Him like we should. Without a vision the people perish.

The woman was told that it was not the time, nor the place, nor the method that God deemed as the main thing. But He said to the woman it is the genuineness of worship that God desires, for He wants it done "in spirit (small s, human spirit) and in truth (sincerity)." In vain they worship.

Nothing any more insulting to God than for us to have a convocation called, and when we get ready our worship is vain because our minds and hearts are elsewhere. While we sit in the service and say, "I wish they'd get this dumb music and stuff out of the way. I want to hear a Bible study."

Worship is the outflow of inner attitude and affection toward God. Worship is the adoration, awe, and love expressed in action. Worship is communicated affection between God and man. Both emotion and motion are involved because true worship is simply love expressed. Worship is love responding to love.

IT'S NOT ABOUT US—IT'S ABOUT HIM

God is the object of our worship and by His own declaration He said, "I change not." If God therefore is unchangeable, our situation may alter. It may become adverse, but God stays the same. Therefore our worship must not and cannot be affected by our circumstance. Job will still worship God with ten dead children and all his resources gone, and boils all over his body. Not because he doesn't feel bad. He feels horrible. He's in shock. But he knows God hasn't changed.

It is not the place. It is not your past. It is the person that matters. And God is worthy. God is deserving. And the beautiful thing is; God is seeking worship. He's like the queen of England riding by the slums, willing to receive anybody's adoration, anybody's gesture that's honest. Doesn't mean they got everything right in their life. Maybe 90% of their stuff is wrong. But for a moment they behold the grandeur of the dignity passing by and they give homage. And the one riding in the coach accepts it. "Thank you, thank you."

And God comes here on the wings of the wind. And He comes just to pick up some worship because all day long it's been GD this and GD that, and GD this and GD that, and He's been cursed and Jesus this and Jesus that. All day long His name's been blasphemed. All day long He's been lied on and lied about. He waits for a few hundred people that gather in this little box we call a building and He just flies down here on the wings and He waits to pick up a little bit of worship. And then we say, "You know I've had a bad day. I'm tired. I got to lot of trouble." And He just flutters and He waits.

WORSHIP—HIS LOVE TO US, OUR RESPONSE TO HIM

Our response to His love, we call worship. Isn't it strange that Paul the apostle could worship God in a slimy, smelly, filthy jail? Why? Cause God didn't change. His situation changed. God didn't change. And if God wanted to, He could have kept him out of that fix. I got news for you honey, if God wanted to He could have kept you out of your mess. He loved you enough and trusted you enough. He trusted you with the mess. A lesser person couldn't have handled it. You ever asked that? I have. "God why do you let this happen to me." "Cause I know you can handle. It'll make you into something. Shut your mouth and go through it." God never sends anything into your life that would destroy you. It is only going to develop you. If it has to break you to make you, let it break you.

God didn't lose control of something because your life seems to be out of control, because chaos has visited you and calm has left you. God has not fallen off the throne. He's still the omnipotent, Almighty God. He's got all power. "The Lord God reigneth, let the earth rejoice." He rules and reigns in the kingdoms of men, sets over it even the basest on men, rules in the army of heaven, even the devils and the demons of the damned regions, they are subject to God.

Don't you ever believe the devil can mess with you any time he wants to. He can't mess with you anytime he wants to. You're sanctified people. You got the name of Jesus on you. You got the Holy Ghost on you. Believe me. I'm telling you what I know. Trouble and chaos, and devils and demons come by to torment you, you can rest assured they got a permission slip in their hand. They have checked with the Dad to see whether, He looked at you and said "Yeah, that is going to help them. Okay. They won't understand it now but two and a half years down the road they going to look back and say 'Now I got it.'"

DON'T TRY TO ESCAPE WHAT GOD ALLOWS TO COME TO US

We're trying to escape this. God's trying to let us go through it because He sees what we got coming up down there. And we're trying to escape this and He's trying to use this to expand our understanding so we can take care of it down there. No wonder David said (you got to learn to say that in your life) "It was good for me that I was afflicted."

Boy, you talk about maturing. You're maturing when you can look at bad and say, "this is good." Look at loss and say, "I gained." Caught your tears in a five gallon bucket and said "the Lord's working this all out for something great," "for all things work together for the good to them who love the Lord, who are the called, according to the purpose of God." May not be able to shout and boogaloo now but all things work together for good and I'm not going to insult God by saying "God this is not fair."

When you say, "God this is not fair" you have just said "You have made a mistake." You going to be honest say this, "I don't understand this but You're smart. I ain't figured this out but you're smarter than I am and I'm going to bow my knee and I'm going to proskuneo."

Isn't it amazing that Paul the apostle not only worshipped in slimy, filthy, dirty, stinky jails but he was a pretty good worshipper on a stormy ship in a place called Euroclydon? He worshipped God in a 14 day fast in the middle of a storm that hadn't seen the sun or moon for days and nights. Don't you see that every time? Because worship is a one on one deal. I can be in the middle of hell and chaos, and crud and garbage and I can worship God.

IT'S NOT YOUR SITUATION—IT'S YOUR PERSPECTIVE

It's not your situation that governs you. It's how you see yourself in that situation. John is put on the isle of Patmos. They think he's forgotten. You know what they did? They set the platform for him to write 22 chapters of the book of Revelation that is being read in 1997 around the world. They thought they fixed him. God said, "Oh they gave him a platform so that he had no distraction. All he could do was get in the Spirit on the Lord's Day and I could visit him and write My will upon his mind." Suppose he'd a refused the mess. We'd a lost 22 chapters of the book of Revelation.

Suppose he'd a been like some of us and say, "This ain't fair. I paid my tithes. I fasted and prayed. I gave to the building fund. I was there when Jesus was crucified. I laid my head on His chest. I talked to Him. He was my friend. I was His beloved disciple. I can't believe You did this to me." You think God would have given him 22 chapters of the book of Revelation? I think not.

He just looked at his mess and said "Can't figure what's going on here but I know one thing, I'm going to get in the Spirit on the Lord's Day. And I'm going to bless Him, and exalt Him, and magnify Him." No wonder the Lord said in His word, "Bless the Lord at all times. Let His praise be continually in your mouth."

WORSHIP IS ABOUT WORTHINESS OF OBJECT WORSHIPPED

Worship is about the worthiness of the object. It's not about the worthiness of the worshipper. It ain't got nothing to do with you except you have a right attitude. That's it. Not if you got everything right in your life. Do you have an attitude "I want to know God. I want to please God. I want to put my past behind me. I want to be an adorer of God?" That's all it is. If you don't do that, it's vain worship.

That's why the leper ran up to Him and worshipped Him. It has nothing to do with the worthiness of the worshipper. Nothing could be any more pitiful and vile and rotten than Matthew 8 with a leper with his face falling off and his fingers falling off. He was defiled. He was an abomination. He could not approach the place of sacrifice. He was not allowed in the temple. But yet he came and he worshipped Jesus. Jesus accepted worship from a leper.

Jesus, In Mathew 15, accepted worship from a Syrophenician woman who was a worshipper of idols, who had a demon-possessed daughter. Why? Because the worship was honest. Didn't mean her life was right. The worship was honest. Got His attention.

There's a method in my madness ladies and gentlemen. I'm trying to get every one of you to a place where you get a concept of God, because when we reach that plateau of real worship unto God, the miraculous will be normal. The supernatural will flow through us just like it flowed through the early church, like it flowed through the man Jesus.

THE WHY & WONDER OF WORSHIP • BOOK TWO

THE
WHY & WONDER
OF WORSHIP

VOLUME FIVE • CHAPTER FIVE

THE WHY & WONDER OF WORSHIP • BOOK TWO

CHAPTER FIVE

ALL THINGS COME FROM GOD

1 Chronicles 29, it is the dedication, the coronation, of Solomon. The scripture says that they made Solomon king the second time. The first time didn't take. They made him king a second time.

1 Chronicles 29:22, "and they made Solomon, the son of David, king the second time." But I just wanted you to get this, because when David begins to...well, let's read Verse 10, "Wherefore David blessed the Lord before all the congregation: and David said, blessed be thou, Lord God of Israel our father, for ever and ever. (11) Thine, O Lord, is the greatness, and the power, and the glory, and the victory, and the majesty: for all that is in the heaven and in the earth is thine; thine is the kingdom, O Lord, and thou art exalted as head above all. (12) Both riches and honour come of thee."

And you thought it was your degree. You thought it was your ability to preach. All things come of God. Yeah, I can tell by the weak response that you don't believe it. (12) "Both riches and honour come of thee, and thou reignest over all..." Over good things and bad things. (12) "...and in thy hand is power and might..." Not the devil's. (12)..."and in thine hand it is to make great, and to give strength unto all." God can make you great, if He sees you can handle it. Watch this; "...now therefore our God we thank thee and praise thy glorious name, for who am I and what is my people that we should be able to offer so willingly after this sort."

I was saving this sermon to preach when we get ready to do our drive for building the new tabernacle, because that's what this was all about; it was putting the money aside, the gold, the silver, the brass, the jewels, and the diamonds, and they just gave willingly and they made this great big pile and was able to build the house debt-free. So I was saving all of this, but I may die before then, so I'm going to talk on it for a little while. Watch what he says, (15) "For we are strangers before thee, and sojourners, as were all our fathers." In other words; we're just passing through time. (15) "...our days on the earth are as a shadow, and there is none abiding."

WE CAN ONLY GIVE WHAT GOD HAS GIVEN US

Here it is; (16) "O Lord our God, all this store...." In other words; the jewels, the money, the gold, the silver, the trinkets, everything that the people had given willingly in the first 6 verses of this chapter he says, watch; (16) "...all this store that we have prepared to build thee an house for thine holy name..." Here it is; (16) "...cometh of thy hand, and is all thine own." So we're giving You back Your own stuff! You gave it to us as currency; we give it back to You as mortar and brick. But You still own it, You just gave it to us to use. Help us not to get intoxicated and think we did something, when it was Yours to start with. That's why tithing and offering is a very dangerous area in people's lives, because you are stealing and keeping something that wasn't yours to begin with. He says, "ALL is thine, and You let us have it."

So God says, "Here, aahhhh, give Me ten, and you can keep ninety." And then we turn around and go, "Now wait a minute." And God could say, "Okay, let's play it your way. Here, I'll keep a hundred and what are you going to do?"

You say, "Well, I'm going to work." "Oh no, I'm going to make sure you get fired." You say, "Well, I'll get a job," "No, I'm going to give you an aneurysm," You say, "Well, I'm going to write...," "No, I'm going to give you arthritis so you can't hold a pen."

Don't you get it, God don't need your stuff! We need HIS stuff! 1 Chronicles 29:17, "I know also, my God, that thou triest the heart, and hast pleasure in uprightness. As for me in the uprightness of mine heart I have willingly offered all these things: and now have I seen with joy thy people, which are present here, to offer willingly unto thee." They were dedicating to build the house. (18) "O Lord God of Abraham, Isaac, and of Israel, our fathers, keep this for ever in the imagination of the thoughts of the heart of thy people, and prepare their heart unto thee:" (19) "And give unto Solomon my son a perfect heart, to keep thy commandments, thy testimonies, and thy statutes,..." Sometimes, prayers of the greatest men and women of God don't work fully. Nobody had a heart like David's heart after God. He prayed earnestly for his boy Solomon and it only went so far. Solomon had to kick in, and Solomon wouldn't kick in. Don't stop praying for your kids. (19) "...and to do all these things, and to build the palace, for the which I have made provision. (20) And David said to all the congregation. Now bless the Lord your God. And all the congregation blessed the Lord God of their fathers, and bowed down their heads, and worshipped the Lord, and the king." We got trouble now; you're not supposed to worship people. Unless you understand the Hebrew word that is translated "worship" here, to mean; give reverence to—to honor. (21) "And they sacrificed sacrifices unto the Lord, and offered burnt offerings unto the Lord, on the morrow after that day, even a thousand bullocks, a thousand rams, and a thousand lambs, with their drink offerings and sacrifices in abundance for all Israel: (22) and did eat and drink before the Lord on that day with great gladness. And they made Solomon the son of David king the second time, and anointed him unto the Lord to be the chief governor, and Zadok to be priest."

Last week we taught on the word "worship"; "Shachah". That's exactly the same word that is translated here in Chronicles. The same Hebrew word—to do obedience, to show reverence, to have honor towards. The New Testament was "proskuneo"—to kiss toward, kiss the hand, to show honor. Worship involves a physical involvement.

WE'RE MADE FOR A PURPOSE—WORSHIP

I want to go on a real great journey. Psalm 22. I'm going to go there in just a minute and I'd like you to be there when I get there, okay? According to Ephesians 1:12, Colossians 1:16 and Revelation 4:11, the scriptures are emphatically plain that we were made for a purpose, and the purpose was the worship of God and the glory of God.

Ephesians 1:12, "That we should be to the praise of his glory, who first trusted in Christ." That's the purpose for which He has called us.

Colossians 1:16, "For by him were all things created, that are in heaven, and that are in earth, visible and invisible, whether they be thrones, or dominions, or principalities, or powers: all things were created by him, and for him:"

REVELATION & PROPER OBJECT REQUIRED TO WORSHIP

Revelations 4:11 says that He created all things for His glory and for His pleasure. (11) "Thou art worthy, O Lord, to receive glory and honour and power: for thou hast created all things, and for thy pleasure they are and were created." Got it? Okay, now watch: Life's highest occupation, therefore, is to be a true worshipper of God. To be a worshipper of God involves a few things; 1) you cannot worship without revelation. Revelation is what makes you understand, it helps you see, it lets you embrace, experience, grasp, comprehend. You have to have revelation to worship. If you don't have revelation to worship, you worship, but you worship ignorantly. You will still worship, but you'll be off base. Paul said that the things that you worship ignorantly—Acts Chapter 17.

The heathens worship devils, they don't mean to, they think they're worshipping God, but Paul says, "Because they worship ignorantly." The object of worship is an imperative, it must be correct. You cannot have pure, true worship if your object is wrong, so you got to have revelation and; 2) you got to have the proper object.

Revelation is what causes the release of worship. Worship releases you—you are awed. Worship is an awe, it's an adoration, it's an overwhelming emotion and feeling that has to be expressed. You have to express worship.
In order for us to be proper worshippers, here it is; acceptable responses to the object are required. You cannot just respond any old flippant way you want. God, who is the object of worship, usually through the scriptures, prescribes for us the manner that is acceptable to worship. You can't just barge in.

ATTITUDE IS EXTREMELY IMPORTANT

God complained of Israel who were offering Him second-rate offerings, but they were worshipping. He got mad at them. Read Malachi 1 and 2: it says, "If I'm a great God, where's my honor, if I'm a Father, where's my honor?" He said, "Go offer your governors these diseased and broken down and lame animals that you are offering to me." You see, they said, "Well, we're going to kill it anyway, why should we give our BEST one away?" We're going to burn it up as a sacrifice, after all...it's the attitude that counts," and God says, "That's right, it's the attitude that counts and your attitude is that I don't count."

And so He just plays a game with me, He says, "Okay, take this diseased thing and bring it to your governor and say, have a gift on us." He'd throw you out of the court. Yet you bring me your lame and your diseased and your broken and decrepit, things that are useless, and then you expect me to just say, "Wow, thanks a lot fellas, I'm so thrilled with your attitude towards me." God never accepts substitutes or replacements for anything He has already previously commanded.

You and I cannot offer Him a substitute when He has plainly laid it out—"I want this." We cannot give Him a replacement for something when He requires something else. You can't come before God and offer strange fire and turn around and say, "Well, fire's fire." God says, "No, fire ain't fire." The sons of Aaron found that out. You just can't come in and mix strange fire and say, "What's the difference?"

SERVICE & BELIEF CAN'T REPLACE WORSHIP

So, service and belief can never replace worship. Here's how it works; belief—worship—service. There are people in this church that believe...they don't think they do, but they do...that study is equal to, or surpassing worship. God will never accept a substitute for what He calls for as priority. We were saved to be worshippers of God. You say, "Well, Bro. Arnold, the Bible says to study to show yourself approved unto God." That's right, that was written to a worshipper!

Now if you are already a worshipper, "Study away, Matilda," and if your study doesn't provoke you into more worship, then you are studying for the wrong reason.

STUDY SHOULD ENHANCE THE MAJESTY OF GOD

If our study doesn't enhance the magnitude and majesty of God, we are not getting the message that we just read. Our study ought to be as we are reading and looking at something, we ought to go, "Oh my God, You are so awesome, hallelujah…!" You get to studying the Word of God with the right attitude, God will bless and anoint your mind and you won't get through the whole passage, you'll stop and you'll just go in your mind…and your mind will reflect…and you'll go down memory lane.

The Holy Spirit will quicken into your mind something that God did for you that is similar to that scripture and you'll just step back and say, "Oh, hallelujah!" That one honest, sincere, "Oh praise God!" …that becomes worship, because God's pronouncement and presence is right there! But if you are reading and I'm reading, so that we can get our 5 chapters in…better to get 4 good verses in and just take time and worship over them. Take time and read them and say, "Well, I don't understand beans about this." "What in the world does this mean?"

WE NEED A HOLY—HUH?

I read stuff and just kind of do it with a holy—"huh?" …a holy huh?…what??? I try to look at it this way, and I look at it that way, and I try to dissect and bisect it and say, "What in the name of Jesus…what is this?" "Huh?" If God can get an honest "huh" from you, He'll breathe on you. If He can just get an honest "huh", instead of you and I just glossing over it and saying, "Oh well, sometime Bro. Arnold will explain it to me." What you don't know is that Bro. Arnold spent two weeks looking at it going, "Huh?"

You ever notice there are some books in the Bible that I don't preach much from? They're there! There's just too many huh's in there for me. You hardly ever hear me preach from the Song of Solomon...man, that thing is kind of sensual. You read that first chapter, or two...man, that thing is hubba, hubba. You want to go to the drive-in movie and do some sparkin' or somethin', man, whoa! That guy is explicit about romance..."Thy hand is under thy head, and thy kisses are sweeter than wine..." and he starts describing body parts and I'm going, "Whoa!" And then I get a holy cough, so then I say, "Well, let's see what the Psalmists have to say about this." You say, "This man's got women trouble." Am I in the Bible?

INTIMACY & ROMANCE IS GOD'S IDEA

Am I the only honest person in this building that has ever read the Song of Solomon and kind of gulped? Kind of just went whoa! You don't read the Song of Solomon when you are away two nights from home; you'll pick up the phone..."Hello, this is the big bubba speaking, I'm catching the early jet and I'll be home, let's go cut the lawn together." Look at my poor wife...she doesn't read the Song of Solomon, either...we've only had one daughter! Better get off that horse right now! Well, I figured I could find you somewhere.

You know what it's telling me, is that as holy and far away we want to make God, God is as close as your heartbeat and your emotion and your affection. What makes our face red, and a little awkward, or embarrassed, will not in any way make God embarrassed, because reproduction, sensuality, intimacy, and romance was all of God's idea within the marriage vow. He invented all this stuff and He thinks it's beautiful. Come on, I'll get your red-face finished here in a second. I think it's a wonderful thing; I'm glad that God didn't invent for a marriage vow a handshake. I'm glad He was more serious than that, I really am. I'm very, very happy that God is a very romantic type God. Hallelujah, let's leave it alone, okay, point made.

SACRIFICE CANNOT BE EQUATED WITH WORSHIP

Service and belief cannot replace worship; neither can study, though study may be very sincere. Neither can sacrifice be equated with worship. You cannot give enough. We have a generation of so-called Christians who pay people in their churches to do their worshipping. That's what the choir does, and the choir director, that's why we have special singers, that's why we have the preacher. Now, I don't think it's really true here too much, but a lot of other places—it's true. When things are labeled a worship service, there ain't no worship going on. It's a paid performance by people who are on staff to entertain people who don't want to worship. You cannot throw money, and God accept that as much as not being able to throw anything in and just in your own way, whispered out loud, "I love You, I thank You, I appreciate You, I'm not what I ought to be, but I know You are great and holy and I ask for mercy and I ask for help...," God will sit down on the pew next to you.

But if you throw a hundred dollars in there, and while they are clapping and singing, you just sort of sit there and pick your fingernails.... You might as well just get your money and stick it back in your pocket. In the first place, God don't need your money, He makes gold! He knows how to make diamonds, He knows where all the rubies are. You hear me! Now we need money to do things, but God don't need any money. What He does want is worshippers, and if He can find people that will worship, it will release Him to be everything that He is and everything that He has promised to be.

FOLLOW A WORSHIPPING LEADER

You noticed the scripture that I read to you in 1 Chronicles 29; it was David—the leadership—that said, "Let's worship." It was David who stood up in front of tens of thousands of people and said, "Let everybody begin to bless the Lord." Can you imagine what a roar that must have been if there were a hundred thousand people in that congregation, and this man without a microphone or megaphone just stood up somehow and said, "Let all the people bless Yahweh!" Can you imagine what a thunder it would be when young and old would just begin in their own way to bless God, some loud, some kind of quiet, some moving, gyrating, some being still, some prostrate; for the Bible says that many just bowed and began to bless the Lord. It got noisy!

You ought to thank God for corporate worship for those of you that don't have a propensity towards loudness—the loudness covers up your stillness. There's nothing wrong with your stillness; it allows you to blend. I never did like being in a church where they said, "Let's all pray," and everybody bowed their head and you could hear a pin drop, you could hear a mouse run across cotton. It would be so still and you're goin'...lookin' around, cuz everybody is wantin' to know if everyone else is finished.

NO EXACT WAY TO WORSHIP KEEPS IT FROM BEING A RITUAL

Here's what the problem is; all these 17 or 18 weeks that I have taught on worship; I have yet to explain to you the exactitude of worship. There is not scripture that we can find that gives an exact definition of worship. We have fragmented pictures, God

gives us word studies and picture studies of different scenarios, of different peoples, of different cultures and different times trying to worship, and He gives us a multiplicity of varied words that are expressed in their worship; and I think there is a reason why. I could be wrong, I'm wrong about a lot of things, but I think I'm right: If God were to give us an exactitude of worship...of what it was, where it begins, what it is and where it stops, we would...being the people that we are...would eventually make it an empty ritual.

GOD WANTS MORE THAN JUST WHAT IS PRESCRIBED

Now watch; we are in danger of that right now about doctrine. We're in danger of that right now about our own types of worship. That we could actually believe that just clapping is worship...no, those are only channels of expression. Matthew 15:8, "This people draweth nigh unto me with their mouth, and honoureth me with their lips; but their heart is far from me." Now watch what happened; God gave to Israel as a nation, a catalog of exactitude and specifics of what was required in each worship, in each burning offering, each peace offering, each trespass offering.

Now God was doing that, not so that they could be accepted, but so that they could see how unacceptable they were and how holy He was, and that unless grace worked in them, nothing could happen for them. But what happened was; their religiosity, and their ceremony, and their ritualism degraded into a level of performance only, so that they did exactly what was prescribed. And if WE aren't constantly challenged, we will think that as we do what is prescribed, that is what God is wanting.

GOD WANTS OUR FOCUS ON HIM

But God went on record and said, "I am sick of the smoke of your sacrifices, and I am sick of the blood of your beasts." He says, "Away with it all," but you say, "Well, You instituted it." Well, God says, "But I only instituted it so that you could understand that the people who draw near to Me must be purified by a substitute and by an atonement, and what I really wanted was you, but you are unacceptable to Me. Because I am holy and you are unholy, so I have to put in between you and Me—a mediatorship." "You have to have a way in which you can approach me, so I've given you this system of bloodletting and blood sacrifices, so that you would understand that I am beyond you and I will not come and play games with you until there is some type of legal justification taken place.

So I gave you this ritualistic system with the altar and the laver and the coming into the Holy Place and the Holy of Holies, so that you could understand that it really takes something to approach Me." "But what I wanted you to do is not settle into your ritual, I wanted you that, when you offered your turtledove, or you offered your ram, or the goat, or whatever, that your eye was really looking towards the Holy of Holies, that you really wanted ME."

GOD WANTS YOU—NOT JUST THE SACRIFICE YOU BRING

That's why the Bible says that the law was weak through the flesh, nothing wrong with the law; the law is holy. It showed us God's greatness and our evil, but it couldn't accomplish what God wanted it to do in us, not because of any frailty or failure in the law, but the frailty in the weakness of our flesh, and that once again we codify what was given to us until it just became an empty ritual. ...So that when the Hebrews began to bring their sacrifices, all they were bringing was WHAT WAS REQUIRED, and they weren't bringing themselves! And God was saying, "I don't want dead rams and goats and turtledoves, I want you. Don't you understand yet? I want you!" And they couldn't get it. So then He gives this statement, "These people draw nigh unto me with their lips, but their hearts are far from me."

Now a Jew could stand up, or a Hebrew could stand up and say, "Well, you required this sacrifice and I gave it to You, what else do you want?" "I did what you said." God says, "No, no you didn't do what I said, I said love the Lord thy God with all thy heart, and all thy mind, and all thy soul and all thy strength." One writer says, "Love Him with all your body, and your neighbor as yourself, on these hang all the law and the prophets,"...this is what I WANT, I want YOU!

VAIN WORSHIP—NO FOCUS ON HIM

Now wait a minute, while we look at this narrowly, or even judgmentally, or unkindly on the Hebrew and the Jew and say, "Yeah, them guys..." let's focus on ourselves. We go through the motions of worship, but our hearts are far from Him. I wonder how many business deals are done here during service? I wonder how many dress patterns are cut out during service? I wonder how many electric bills and bank accounts are balanced here during service? Whoops! Have I become your enemy because I tell thee the truth?

Matthew 15:9, "But in vain they do worship me, teaching for doctrines the commandments of men. (10) And he called the multitude, and said unto them, Hear, and understand:" So they do worship, but it's vain. All He is trying to tell you is; be careful, lest you begin to emphasize the mechanical and not the devotional and the emotional. Clap your hands, lift your hands, get loud, sing, cry, weep, dance, rejoice, leap—all are a part of expressing worship.

WORSHIP IS EXPRESSED, BUT IS *NOT* THE EXPRESSION

My Bible study tonight is about the expression of worship, but worship IS NOT expression, worship is expressed, but if we are not careful we will get married to a concept that the expression is now substituted for the worship…so…we can be very critical and judgmental of anybody that doesn't express like us. Now I am for demonstrative things, I am for expression, we need somehow to physically let off Holy Ghost steam, but if you don't have a propensity towards gymnastics for Jesus, and you're not one that is going to take off and run around the aisle—fine; what are you going to do?

DON'T DECEIVE YOURSELF

A cold heart can't produce hot, boiling worship. Kind of hard for a lukewarm heart to produce boiling worship, and if you're heart is not on fire for God, it's so easy to say, "I'm just not emotional." Fine, you're not emotional, are you a worshipper? So you say, "Well, I express myself differently." Fine, you have a right to do so, as long as you are expressing and you are not deceiving yourself—then go for it, but don't lie to yourself. Don't say, "Well, I'm just sort of a more quiet spirit." Fine, God's got millions of wonderful, quiet spirits in the kingdom of God that probably will not boogaloo and jump around the place, but don't deceive yourself by not doing something with what you feel in your spirit. You need to express something. If you can find a release through tears and a quivering lip, then you do that, but don't sit and do nothing and lie to yourself and say, "Well, I'm not emotional." That's not the issue. Worship must be expressed.

DON'T LET WORSHIP BECOME MECHANICAL

Now watch, the flip side is that the expression does not necessarily mean you worshipped, because you can learn the ritual just like Israel learned the ritual. We laugh and complain and joke and probably are very unkind to people who come out of Catholicism…my mom was Catholic, all my relatives were Catholic, I knew how to pray the rosary. I prayed the rosary lots of times, and we laugh and say, "Well, they're praying their beads; they're going through a ritual." We've got our beads! We've got our ritual! I'm just trying to help us here. Beware the emphasis is not on the mechanical; it has to have some type of devotional and emotional content.

The other side of the aspect is Mount Carmel; all their emphasis was on emotional. The false prophets of Baal…they were much more emotional than Elijah. You didn't see Elijah jumpin' up and down on the altar and boogalooin' all afternoon and cuttin' himself and carrying on and screaming and acting like a crazy man from a carnival. These cats were emotional, but they were not factual. They were not locked into truth. They couldn't produce fire. The desire is fire, however; we can get the fire to come down as long as we don't make an affront to God. We need fire! We need God to answer!

WORSHIP MUST FLOW OUT OF AN ATTITUDE OF ADORATION

See now, there is another aspect to this; there's a problem with the Athenians in Acts 17, Mars Hill. Their problem is that they are married to their statues, their idols, and their concepts, and not to the person of God, and they're just as diligent about what they are doing as we are. Get what I'm saying? Okay, let's everybody clap…. Stop! Everybody wave their hand…. Stop! Everybody say, "Praise God…." None of that was worship. But wait a minute; any one of those avenues can become an expression of worship, if they flow out of an attitude inside that adores Him.

These things; clapping, dancing, shouting, crying, singing, leaping, getting loud, they are forms of expression, but they are not the worship itself. They are the channels of the containers through which worship comes to fruition. They are the avenues by which the adoration of my heart, the overwhelming awe that I feel towards God Almighty, finds their expression and manifesting.

WORSHIP IS CLOSE UP—NOT LONG DISTANCE

Let me try it again. Any happily married people in the house? Okay. Now watch: hopefully, you husbands and wives… hopefully frequently, embrace each other, touch, hug, and kiss. None of those things are love. They are forms of an expression, hopefully, of something deeper within you. They are gestures; they are expressions. If the kiss is it, you're in trouble. If the hug is the end of the road…if there's not more steam behind that engine…you've got trouble.

Watch, let me try it again: Husband and wife are separated, because of a business trip, or whatever. Husband misses his sweetie-pie and sends her some flowers…maybe sends her a little box of candy, or gives her a call on the phone…that's not the love he has for her. That's the expression of the love that he has for her. The love that he has for her, hopefully, is much richer, and much deeper, and much purer than a box of candy and a dozen roses. But it's all he can do, because they are separated geographically. Now, when he gets off the plane, or gets in a cab, or comes home on the bus, he hugs and embraces and kisses his wife. Those are also expressions, but of a higher level, because he is now able, closely, to be intimate with her.

REAL WORSHIP IS USUALLY A DEEP RESPONSE TO HIM

Clapping is not worship; it can be an expression of what I feel, but the worship will take place when He responds to my gesture. You can't worship "absentee." Both parties have to be in the area, and when God begins to respond to our gestures of thankfulness and gratefulness and praise, so that now we're in His very aroma, we're in His presence Himself, then we begin to exchange our "love you's" and worship takes place. Watch me now; …and most of the time when real worship takes place there will not be a demonstrative clapping or loudness, most of the time there is a stillness that comes out of our soul. You'll probably become more broken than you will loud. All of a sudden there will come a pure stillness, there'll be some whisper out of the deep of your soul that will just come out of a trembling lip, or a coursing tear that will say, "I love you Jesus." And there'll be such an intimacy, and you'll say it slow and low, because it's so pure, and intimate, and sacred, and precious that you don't want three "boogaloos" sittin' on the bench saying, "What did you say?" You don't want them to hear that, because this is kind of an "I love you" to someone that knows every secret about your heart and every fear that you have and every failure that you've experienced and every anguishing feeling that you have towards the future.

YOU CAN WORSHIP ANYWHERE

There are times that I've been riding in the car, or walking down the street, or listening to a tape, and I'll just be thankin' God, and all of a sudden, whoa! Hallelujah! Praise God! I'll just hear something real good, and goose bumps will run up my neck and I go, "hallelujah, that's beautiful," and it seems while I am in that time of thanksgiving and praising God, it's like He just kind of like, He manifests His holiness. He just comes up, and you just go, "oooh, Jesus, Hallelujah, Jesus." And you just slow down, and it's almost like it's the fulfillment of that song, "I come to the garden alone while the dew is still on the rose, and He talks with me and He walks with me and He tells me I am His own, and the joy we share...." Something happens in there. It's a worship service. And from that worship service, my study, my sacrifice, and my work will have power in it. That's why church doesn't work for a lot of people, because all it is, is church.

WORSHIP CANNOT BE TAUGHT OR ORCHESTRATED

Are you hearing what I'm saying? Praise can be taught and practiced. Oh yes, we can teach you praise things, and sing praise choruses, and praise. And that's fine and we need it, and prayer can be taught and practiced. And singing can be taught and practiced. And a service can be taught and orchestrated and structured, but NOT WORSHIP! Because worship, like real love, carries with it one thing that nothing else that I just mentioned carries: spontaneous combustion—of which you have no control!

YOU LEARN TO WORSHIP BY WORSHIPPING

About these nincompoops; and I mean all respect to these nincompoops; these nincompoops that write all these books on love...do you know that every time they keep writing on love they're messing it up? The more you try to explain love, bring it down to exactly right, to a formula, to a code, to what you got to do, and what you shouldn't do...I know they are trying to help people, but love is like worship: spontaneous! It just happens! It flows! It's better experienced than told. Better to embrace the author than read His book. Worship is, indeed, love responding to love. The more you try to teach on it and explain really what worship is, the more you mess it up. You learn worship by worship.

EVERYTHING SHOULD LEAD TO *HIM*

Worship is responding to God, it's interaction between the person and their God. It is intimacy of the highest level. It is emotion expressed. That's why our churches have more singers and praisers than worshippers. Now we need singers and praisers to help bring us to God, but once you sing and praise; worship is what you do once you get there. That's why I say everything in the service should be leading to Him. Worship should be a celebration for who God is and what He is—Psalm 150:2.

MAKE THE VOICE OF PRAISE HEARD

Psalm 122:1, "I was glad when they said unto me, Let us go into the house of the Lord." Now watch; worship should be a celebration, it involves emotion. I was G-L-A-D. Now lots of time we can say, "I was sad, but I did my duty." You might as well stop lying to yourself, you ain't going to be glad all the time. There's sometimes you carried your carcass here you wished you'd of let your carcass stay home. That doesn't make you a bad person—that makes you a person.

Psalm 100:1&4, "Make a joyful noise unto the Lord, all ye lands. Serve the Lord with gladness: come before his presence with singing." (4) "Enter into his gates with thanksgiving, and into his courts with praise: be thankful unto him, and bless his name."

Psalm 66:1, "Make a joyful noise unto God, all ye lands: (2) Sing forth the honour of his name: make his praise glorious. (3) Say unto God, how terrible art thou in thy works! Through the greatness of thy power shall thine enemies submit themselves unto thee. (4) All the earth shall worship thee, and shall sing unto thee; they shall sing to thy name. Selah. (5) Come and see the works of God: he is terrible in his doing toward the children of men. (6) He turned the sea into dry land: they went through a flood on foot: there did we rejoice in him. (7) He ruleth by his power forever; his eyes behold the nations: let not the rebellious exalt themselves. Selah. (8) O bless our God, ye people, and make the voice of his praise to be heard:"

WORSHIP—A JOYFUL RESPONSE

Apparently worship involves noise. Hear what I'm telling you. Israel's sacrificial system was designed by God to induce them to a joyful response. When they brought their sacrifices to the priest and they saw that sacrifice slain, they, in essence, experienced a spiritual liberty, for the substitute died for them; and atonement was made for them; and the blood covered their errors, trespasses and mistakes. So they experienced a liberty from the very law that was destined to kill them, and so that very experience of bloodletting and sacrifice and atonement, was really designed by God to make the sacrificer of the animal a joyful worshipper—"...Look what just happened for me...bless the Lord...!" But they missed it! It wasn't because they were evil, it was because they were like us—people. So that when we come together, we have to always constantly rehearse..."Look what the Lord's done for us..." and it gets to be old hat..."Oh, I heard that story....."

Psalm 95:1-6, "Oh come, let us sing unto the Lord: let us make a joyful noise to the rock of our salvation. (2) Let us come before his presence with thanksgiving, and make a joyful noise unto him with psalms. (3) For the lord is a great God, and a great king above all gods. (4) In his hand are the deep places of the earth: the strength of the hills is his also. (5) The sea is his, and he made it: and his hands formed the dry land. (6) O come, let us worship and bow down: let us kneel before the Lord our maker."

REJOICE—WE HAVE A BETTER COVENANT

Now, if these scriptures are all telling the Israel people to bless and be glad and enjoy God for what He has done for them, how much more us? For their sins were just covered, our sins are taken away! Totally cleansed! Totally pardoned! If you read Hebrews 10:1-4, it says, ...with those sacrifices there was always the conscience that accused, and caused them to remember. Even though atonement was made, the conscience was not totally purged. There was a remembrance of sin in those sacrifices, for it is not possible for the blood of bulls and goats to take away sin. You cannot take something inferior and cleanse something superior. Man is superior to the animal kingdom. You can't take something lower, and make something greater—better.

That's why God incarnated Himself. He took something superior and helped something inferior. That's why the blood that was in Jesus was sinless blood. It was indeed the blood of God! It was sinless, precious, holy blood. It was the only blood that could buy our redemption. Something superior came down for something inferior and gave us something that was superior to anything else.

EMOTION IS NOT WORSHIP—IT'S THE EXPRESSION OF WORSHIP

So why aren't there more worshippers in Pentecost? What's our problem? We don't understand. We've been sidetracked with emotion. Yes, we have. And I'm for emotion, I believe emotion has its place in the kingdom, but I'm not going to be stupid enough to say that emotion is worship. No, no! It's an expression of my worship, but it's not my worship. My worship is how I feel about Him, what I see in Him, what I think about Him, how I adore Him, and I've got to find a channel and avenue by which I could express what I feel.

WHAT YOU THINK OF *HIM* YOU WILL EXPRESS

If you don't ever express anything, is there a good chance you don't feel anything? You don't think much about Him...He's not a high criteria in your life...He's not a high priority.... Is it not true that our low vision and view of God is what births small lives? Is it not the curse of Christianity? It's not doctrine so much as it is the loss of the vision of the majesty of God. If we could get God to wash our eyes, so that every time we went anywhere, or wherever we worked, we would sanctify our work place, we would sanctify our schoolyard, we would sanctify places we eat breakfast or supper...when we walked in..."Listen, I'm bringing God in this place...."

It doesn't mean you have to pass out tracts and talk in tongues in the men's room. That's not what it means; it means that you have a vision of God and you look at people through that vision. "...I can help this person God, let me be a vessel, let me be a channel, help me to touch this person, let me be an ambassador...."

IT'S ALL ABOUT RESTORATION TO WORSHIP

I don't think we understand what the incarnation was. I've preached it until my tongue has fallen out—the incarnation was more than; "To wit God was in Christ." The incarnation is a lot more than the Baptist, and the Presbyterians, and the Episcopalians, and the Catholics, Jehovah Witnesses, and the Mormons, and all the rest of them, and the Charismatics, and the Pentecostals; it's a lot more than we have said it was.
We say that Calvary and the incarnation was the royal rescue mission of Heaven. That is not the full truth! It wasn't a rescue mission; it was a rescue mission with ONE desire: Restoration! It wasn't just to pay man's debt; it was to buy man out of sin's hostage-holding pattern, so that man could be restored to the place of a worshipper of God.

NEW JERUSALEM IS ALL ABOUT WORSHIP

Now, you know a little bit why I'm always bent out of shape about this signing a card and believing in Jesus stuff. It's so sickening! Not only because 1) it's erroneous and false doctrine, but 2) it doesn't give the person a chance to be a worshipper. "...Sign a card and put it in your pocket..." well, let me tell you what's almost as bad as that: talk in tongues and sit down. Talk in tongues, give you a list of what to wear, what not to wear, what to watch and don't watch, where to go and where not to go, what words you can use, what colors you can't wear, and then sit down and hope the preacher gets you to the City.

What are you going to do when you get to the City? If you don't worship here, you aren't going to all of a sudden magically worship there. If you're not excited about Him here, you don't have to worry about getting excited about Him there, because He's going to be no different there than He is right here. He's not going to get any better! You say, "Oh, well, I will worship in that day, because I will see Him." "You can see Him now!" Don't you get it? God was trying to restore the human race through the plan of redemption to the place that man had in Adam in the garden before the fall. Now if you can get that, then you are ahead of most theologians. God is trying to get us back to where we were in Adam.

BECOME COMFORTABLE IN GOD'S PRESENCE

Where were we in Adam? Comfortable in God's presence; looking forward everyday for the visit of "my best friend." I've told you before, it bears repeating; Adam was the world's greatest worshipper, because he didn't have to deal with rejection and fear and guilt and shame. He didn't have to deal with peer pressure. He didn't have to worry about whether God would accept him. He knew when he blinked his eyes that God would accept him. Oh, I wish I could get this assembly...that if you believe and if you are honest in your worship, you will be accepted! Get back to the place we were in Adam where there weren't two agendas—we won't worry about the time.

Do you realize; in Adam there was no such thing as distance between him and deity? "That's my Dad."—"That's my boy." "That's my Father."—"That's my son." "He is my Lord."—"He's my child." "I have such a peace in His presence, I'm not afraid of Him." Adam found fulfillment in God—God found satisfaction in Adam.

The animal level could only reach so high, but here was someone in His image that transcended angels; for angels were never given the privilege to bear the nature of God. Angels never bore the image of God. No wonder the scripture says, "Angels desire to look into those things." It's not just a salvation issue, it's the whole issue of; "What's going on with God, why is He so turned on with these humans? I saw Lucifer and his gang make one bad move and God wrecked a whole universe to throw them out, these guys keep falling in the mud every week, saying something about, 'I'm sorry', and God just bends His ear as if He is straining to say, 'What did you say'?"

SELF WORTH IN GOD—IMPORTANT

Angels desire to look into this thing. We are a dilemma to the angelic hosts. They can't figure out what makes God move towards us. We are such weaklings. They move at the speed of light…greater in power…can't die…can move through the universe with thought. I'm taking hours to get to Orlando! God let's them take a trip by themselves—and He gets in the car with me! Man, do we need a lesson on self worth, or what?

SACRIFICE OF PRAISE—THE BEGINNING

Hebrews 13:15, "By him therefore let us offer the sacrifice of praise to God continually, that is, the fruit of our lips giving thanks to his name." See, that's the sacrifice of praise, the fruit of our lips, giving thanks to God. That's the beginning of what you do. Hosea said…let's offer up the calves of our lips, it's a sacrifice.

1 Peter 2:5, "Ye also, are lively stones, are built up a spiritual house, an holy priesthood, to offer up spiritual sacrifices, acceptable to God by Jesus Christ." That's what we are supposed to do; offer up spiritual sacrifices to God and the medium of that channel is Jesus Christ.

1 Peter 2:9, "But ye are a chosen generation, a royal priesthood, an holy nation, a peculiar people; that ye should shew forth the praises of him who hath called you out of darkness into his marvellous light:" Who are not a people but now are a people. One time you didn't have covenant, now you got covenant.

We are called back, to be converted back, to be restored back, so we can come back, to learn to do, and to be, what we were created to be at the beginning; to worship God, glorify God, enjoy God, manifest God.

THE WHY & WONDER OF WORSHIP • BOOK TWO

THE
WHY & WONDER
OF WORSHIP

VOLUME FIVE • CHAPTER SIX

THE WHY & WONDER OF WORSHIP • BOOK TWO

CHAPTER SIX

A BRIEF REHEARSAL

Let's just see if we can begin to tie up some of the loose strings from last week's Bible study. 1 Chronicles 29:10, "Wherefore David blessed the Lord before all the congregation: and David said, Blessed be thou, Lord God of Israel our father, for ever and ever. (11) Thine, O Lord, is the greatness, and the power, and the glory, and the victory, and the majesty: for all that is in the heaven and in the earth is thine; thine is the kingdom, O Lord, and thou art exalted as head above all. (12) Both riches and honour come of thee, and thou reignest over all; and in thine hand is power and might; and in thine hand it is to make great, and to give strength unto all. (13) Now therefore, our God, we thank thee, and praise thy glorious name. (14) But who am I, and what is my people, that we should be able to offer so willingly after this sort? For all things come of thee, and of thine own have we given thee."

Remember what we talked about that last week? "All things come of thee...," we are only returning to God what God gave to us. That's why it's really a call to stewardship, that's all it is. God in His kindness and His benevolence just gives to us and then says, "Now, I'm trusting you to be good stewards." He doesn't have to give us anything, but He does. And then I think He is very disappointed when we become very selfish and self-centered and stingy and we don't give anything back, because the Lord looks at it and says, "You really didn't give Me anything, it was Mine, I just let you have it." Kind of like a little child that crawls up in her daddy's lap and says, "Daddy, let me have a quarter," and daddy says, "Why?" and she says, "Because I want to buy you a birthday card." So daddy gives her a quarter and she buys the birthday card and scribbles a few notes in it and when he gets the card he is so thrilled and elated over the card even though he bought it. Get the picture?

Can you imagine how condescending God is that, when you return, or I return, part of my income, or my life, or whatever I have—gifts, or time, or talent, or anything—that He actually condescends to us and says, "Oh, thank you!" That's what He says, "Oh, that was so nice of you to give that!" He never says," Give My stuff back to me!" He says, "So nice of you to give that to Me, you didn't have to, that was so sweet, in fact I think so much of it, I'm going to bless you." I think God has such a great sense of humor. I'm sorry if I offended you spiritual people. Well, okay, I'll just skip that and just get into the message....

(20) "And David said to all the congregation, Now bless the Lord your God. And all the congregation blessed the Lord God of their fathers, and bowed down their heads, and worshipped the Lord, and the king." (21) And they sacrificed sacrifices unto the Lord, and offered burnt offerings unto the Lord, on the morrow after that day, even a thousand bullocks, a thousand rams, and a thousand lambs, with their drink offerings, and sacrifices in abundance for all Israel: (22) And did eat and drink before the Lord on that day with great gladness."

There are a few things I want to talk to you about tonight. Last week we were dealing with the worship expression; the various things that we demonstrate—clapping, singing, praising, crying, sighing, running, leaping.... Those are not acts of worship; they are acts of expression of worship. It's really important that you understand that, because clapping is not worship, it is an expression of what we are feeling in our heart, because worship is to feel in the spirit, or in the heart, an adoration or an awe towards God; and finding an outward expression of that.

That's why it's very easy for those of us who are *quote* "Pentecostal" by choice, to be very demeaning and unkind to people who are non-expressive. It's very easy to say, "Well, they don't worship God." Well now, you better be careful. They may be worshipping God. They may not worship God as well as you do, but then again, they may not have as much light as you have. They may not be as exuberant as you.

WORSHIP MUST BE DEMONSTRATED

Expressions of worship are not worship; they are the channels through which worship comes, but worship must be demonstrable. For a man to tell his wife he loves her and then goes to live with another woman...I may have my doubts. For a man to say he loves his wife and has two gals on the side, and slaps her around all the time, and doesn't pay the light bill...I have an indicator that there may be a problem here. For a woman to say that she loves her husband, but doesn't like to be around him...well, I'm not goin' by the Song of Solomon, I left that one alone. But...but if you say you love somebody in an intimate way...you are related in a matrimonial type thing...there ought to be some type of huggin' and kissin'. You really need to do more then handshakin' and "I'll buy you an eggbeater for your anniversary...."

I don't know why we have such a problem with that. I don't know.... Did this church preach against kissin' before I got here, or something? Was it a cardinal doctrine here? Is there something wrong with a man and a woman holding hands, or embracing, or just hugging, or enjoying without having to be sexual and sensual? Is there anything wrong with a woman giving her husband a peck, or a hug, or a big ol' sloppy kiss? Is there something wrong with that? An expression? ...I'm going to find you. You can stay out of the Song of Solomon all you want to, but I have a real problem with people who are just kinda Pentecostal librarians and never express anything.

"Yeah, you know I love you, I come home every night."
"Well, so does the dog!"
"Well, I washed your clothes. Doesn't that I show I love you?"
"No, it means that you don't like the smell, that's why you washed the clothes."

WORSHIP IS TO BE A CELEBRATION

Worship is supposed to be a celebration of who God is and what He is. That's what worship is supposed to be, therefore; if we celebrate God, we have to be glad. I think there is enough scripture to prove that we are supposed to be joyful. We are to break forth in rejoicing. We ought to be thrilled with the fact that God loved me enough to adopt me and let me become a part of His family. He didn't need me; I needed Him. He could make more worlds; He may be making more worlds now! He most likely is!

GOD IS MEASURELESS

You know, we don't know how far the universe is, we could be the furthest outpost on His universe, we may be the smallest mud ball, He may have billions of other types of civilizations other than you. You have no idea. I mean, as brilliant and magnificent and awesome and powerful and measureless as God is, how could we ever say, "Well, He is confined to this little mud ball spinnin' around out of control down here"? I don't think so. I've never been able to get over just the little bit of study I've done on Seraphim's and Cherubim's; I haven't got that clear in my mind, but it's so awesome—that it can't be numbered. It says that there is a company of angels—Innumerable. That means that you can't use a computer to find the answer. It will go the end of your screen and say...patent pending—patent pending.

Innumerable! What's He need all them angels for? Truly, not enough to take care of this little mud ball; one angel killed a hundred and eighty-five people in one night for Hezekiah. He doesn't need a company of innumerable angels to take care of a few billion people. If you equate that out, if one takes care of a hundred and eighty-five people, a few thousand can take care of the whole thing. It's awesome! What is He doing? What's He doing right now?

That's why, to me, it should be so easy to worship God when your mind gets short-circuited to how awesome He is and how you can't calculate how great He is and that He would condescend to just step down unto this platform and say;

"I love you, and I want you to be My family." "Would you let Me adopt you?"
"Oh, no, I'm busy."
"Would you let Me forgive you of your sins, and would you let Me move into your body so that your body could be My house, My temple and My headquarters?"
"No, I'm, not...not religious!"

GOD'S BLESSINGS ARE UNLIMITED

You know how mind-boggling that is, that every day His blessings and His mercy are fresh and new every morning? That I wake up every day and I've got a right mind and my body is still functioning? It may ache, it may move a little slower, but it's still functioning.

I was talking to someone yesterday and they were grumbling to me about…in fact I was at the coffee shop and I said, "Hey, ol' smiley," and she said, "Oh, I hate being here, I just hate working." I said, "You need to go with me today." She said, "Where we going?" I said, "We're going to the children's ward at Shands, I want to show you kids that have hoses up their nose and wires down their neck, and several kids sitting in Cerebral Palsy wards that can't walk and other people with Emphysema that can't breathe, you'd be very, very happy to sell these bagels and have a cup of coffee." It took the smile right off her face and I ruined her day. She was wanting someone to say, "Yea, you're right, you should just shoot yourself." That's so crazy! We are very blessed!

WORSHIP—BEING COMFORTABLE IN EXPRESSING LOVE

We need to understand some more about worship's expression. We need to express ourselves in thanksgiving and praise unto God. My last point last week…we were called and converted back, and restored back—to come back—to learn what we were originally created to do at the start, and that was to worship God, glorify God, magnify God, and enjoy God. We have a generation that has been taught that they should enjoy God, but they have not been taught that the way to enjoy God is to worship Him. They've been taught that the way to enjoy God is to get some pet scriptures and to praise Him until you annoy Him half to death and He gives you what you want. That is a self-centered religion. That's not what God wants. God wants to be at the center of our lives. He wants to be THE center of our lives and He wants us to be able to express ourselves. …You are either not hearing me, or I am not talking very well.… The American churches have literally, totally, missed the message of worship.

We were not saved to serve. We were saved so that we could worship God, and in worshipping God we could become fulfilled, and by worshipping God we would have a natural drive and inclination to serve God and help my fellow man. The only reason that church becomes a pain in the neck and that in asking you to do things and adjust your life, it's a pain in the neck, because we are not really worshipping to the level or depth that we need to be doing. Because if we are taken' up with Him, anything He would like for us to do is simple.

How many husbands have ever been confronted by a preacher, a priest, a rabbi, a friend of the family, and are totally devastated when confronted with the statement that their wife doesn't feel like they love them much, or care for them. Now get what I'm fixin' to say: How devastating when a preacher has to sit down with a man, 'cause I've talked to the wife, and say, "We've got a little problem here, your wife is having a problem with knowing whether you love her or not, and she feels like you don't care." Now nine times out of ten, it's not right, it's handled in a few minutes. But, the husband is devastated, because deep within his heart he loves that woman better than sunshine and rain. What the problem is, he has trouble expressing it. It's not that they don't love, but they're awkward in how to express what they feel. They feel deeply within; they love, they adore, they appreciate, but they don't know how to outwardly let a flow of expression be demonstrated. Sort of like a young fella that falls in love with a gal, or visa versa, and they get all tongue-tied and don't know how to look them in the face and how to talk to them and say how they feel.

You ever feel something so deep, but you can't say it? You ever notice when we go to different funerals how you gather around people who have lost a loved one and you feel deeply…empathy, pity, sympathy, compassion, hurt, not to the level that they are, but you are hurting for them, and you love the person that they lost, and yet, you walk up and you almost don't want to say something, because you don't know how to say; and you're hoping what you say will fit and it will help…and you almost make a mess out of trying to be kind. And sometimes, you don't say anything, and you stay away and the person will read into that, "You didn't care." And all the while, if the truth was known, you cared so deeply and

THE WHY & WONDER OF WORSHIP • BOOK TWO

so purely, but you didn't know how to express it, and you didn't want to make a fool out of yourself, so you didn't do ANYTHING.

How many times have parents been shocked? ...To be told by somebody else outside their family, things that their child told *them*. To be told by someone outside the family that your child feels like you don't love them, and your first response is, "What?" And you immediately defend yourself and say, "Wait a minute," and you go down the litany of things.... And you go clear back when you were changing diapers and you played dinosaurs and purple pie man and you read books and coloring books and we took trips and we played in the little pool together and we played games and we did magic tricks and..."What? I don't love you?"

And what you're saying is that somehow you have not been able to express to that child something that they can comprehend. But you really do love them, and you'd cut your right arm off for them. And you'd move Heaven and Hell for them, but for some reason they read into something, or they missed the signal, and they think you don't care. Well, I'm just trying to get to a level so that you can understand what I'm saying. You feel deeply, you really do love. You've sacrificed, you've given...that thought has never been in your mind. The sun rises and sets in them. And you are shocked when someone outside your family says, "You know, your son doesn't really feel like they're loved, and they feel like you'll be glad when they leave." What? And you wonder, "What are you snorting?" "How much glue is up your schnozzola?" And you want to confront the issue and say, "Where did you get that from?"

I've said that to say this, ...how many times have we wanted to worship God and in the depths of our own spirits, and our souls, and our minds, and our hearts, we do love God. And we love Him sincerely and deeply, and yet, at times, we find an inability to express that feeling to God in a comfortable way so that we don't feel like loony-tunes, or we don't make a spectacle out of ourselves, but we do bless God and we do love God, and yet maybe we don't know how to express it properly. And you can be frustrated, though you are in love with God.

# THE WHY & WONDER OF WORSHIP • BOOK TWO

When my mother died, I can remember as vivid as I am standing here, the total shock that came across my father when my grandfather sat across the table that very evening after we buried my mom; and my grandfather sat with my dad and just confronted him with his sternness and said;

"Now look, Mildred's gone. Bruce…" (who is my brother) "…has nobody to protect him against you." And I can remember my father's mouth just dropping open;

"What do you mean protect him AGAINST me?"

"Well, for crying out loud George, everybody knows on planet earth that Millie protected him from YOU! You could yell and rant and rave at your other two boys; fine, but Bruce was tender and soft and easily broken and so Millie always protected him so you wouldn't whip him and you wouldn't yell at him and you wouldn't do this to him, but she's gone now and the whole family is scared to death what's going to happen to Bruce, so we just want you to know that we're willing to take him and let him move in with us." My father was devastated, because my father could not accept the fact that Bruce was afraid of him. And of course, with the congenial and warm manner of my father, he yelled;

"BRUCE!" and Bruce came out;
"Hello."
He said, "SIT DOWN HERE! ARE YOU AFRAID OF ME?"

And I was sittin' at the other end of the table sayin', "…well if he ain't, I am." Yet I never had a whippin', we were never molested, we were never beaten, we were never berated, we were never verbally chewed out, it's just that he was stern. Bruce was always scared to death, but it shocked my father that after this boy being twenty-five years old, at that time, that he had never expressed to him, somehow, how deeply he loved him. …I hope I'm finding you.

THE WHY & WONDER OF WORSHIP • BOOK TWO

FROM YOUR HEART TO YOUR MOUTH—LOVE EXPRESSED

What I'm trying to say is that sometimes in the avenue of worship we are sadly lacking in our pathetic performance to convince God, by our expression, we love Him. We can turn it around and say, "Well, God knows my heart." Yes, but He wants your heart to come through your mouth and your body. "Out of the abundance of the heart the mouth speaketh." The body gestures—tears speak volumes of messages. God's not in here looking to read into your heart, He knows the secrets of everybody's hearts. There's something about God that says, "I want to see it, I want to hear it!" "I have a RIGHT to hear it!" "I have a desire to hear." "I want to hear, because I derive pleasure from your expression."

That's why I don't think God has much delight out of any of us going to a service, or coming to a service for an hour and a half and sitting as a sourpuss, or a clay pot. I just don't believe it. How would you like sitting at your family dinner with all your family members around; you work three hours, you cook a wonderful roast and vegetables and nice dessert and everything, and then everybody sits with their face down at the table. After awhile you're looking around...;

"Is it any good?"
"It's great."

Am I finding you yet? There's something about a mother after she labors for hours, and you turn around and say, "Hey, boy, that's some vittles, man that's some cornbread and hash, I loved it!" It doesn't matter that they have to go in and wash dishes for two and a half hours, they are just thrilled that you've expressed to them your appreciation of what they have just partook of. If we do that as people fixin' vittles, or fixin' a house, or buyin' somebody something, what do you think it does for God when people turn around and say, "Oh, thank you for the bread of heaven, thank you for the water of life, this has been such a wonderful thing that you are my Father, my Daddy, my God, my Priest, my Sacrifice, my Lord, my Savior, my soon-coming King." "I appreciate You, and I want to bless You, and I'm not tired of it, and I'm not in a hurry to get out of here." You get what I'm sayin'? If worship is indeed the celebrating of God, and the exalting of God, and the adoring of God, ask yourself this simple question, "how long has it been since you've been in a real worship service?"

HOW DO YOU EXPRESS WORSHIP?

Mark 12:30, "And thou shalt love the Lord thy God with all thy heart, and with all thy soul, and with all thy mind, and with all thy strength: this is the first commandment."

Real worship, there's a good definition of what real worship is, because worship is love responding to love. It is relationship being expressed. If we are not good worshippers, either we do not love God, or we love God, but we are not quite comfortable and we are somewhat awkward in how to express it. Let me go to the third point: And sometimes we become intimidated by people around us who feel like; unless we express like they express—we don't worship. Now I know that I am very...I guess, boisterous would be a good word...demonstrative, loud, vocal, physical, intense; I own the microphone; I can scream loud, and ah...I WANT people to respond and react and, maybe in my own way, in trying to get you into a relationship with God I intimidate some of you, because you just are not given to loudness and extremes! And I'm trying to cut as much slack as I can, I just want to know then, what are you given to?

Because sitting and staring is not worship, and meditation is not worship. It may be an aspect that will lead you to worship, but you can't take meditation and sit out in the woods somewhere, or by a babbling brook and just adore God's creation; that's not worship—you can do the same thing listening to classical music. ...It has to be expressed. I'll tell you what you can do; you can ride down in your car and God will let the Holy Spirit quicken a thought in your mind of something God has done for you, or just a feeling....

Have you ever just had a feeling just blow in the car, or blow into your house somewhere, and your mind is quickened, and all of a sudden a tear will just swell up in your eye, and out of the depth of your soul...just lip quivering, and just say,

"Oh, thank you." ...You've just started worshipping! See, it's just that sometimes it's easier for some of us to do it in private than in public.

WE MUST HAVE PRIVATE WORSHIP

Now my argument is; if we can do it in private, it ought to spill over into public. Maybe, many times, the terrible burden we put on our praise singers and our musicians and our choirs is that they're trying to sing unto the Lord through a medium of a non-worshipping body to try to get them to worship—because they haven't worshipped before they got here. That's why we need private worship. We need personal prayer. We need to learn how to worship God for ourselves.

IT'S NOT HOW LONG BUT HOW YOU RESPOND TO HIM

I'm going to go a little further; a worship service doesn't have to go fifteen minutes—It can go fifteen seconds. You can just begin to meditate on the goodness of God and think how good He is, and His presence comes near you and: BOOM! Your heart will be on fire and you'll bless Him and love Him and then go on your way; it doesn't have to be where you fall out and get run over by the lawn mower and then God heals you instantly and you get back up and speak in tongues. That's not what it's all about—it's about a relationship; it's about expressing myself to God.

HOW DO YOU EXPRESS LOVE?

My wife doesn't like it, but I kiss her in public. I act crazy in public; I like her, she smells good, kisses good...I like her. Now, there are some things that I don't do in public and I usually don't sweep her in my arms and put a big lip lock on her, but I'll hug her and just tap her and smile at her and act kind of crazy, and you know how wives are...she'll say, "Jeffrey, stop that!" And I'll just act crazy; I'll say, "Oh, come on baby, give yourself to me, come on honey, just me and you, let's go." And she'll get so embarrassed, her face will get so red, I don't give a flip about people over there by the beans and the carrots and the string beans, they ain't paid none of my bills, ain't fought none of my devils, I don't care about them. I know you are supposed to protect your image—I ain't got an image. Everybody in this whole church thinks I'm crazy. Everybody in the whole world thinks I'm crazy. Us crazy people can have a lot of fun, my friend. We can get by with stuff that other people can't get by with; it doesn't matter.

There ain't nobody's opinion that matters to me but J E S U S! That's the opinion that matters to me. He found me, He brought me out, He redeemed me, He forgave my sins, He gave me the Holy Ghost, He is coming back for me, He matters to me!

And I'm very happy with my wife in private, and I'm very happy with my wife in public. Now, I probably know that I need a class in being classier—in being more subtle. It is embarrassing to be standing in the produce aisle going, Come on baby...hubba, hubba, come on." She just runs away from me with the cart. And I'm not planning on putting no big lip lock on her; I just want to have fun with her. I remember when we first got married...in Kansas...we didn't have a washer in those days—we weren't uptown, we went to the washateria all the time. I remember just playing around when we were folding clothes and just kidding around and lollygaggin'. We didn't do anything immoral, just kind of...fun. I remember huggin' her and she would say, "Oh, Jeffrey put me down." ...I would do worse if she didn't run so fast.

Maybe I got that from my mother, because my mother used to kiss me all the time and she used to kiss me in public all the time and I used to hate it when I was in front of my buddies. My mother would come up...and I was a little, fat, roly-poly kid...she would call me little jelly belly, little roly-poly, she would just shake me and kiss me and I'd say, "Oh, come on mom." So I inherited a genetic sickness.

WORSHIP MOVES GOD—IN YOUR DIRECTION

I'm trying to help you understand that worship has to be expressed; it HAS to be expressed. You can't just assume..."here God, read my resume." I'm going to tell you something else, when you express worship when you are hurting, when you don't feel anything, when you feel like a loser, when you sense like you're behind the eight-ball, it means so much to the one that you express it to. Because the one that we're dealing with knows our dirty hearts and thoughts and intents. When He knows that we're reaching for Him through trembling lip and weeping eye and breaking heart, it moves God. Worship moves God!

Real worship releases all our heart's adoration and our abandonment, it lets our soul's attitude be manifest, it moves our mind and thoughts and it moves the strength of our very body. That's what Mark 12:30 is saying; "Worship the Lord with all your heart, mind, soul and strength." I know it says "worship", but that's what love is. Love and worship, that's what they are, because worship is love responding to love.

THE STANDARD FOR WORSHIP—MARK 12:30

If Mark 12:30 is the standard for a real worshipper, then the pathetic performances and pitiful praises that we offer during a service...our whispered little thanks...surely must be insulting. If this says, "Worship the Lord with all your heart, your mind, your soul, your strength," get your body involved, get your emotions involved, get your thoughts involved, get the depths of your spirit involved, let abandonment...just go after it, just bless God. So when we do this little, "praise the Lord", God appreciates the "praise the Lord", but that's a long way from, "...all your heart, all your mind and all your soul, and all your strength." If that's the biblical criteria for worship, then that tells me that I've never seen a worshipper. If that is the standard for a real biblical worshipper, then I'm sure a long way from that. If that really is the standard for a real worshipper, then I've got news for you; a real worshipper would be banned from this church. We would not tolerate anybody that did that all the time, because it would be so disruptive to our plan. Isn't it funny that a real worshipper may be banned from our services, but welcome to the game. Not much difference between a worshipper and a fan; except, the fan is allowed to worship and the worshipper is NOT allowed to worship. Worshippers—not allowed at the church service, but the fan is allowed at the game. Apparently it is okay for the worshipping fan to celebrate team's performance, but the same celebrator will give God nothing but leftovers. You'll jump up and down at a race track to yell at a horse, scream as your team plays soccer, or football, or baseball, or whatever it is, and then come and sit in church and barely raise your voice to praise the Lord?

CHANGE YOUR OBJECT OF WORSHIP

In Acts 17:22-24, Paul says, "For as I passed by and beheld your devotions...." Now what is he saying? He said, "I found an altar with an inscription, TO THE UNKNOWN GOD." But that's not what he's talking about, he said, "I passed by and I beheld your devotions." You can't have devotions that are not seen...not expressed. He said that; I WATCHED the way you worship your false gods and I want to explain something; that with the intensity with which you are doing it, it is to be commended, but the object is incorrect. I want to explain to you; just change your object, don't change your intensity, just change your object.

If we can worship God with the same excitement and intensity that we use to think about going out Friday night and grabbing a bottle and drinking all night...isn't it funny...we...is there anybody here besides me that used to go honky tonkin'? Only three people? Uh huh. Did you ever notice when you got a few belts under your belt you could do *some kind* of serious boogalooin'? You could get out there and dance in front of everybody and didn't worry about the critics. Ever notice it didn't bother you how far it was from your seat to the dance floor? But people have a problem between the pew and the altar! "...Boy, that's a long way to go!"

Maybe the issue really was; you never did do much dancin', or carryin', or raising your voice, until you had a few drinks. You see, the more you drank the less conscience you got of everybody else. When you get a good snoot full, you get belligerent. You'll start going over to other people's tables and sayin', "How are you doin'? "You're beautiful!" "Is that your husband?" "Oh, it's your dog. I see."

Now you just laugh, but I've done it all my life...dance with people you don't know. I've bought drinks for people I didn't know; "Give the man a drink, you're my kind of man!" ...Don't even know the man's name! Because...there's this euphoric feeling that comes over you when you're boozed up, or you've been snortin' drugs, or somethin', you just...everybody's wonderful.

BE FILLED WITH THE SPIRIT

Now wait a minute, that is typical of the Holy Ghost where the Bible says, "Be not drunk with wine wherein is excess, but be ye filled with the Spirit." If we were really filled with the Spirit, we'd be like; "...Come on, let's dance a while, come on let's praise God!" If you really came in here half bagged on the Holy Ghost, you'd have a plan, you'd get on your row and say, "Come on honey, let's mess up this whole row!" You wouldn't care what was goin' on, but you're so sober....

When you read in Acts Chapter 19; they chanted for two hours over the goddess Diana. They chanted for TWO HOURS; "Great is the goddess Diana!" For TWO HOURS they jumped around and acted like a bunch of fools for something that never happened. If we have a song service for more than fifteen minutes, people are checking their watches and thinking, "...Now what's happenin' here?"

We are to express through our bodies, through our minds, through our voices, through our eyes, a desire to bless and embrace God, but if that expression does not finally result in obedience to God, you have not worshipped—you just got sweaty; because this is just an expression of something that's inside you. Am I makin' sense, or are you just bored? We have no problems with petitions, and no problems with prayers, and no problems with praising for answered prayers, but sometimes we are very, very prohibited in expressing our deepest feelings to God. It can be very, very frustrating if someone tries to make you worship, or you want to worship, but don't know how to worship.

CORPORATE WORSHIP—MULTIPLE EXPRESSIONS

Psalm 22:22, "I will declare thy name unto my brethren: in the midst of the congregation will I praise thee. (23) Ye that fear the Lord, praise him; all ye the seed of Jacob, glorify him; and fear him, all ye the seed of Israel." Now here's the reason why: (24) "For he hath not despised nor abhorred the affliction of the afflicted; neither hath he hid his face from him; but when he cried unto him, he heard. (25) My praise shall be of thee n the great congregation: I will pay my vows before them that fear him."

One of the blessings of corporate praise and worship is to allow you to be in the midst of a multiplicity of expressions. For one person alone can never express and worship God fully. You may sing, you may cry, you may talk in tongues, you may dance, you may leap, you may shake; fine. But you won't do all of them. God has shown us in the scriptures that all of these channels and avenues are acceptable forms of expression. So the blessing of corporate worship is that while one person is not able to fully worship God, when you have a few hundred people together, there'll be so many different expressions of worship, God will have fully been worshipped.

So it makes room for us in the service, that if we are not emotionally prone, if we are not demonstrators, if we are weepers, if we are whisperers; fine, but as the corporate worship begins to go up to God, you find your niche and your place in that corporate body, and all different types of expressions are going up to God.

Some people are gong, "Hallelujah," some people are quietly going, "I love you Jesus," other people are shouting, some people are running, clapping, dancing.... That's the blessing; that's why he said, "I'm going to bless God and praise God and worship God in the great congregation." "I'm going to pay my vows that I made to God in private and pay them in public." That means sighing and crying and hand clapping and dancing and rejoicing and leaping and shouting—all forms of worship are being expressed. Thus, God is completely and fully and totally worshipped while you may have only worshipped God with a weep, or with a sigh, or with a whispered praise. That's why there needs to be room in the corporate body for a multiplicity of expressions.

GOD ENJOYS DIVERSITY

I am not trying to make everybody be like me, that would be boring, that would be horrible, that would be crazy. God is into diversity. He didn't paint everything gray or green. He didn't make everything look the same; He gave every type of creature a different kind of voice and He apparently enjoys all of it coming up in one day. So when we get together, He knows that some of you are never going to get up, unless the Holy Ghost literally throws you six rows…you're never going to get up and just run the aisles around this place—it's not your make up. And you'll maybe have no desire to, unless God would just all of a sudden yank you up and move you, which it may happen, but I don't think it will happen, so God knows that there is a propensity in each one of us to do certain things towards Him.

It's like God sits enthroned here as we begin to exalt and magnify Him, it's almost like He looks at these angels and says, "Now, boys, you guys do your thing; watch my kids do their stuff." You that have more than one child, two, three, four children; every one of them has their own little way to say they love you, and coming to you, and embracing you. Although each one is different, one's high and one's low, one's this and one's that, every one of them is accepted by you. So it is with God. All God wants is for you to express it, and I think that this church has given you a platform whereby you could express it. Nobody is trying to make everybody shout. I am not! If you read that into what I have taught, you have misread everything I have said. I am not trying to make you shout, I am not trying to make everybody just scream and rant and rave.

I am bothered when we are trying to bless God, and praise God, and worship God, that you sit with folded hands, and crossed arms, and crossed legs, and then try and tell me how much you love God…. …not in the coldest day in Hell, I'll never buy it! It ain't got nothin' to do with emotion—it's got to do with your depth of love; or you inability, or your fear, to express that you love Him.

Let me tell you something, if you can bless and praise and magnify God in private worship, it'll become much easier in public. You can't learn it in public, it has to be developed in private, and then you use this as a trial grounds. I have great times in my office at my house. I talk in tongues, I cry, there's sometimes I moan, there's sometimes I just kneel down at my recliner and pray for 45 minutes or an hour and I don't hardly open my eyes and I'm just talking to God and waiting on God; there's other times I'm just dancing around and thanking Him for this…. I didn't just get here so we can strike up the band—so that I can turn around and get my motor cranked; my motor was cranked before I got here. All I did was come to get an oil change.... Don't you get it? This is a place where we can all express an explosion!

It ought to be exciting that you can go to a place called a church building where you can go and feel comfortable. You can lift your hands if you want to, you can clap, you can bow your head and say, "God I love you with all my heart, and I praise...," you are welcome to do that, but you are not welcome to sit and stare. Now I am taking a position on that: that's not doing you any good. You've got to express.

Let me tell you something; I am not a good counselor. My things are so crude, my answer is usually, "Oh, for crying out loud, go pray! Who's next?" There's nothing that cannot be handled if you won't take enough time to stay in prayer and break through to the realm of the supernatural, and God will give you an answer that will be a thousand times better than mine. Because all I'm doing, unless I get a word of knowledge—is guessing; and the other problem is that I am measuring my answer by what works in my life—and it may not work in your life.

YOUR CITY IS AFFECTED BY EXPRESSED WORSHIP

Matthew 21:6, "And the disciples went, and did as Jesus commanded them, (7) And brought the ass, and the colt, and put on them their clothes, and they set him thereon. (8) And a very great multitude spread their garments in the way; others cut down branches from the trees, and strewed them in the way. (9) And the multitudes that went before, and that followed, cried, saying, Hosanna to the son of David: Blessed is he that cometh in the name of the Lord; Hosanna in the highest."

Did you get the picture that he was just saying? Those that went before and those that went behind cried the same thing, and Jesus was in the middle. Worship—those that are ahead—those that are following—Jesus in the middle. What's all the noise about? The one that's in the middle. They are exalting and blessing the one that's in the middle. Watch this; when you start exalting, blessing and magnifying the one that's in the middle, it moves the whole city. When you exalt and bless us, it just moves us.

(10) "And when he was come into Jerusalem, all the city was moved, saying, Who is this?" See…see, now the city didn't know, but the worshippers knew. (11) "And the multitude said, This is Jesus the prophet of Nazareth of Galilee."

A MESS BEFORE A MIRACLE—JESUS DEALS WITH THE HYPOCRITE

Now watch this, because this is powerful: You can't just have a cause without an effect. If you are going to have worship, there's going to be an effect *from* worship. One of the first effects is that the false has got to go, the fake has to leave, the charlatan has got to be exposed, the religious wise guys that don't have any relationship with God has got to get out of the temple. Notice that when you start ushering Jesus in between worshippers, the first place He is going to go to is where His name is placed, and He is going to clean house. He went right into the temple and started dealing with the people who should have known better.

When the Lord of the temple shows up, He is going to kick some tables over. He is going to make a mess before He brings a miracle. He made a mess before He did any miracles, because He's not going to do miracles for fakers. He does not even want the praise of dishonest people. He does not want the verbiage from hypocrites.

(12) "And Jesus went into the temple of God, and cast out all them that sold and bought in the temple, and overthrew the tables of the moneychangers, and the seats of them that sold doves." He cast out people that were not worshipping. (13) "And said unto them, it is written. My house shall be called the house of prayer; but ye have made it a den of thieves." The minute He cleaned house He set the table for the miraculous. (14) "And the blind and the lame came to him in the temple; and he healed them."

THE WHY & WONDER OF WORSHIP • BOOK TWO

THE KINGDOM—JESUS ENTHRONED IN PRAISE & WORSHIP

He won't show His stuff while the charlatans and the fakers are sitting in the temple playing church games. Please notice that when Jesus Christ is enthroned in praise, thanksgiving, and worship, you have the kingdom. When you have the kingdom, you have the aspects of the kingdom, which is supernatural, miraculous, Holy Ghost, power, authority on display. All these weeks I have been trying to share thoughts with you about worship. I confess to you, I have an ulterior motive; I'm trying to get to where I'm going right now, because the end of all this worship is the magnifying of God and the ministry of God among us: You don't have to learn three steps and read two books and do all this stuff. You don't have to do that. You just have to be a worshipper and a lover of God and let your soul be a sanctuary for the truths of God, and God will throw His own weight around.

WORSHIP BRINGS THE SUPERNATURAL

Listen, there is no way that anything can stop the supernatural display of God when people decide to worship God and let God get rid of the trash and the junk and the counterfeit out of our lives. God is too smart for us, He is called the all wise God, He is the all knowing God, He's not going to do a bunch of stuff for us so that we can flaunt our own pride and religiosity and take credit for it because we're the Pentecostal church. That don't mean nothing to Him, He is going to be enshrined among the humble and the contrite, and the pure and the transparent, He's gong to be enthroned among people who say, "We want YOU in the middle!"

(14) "And the blind and the lame came to him in the temple: and he healed them. (15) "And when the chief priests and scribes saw the wonderful things that he did, and the children crying in the temple, and saying..." Notice, watch what happens once Jesus gets rid of the mess and the miraculous starts; the critics are still there, but the praisers are increasing. Now the children are blessing and exalting and magnifying God. In other words, once God starts showing His stuff, worship and praise literally just explodes. There was nobody directing these kids

to bless God and magnify God, it was the wonderful worship that set the stage and it upset the critics, because they're never going to get honest.

(15) "...and the children crying in the temple, and saying, Hosanna to the son of David; they were sore displeased." Sure, not everybody is going to be happy when the miraculous takes place. Everybody is not happy when worship takes place.
(16) "...and said unto him, Hearest thou what these say? And Jesus saith unto them, Yea; have ye never read, Out of the mouth of babes and sucklings thou hast perfected praise?"

WORSHIP FOLLOWS GOD'S MAJESTY CONFRONTING US

Watch; as God's majesty and mystery and magnificent confronts us, worship must always be the result. In Exodus 33:12-23 and Exodus 34:5-8, where Moses says, "Show me thy glory," and God turns around and says to him, "No man can see My face and live," He says, "But I'll make all my goodness to pass before thee and I'll put you in the cleft of the rock, put My hand on you when I pass by, I'll take My hand off and you'll see My hinder parts." If you read it in the original it says, "You'll see the afterglow."

And the scripture says when the Lord begins to proclaim His greatness, the Lord good and mighty, kind and full of longsuffering and on and on...the Bible says that Moses just falls down and worships, because worship is always direct result of beholding the majesty and the greatness of God. You don't have to be provoked and prompted to, it will automatically happen! That's why we need song service, that's why we need singers, and praising, and audience participation, so it creates an atmosphere, so we get divorced from the days activities...we step into the sanctuary where God can show His stuff. And when God shows His stuff, we'll leave the area of spectatorism, and even thankfulness and praise, and we'll step into a realm of worship, which will cause us to fall down, and when you fall down you're not taking credit for anything. Then God will start showing His stuff, because right after that, God turns around and says, "I'm going to show signs and wonders that you've never seen before." See, that's the real thing that we're going after for worship—is that we might extol Him and magnify Him and just somehow enshrine Him in our hearts and our emotions, so that He is everything, so that He is allowed to be what He is, G O D!

WORSHIP—THE OVERFLOW OF A GRATEFUL HEART

Worship is an inner attitude expressed—a communicated affection. Worship is the outflow of inner affection of attitude. Worship is the overflow of a grateful heart. Psalm 45:1, "My heart is inditing a good matter: I speak of the things which I have made touching the king: my tongue is the pen of a ready writer." If you read it in the original when it says, "My heart is inditing a good thing...," it says this; "My heart boileth over." Why? ...I'm meditating on the greatness and the goodness of God and the kettle is boiling! You don't have to sing 35 songs to get you in the mood. All we have to do is get you to meditate on the good things of God and let your spirit boil over, you already have the nature of God inside of you—it just needs to spring up.

Here's why we have problems with trying to orchestrate worship; because worship is spontaneous. It explodes of itself. You can't MAKE worship happen. You can orchestrate a song service, have praise and thanksgiving, have testimony, but worship is when all of a sudden I step into the raw presence of God and His Spirit touches my spirit, and something happens. When you really meditate on the wonder and the greatness of God, something happens inside and it boils over inside—it has to be expressed. Is that honest then to say that many who never open their mouth—there's no boiling? Or you have a cork on that's really tight?

Worship is the outpouring of the soul; it is the soul that rests and, yet, rejoicing in the presence of God. Worship is the occupation of the heart, not with needs, or blessings, but with God Himself.

WORSHIP SHOULD HUMBLE US

2 Samuel 7:18-22, "Then went king David in, and sat...." It is possible to have a great worship service and not have to stand up. You can sit...you can have a worship service sitting in your car. You can have a worship service sitting in the

recliner of your house somewhere. The only other ingredient is; make sure you are sitting before the Lord, not NBC; before the LORD, not the OSCARS. The LORD.

(18) "...before the Lord, and he said, Who am I, O Lord God? And what is my house, that thou hast brought me hitherto? (19) And this was yet a small thing in thy sight, O Lord God; but thou hast spoken also of thy servant's house for a great while to come. And is this the manner of man, O Lord God? (20) And what can David say more unto thee? For thou, Lord God, knowest thy servant. (21) For thy word's sake, and according to thine own heart, hast thou done all these great things, to make thy servant know them."

You get what David is doing? He is sitting before the Lord and he is bragging on God, and he is telling God, "I know that I am not worthy, but You are wonderful, You are great, You've been so precious to me, and You've promised me things about tomorrow that I'm not worthy to have and my home isn't set in order like it ought to be, but You've been so precious to me, and what else can I say?" I'm telling you, you can have a worship service without having to even sing, you can just speak!

(22) "Wherefore thou art great, O Lord God: for there is none like thee, neither is there any God beside thee, according to all that we have heard with our ears." Did you get it? David just had himself a personal worship service that took him about six verses. He just went in and sat down and was just overwhelmed with the goodness and greatness of God. Worship, if it doesn't humble you, has failed to do what it should do.

THE SPIRIT—HOLY GHOST—COMES DOWN, FLOWS THROUGH AND BACK UP TO GOD

In John 4:13-14, Jesus talked about putting a well into people who believed. Scripture says it would be in them a well springing up into everlasting life. Now I want you to understand this; here's what worship is: God seeks worshippers, He knows that we don't really know how to worship, so here is what He does according to John 7:37-39, "In the last day, that great day of the feast, Jesus stood and cried, saying, If any man thirst, let him come unto me, and drink. (38) He that believeth on me, as the scripture hath said, out of his belly shall flow rivers of living water. (39) But this spake he of the Spirit, which they that believe on him should receive: for the Holy Ghost was not yet given; because that Jesus was not yet glorified."

So what He is saying is; "I want to be in you a river of living water springing up, but you don't have the river in you, so what I am going to do is put the river in you." That's the baptism of the Holy Ghost, that's the river of life. Now watch; it comes in and then what it does as we begin to open up in praise and worship is, it flows through us...springing up. Why up? Because that's where He is...up! See, the Spirit came down, comes through, goes back up. It makes a complete cycle. The beautiful part is when the worship is springing up and flowing through me I'm becoming purified, I'm getting better, I'm getting cleansed, refuse and junk is coming out of me.

IT'S A SPIRITUAL CYCLE

We don't know what to do, we don't know how to pray, howbeit the Spirit helpeth our infirmities, with groanings and utterings that we don't know what to say. The SPIRIT moves through us! What crazy kind of people don't want the Holy Ghost?

So, the Holy Ghost flows out of us in worship, and out of us into service to man. So true worship is actually receiving living waters, living waters rising up in me, and then living waters returning to its source.

Watch this; Ecclesiastes 1:7, "All the rivers run into the sea; yet the sea is not full; unto the place from whence the rivers come, thither they return again." See, God is the initiator of worship, He enables us to worship, He manifests Himself, He literally imparts a part of His own essence, nature, and being, into us so we can worship, and then He receives it back. Don't you see, the whole thing is a kind condescension of God, because we couldn't do it if He didn't help us. The beautiful thing is that He puts it in us, we're not worthy to have it, it purifies and works through us, it comes back and then He acts like He is so thrilled that He got it.

PURE WORSHIP HAS NO PETITIONS

Last point: worship is actually ascribing worth to somebody. In Revelation 4:8-11, Revelation 5:8-14, it is interesting to note that the living creatures, the beast, the elders, the multitude, which no man can number; in these two passages of scripture they are blessing, exalting, magnifying, and worshipping God and there is no point in these two verses where a single petition has been offered. The purest form of worship has no petition—it is all praise and blessing of God.

Learning worship is so needful for us; it will help us. I don't want you going home frustrated, saying, "I'm not a good worshipper." Fine. Learn how, God is a great teacher, He is very patient. Nobody ever flunks His tests; He stays overtime to help you.

THE WHY & WONDER OF WORSHIP • BOOK TWO

THE WHY & WONDER OF WORSHIP

VOLUME FIVE • CHAPTER SEVEN

CHAPTER SEVEN

Luke 7, Verse 36-39, "...And one of the Pharisees desired Him that He would eat with him. And He went into the Pharisee's house, and sat down to meat. And, behold, a woman in the city, which was a sinner, when she knew that Jesus sat at meat in the Pharisee's house, brought an alabaster box of ointment, And stood at His feet behind Him weeping, and began to wash His feet with tears, and did wipe them with hairs of her head, and kissed His feet, and anointed them with the ointment. Now when the Pharisee which had bidden Him saw it, he spake within himself, saying, This Man, if He were a prophet, would have known who and what manner of woman this is that toucheth Him: for she is a sinner."

GOD DOESN'T TELL EVERYTHING HE KNOWS

I wish I could add a little comment in there. Apparently, the Pharisees concept is; you might as well say everything you know, because the Pharisee says, "If He knew...," as if to say—if you know, you are supposed to talk. God knows lots of stuff He stays quiet about, thank you Jesus! It's kind of like the devil saying—you know, if God knew about you what I know.... He knows! He is just keepin' quiet! You ain't got to spill the beans on everything you know.

PRACTICE WHAT WE HAVE HEARD

We have, hopefully, been exposed to a lot of facets of worship. We ought to, sooner or later, start becoming better worshippers. A couple of weeks ago, we studied a message that I taught on expressing our worship, and that sometimes the expression of our worship is really the hardest thing for us to do—Being able to say, or demonstrate, how or what we feel within us. It's so easy to get tongue-tied trying to express to someone you love very deeply what you want to say, not just a romantic emotional expression. Sometimes, you can have a friend who has been hurt very deeply, or had a loss in their family, or devastated by something, and you feel empathy and compassion and sympathy towards them, and you walk up to them, wanting to express to them that you understand how they feel, and you can hardly talk for crying. And you feel like such a jerk when you leave the conversation cuz you walk away saying, "I could never say what I felt." And I really think sometimes, that one of the bugaboos about our trying to worship God, is our inability to express what we feel, and too, we lack the feeling.

SELF-WORTH MUST BE BALANCED WITH TRUTH

Now watch! If you lack the feeling, and you are forced, because of peer pressure, or because of where you are, to express—then you become a fake. Wow! In the day and the time that we are living, there has been such an overwhelming out-of-balance emphasis on *self*. There is so much self-acceptance, self-development, self-improvement, positive confession, self-esteem, self-love, "...accept yourself for what you are." But what they're saying is not what the truth is. They're not asking you and I to accept us for what we are; lost, damned, and undone, with no way to approach God, and hopelessly lost. What they are saying is, "You are not so bad, you can help yourself just by believing in yourself."

Well, let me see...if you're dead, and you believe in yourself, you're still dead! If you're a sinner, lost and undone without God, and you believe in yourself, you're still a sinner, lost and undone without God...you're just believing in yourself!
Now don't misconstrue what I am saying. I do believe in self-worth. Oh, yes I do...if it's in the eyes of God, balanced in the scales and truths of God. But you got to understand something; when this world that we're livin' in is talkin' about believing in yourself, and "you're better and you can do all this," it's not the same statement that the Bible is making. The Bible is saying that self has got to be buried, killed and crucified, because self is not going to impress God one bit!
If you can improve yourself, then God has messed up the whole thing, because He thought that you and I were in such bad shape that He had to die so that we could be saved!

SELF-IMPROVEMENT—AFTER SELF-CRUCIFIXION

See, it's not "self-improvement'." I am for self-improvement once *self* has been crucified, kicked in the teeth and buried awhile! Then I believe the Savior, Who wants to save *self*, can improve *self*. But you can't just make up your mind—"I'm going to be better." I hear that all the time; "I'm going to be better than this." No you're not, you dope; you're going to be worse than this, cuz you're going to start believing you're own press reports! You are already a dodo, and now you're going to believe that you are a good man, but you're really a dodo who thinks he is a good man!

And then you're going to start running with a bunch of dodos who are as dumb as you are and you got a Dodo club. And you're going to tell each other, "We're not dodos, we're good people." Don't you understand? That's what the Nazi's did. They told each other that they believed in their cause, and that they were the Arian race, and we're good people, and the Jews…the Slavic…the Gypsies…and the Negro were substandard people, and they needed to be obliterated from the planet. You tell me—and I'll tell you—and we'll tell each other, and after a while you believe that damnable lie! And you'll have on your hands a Holocaust.

LET GOD KILL AND THEN RAISE UP

Hear what I'm telling you! It's a dangerous posture that the world is taking, this self-help stuff. I'm not saying that you can't improve your lot by studious endeavors, or by working better, or trying to be honest. I'm talking about spiritual things, and you cannot improve yourself spiritually if God doesn't originate something in you and I… If God doesn't step in and say, "You're damned and lost; do you want help or not?" You got to understand, when God walks into your face and my face, He doesn't say, "I'll fix you up." He says, "I'm going to kill you." "I'm going to destroy everything you have." "Will you let Me kill you?" "And I promise to raise you…."

I think, sometimes, the biggest problem that we have in church is that too much of us has never died! We surrendered some areas, but we've kind of took our own evaluation that the other areas weren't that bad. Like the doctor that wants to amputate "so far" and you say," Well, one finger would be fine," but he knows the poison is up here, but you are lookin' and saying, "Looks okay, don't feel nothing." He says, "Let's cut it off here." So when you get up to God, God just looks at you and I, and He pulls the sword of judgment back and says, "Ash, let's just kill the whole putrefying mess," and instead of responding to that, we find a church of our choice. We go where they are not so hard, and where there are really nice people.

YOU CAN'T HAVE TWO CENTERS IN YOUR LIFE

The emphasis on this self-help stuff is that *self* is always allowed to stay at the center. And the reason why most churches, and a lot of Pentecostal churches, are not good at worship is because worship puts God at the center, and you cannot have two centers and be in balance! ...Somebody's got to get off the stage! This whole success stuff; this whole pyramid thing...these business schemes...it's all *self* at the center. These guys that get on TV and the radio; I hear them—I don't see them on TV; but I hear them on the radio...

"This is ol' Bro. Bob here; down here at Bob's car lot down here at Micanopy. Life's been good to me and I just want to give somethin' back...."

"How can you sell these cars for such a cheap price, Bro. Bob?"

"Well, life's been good to me; the good Lord is kind and I just want to give somethin' back."

"Well, why don't you just give them away? Why don't you just give us the car that you are driving?"

THE GREATEST THERAPY—WORSHIP

You didn't hear me! You see, the beautiful part about real worship is worship has the ability to lift you and I out of the mess of all our tangled junk. It lifts us beyond our problems and our human limitations, and really, true biblical worship is the world's greatest therapy. "...I got to go talk to my therapist," "...I got to go talk to my psychoanalyst," "...I just bought another couch, so I can be more comfortable...." You get in a real good worship service and you'll get healed of that—that laying on somebody's therapy couch. I'm going to mess with your minds tonight. I really am. You don't need therapy from the outside in. You don't need an unregenerate person taking a walk through your emotions and your mind. What you need is the Regenerator to step in the middle of your puke and mess, and just clear the whole thing out, evaluate the thing, and just say, "Worship me."

GET BACK ON THE SEAT

You see; worship is such great therapy, because when you and I worship God, we first behold God—now that's enough to heal you of worry. And secondly, when you behold God and you are caught up in that realm, you begin to see things through His perspective. We are seated "with Him in heavenly places." You know what that means? That means that we are supposed to be looking down on situations. That's what it says; Ephesians 2:6—we are seated with Him in "heavenly places." Well, if you are in "heavenly places," that means that you are not under the situation, but you are on top of the situation! Too many of us have gotten up and left our seat. We went for a walk in the world, and the world came crashing down around our shoulders and we say, "h-e-l-p!" It's almost like God saying—What are you doin' down there?

TRUE WORSHIP IS THE FLOW—NOT THE FORM

There is not a doubt in my mind that true biblical worship is the greatest mental health treatment available. Oh yeah, I'm going to find you in a second. Now worship, remember, is emotion expressed, communicated affection and adoration at its peak. This requires knowledge, revelation, as well as experience. There is a danger that worship can become mechanical and not devotional; ritualistic, and not real, not really genuine. For true worship is not in the form, but in the flow, regardless of the form. You can't make everybody in a church worship, or praise, or give thanks exactly the same way. But you can express to people the great diversity of worship forms, and they should find one, or two, or three, or four, or five, or six, or seven, or eight that help them.

FIND YOUR WAY TO EXPRESS WORSHIP

You may have a person that has a very good singing soprano voice. You're going to frustrate the dickens out of her, and drive the choir director crazy trying to make her sing bass…"Well, if you love God, you'll just adjust." She can't adjust! It's not within her framework! She's got a falsetto voice, or a high tenor…way up there. She can't do it, and it would be stupid to walk up and say, "You know, if you loved God you'd sing…." Well, she does love God, but you are trying to make her sing and it's awkward for her. So she's got to be able to find a plateau, an avenue, a channel, where by she can express herself.

That's what this whole series has really been about folks. It's trying to expose the multiplicity of ways that we can find an expression of worship unto God, because worship must be expressed. You cannot tell a woman, or a man, you love them, and never express it. You cannot say something in words…just words; and have no action. Hear me; worship is not the action.

THE VERY HEART OF WORSHIP—RIGHT ATTITUDE

The true picture of worship is the attitude that caused the action. Worship is the celebration of God; it is the outpouring of ourselves to God in thanksgiving, in praise, and adoration, in love. But the core to all worship; it has taken me 19 weeks to get here; is attitude. See, that's why it's dangerous to try to teach people choruses and gymnastics, and never teach the core behind it all. The result is that you fall in love with your gymnastics.

Some people are just kind of like a freight train…"give me room, I got to move." They have no idea why they're running; they're just comin' down the track….

"I'm going to dance a while…."
"Fine, any particular reason?"
"I like the beat…."

THE WHY & WONDER OF WORSHIP • BOOK TWO

Did you ever notice; we hardly have any dancers in this church when the music stops? You notice we don't do very well if someone doesn't keep banging and screaming into this mike. Audio Apostolics! God's main complaint with Israel was very simple; Matthew 15:8, Malachi 1:6—they have the actions, but they are missing the attitude.

Is it possible, then, to have the proper action...the proper demonstration...and not have the proper attitude? Sure! Now wait a minute! Is it also possible to have the proper actions...be void of the proper attitude...and possibly be unaware that the attitude is missing? Yes! That's why worship is so resisted and resented by the enemy of our soul, because there is such a fine line between performance that's real and pretense that's real.

WORSHIP IS FOCUS, INTIMACY & GENUINENESS

Everything is focus. Everything is intimacy. Everything is genuineness and reality with God. I'm going to tell you something; you do not have to take 4-1/2 hours to finally get into a worship mode. You can worship before your glasses hit the ground, if your attitude is full of gratitude...if your attitude is full of awe and full adoration...if your attitude is full of love. It doesn't mean your life is perfect and that things are right. It just means your attitude is right.

Am I the only one that can walk down the street and just get to thinkin' a thought in my mind, or a feeling, and I'll think about God, and before I've taken 10 steps, I feel a witness of the Holy Ghost. You know what happened? I just got "in tune." You ever been sittin' there and talkin' to someone about the Lord or somethin', and just a "whoosh" of the Holy Ghost sweeps down, and your hair stands up and goose bumps run down, and tears get in your eyes and you turn to someone and say. "Boy, I feel the Holy Ghost!" Guess what? You're in an experience right then—you're focused.

DOCTRINES OF MEN BRING VAIN WORSHIP

"In vain do they worship Me..." Mat. 15:9.

So it's possible to have worship that's vain.

"...teaching for doctrines the commandments of men..."

Because vain worship comes from doctrines of men, not of God, replacing the truths of God with traditions. That's why traditions can be dangerous. They are very beneficial at times, but they can be dangerous, because they can be substituted for ongoing truth.

WHAT ROLE DOES GOD HAVE IN YOUR LIFE?

It's the man that looks over his shoulder and says to his wife, "I gave you that wedding band 25 years ago, and here is our marriage certificate. What is your problem? Of course we are happily married!" That's as dumb as a man comin' home from work and sayin', "Of course I love you, I come home every night." Where else are you going to sleep? Oh, oh, I'm messin' with people right now, and I feel a whirlwind just swinging up here. I'll leave it go.

Malachi 1:6, "A son honoureth his father, and a servant his master..."

Yeah, a son and his servant...

"...if then I be a father, where is mine honour?"

Yeah, where is mine honor?

"...and if I be a master, where is my fear?"

Yeah, where is my fear, my reverence?

"What do you mean, you're tired? What do you mean you had a bad day? Am I a father?"
"Yes!"
"Am I a master?"

"Yes!"

"Then where is my honor, where is my reverence, where is my fear, where is my dedication, where is my commitment? If I hold these roles, what's your problem?"

WE MUST BE PRIVATE WORSHIPPERS

Wait a minute! That's why you can't always wait to come into a church service to be a worshipper. That's why we have to be personal, private worshippers. We have to learn how to walk with God when we're *not* in church. Guess what, folks? We is "the church"! "The church" just gathers in this building. This *building* ain't "the church"! *We're* "the church"! If we don't have a private walk with God, this public stuff is a sham. If the only praying we do is what me and Bro. Hinote do for you guys—we're in trouble! If you don't ever feel the quickening presence of God somewhere during your day, or your days, or your week, except when you get here...honey, you ain't prayin' enough! You haven't got a vision of God like you need to have.

You got to hear me! I'm all for good church, what I call good church...let's bless God, let's exalt God, because there is power in corporate praise and thanksgiving that will lead into worship. But if this is the only time I'm excited, then I'm in bad shape! I've had a disease since I've been in Pentecost—I can hardly wait to get here. But I'm going to go a little further—I don't need to be here to walk with Him. I walk with Him during the day. I walk with Him during the night. I read the Book whether I'm preaching, or not. I love Him. He saved me...a drunk. He brought me out, He put my life back together. My dedication is to Him, and I'm glad I have a chance to express it here, but if I don't get to express it *here*, I'll express it on the couch, I'll express it laying in bed, I'll express it driving a car. I'm going to make my way towards God. I'm going to tell Him that I love Him. I'm not going to wait to come here to repent. I'm going to apologize when it happens, and if you're not a good praiser and you're not a good worshipper, you'll let sin build up until you can't hardly shake loose of it.

If you worship regularly, even if it is only 5 minutes a day, you'd be surprised how sensitive you become to being offensive to people and having sin reign in your life. It will quicken in you so bad, it'll make you feel ashamed to pull off some shenanigans. Worship has got to be a lot more than us having a boogaloo-time around here.... Worship's got to do with transforming my attitude, my life, my spirit, my desire, and it helps me to measure what's important and what's not important. I'm talkin' about worshipping God!

FOCUS, FOCUS, FOCUS—ON GOD

We got to keep being reminded about focus. Why? In the Old Testament, when they brought their sacrifices to God, the fire fell and consumed the sacrifice. It gave a sign...a witness that God was pleased. And in the New Testament, when we offer up praise and worship and sacrifice to God, the fire of the Holy Ghost burns away from us falsehood, and fakery, and pretence, so that we are purified. You're not going to get purified...listen to me; I don't care what all your little Bible studies are saying, and all these nincompoops you listen to...you are not going to get purified just by studying the Book. You've got to get in to the white-hot presence of God and let Him talk to you. You've got to let Him make the Book come alive! He is the author. You and I have a propensity to read something and perceive it, and then the author will say, "No, no, no, no, that's not what I meant, this is what I meant...." "...and if I be a master, where is my fear? saith the Lord of hosts unto you, O priests, that despise my name."

YOU PRIESTS—HOW ARE YOU DOING?

Now notice, His argument was not with the nation. His argument was with the people who were *leading* the nation. You priests, because the people follow your lead, guess what? We got more trouble than them. We are all priests. Well, who is following our lead? The lost, the doomed, the damned, the discouraged, are following our lead. How are you doing, priests? He complained to them, because they complained about church being too long, too often, cost too much, pain in the neck, interrupting my schedule. Sounds like us! How we doin' priests? It was the Lord who said, "I've chosen you to be priests, you can come near Me." See,

THE WHY & WONDER OF WORSHIP • BOOK TWO

we've never got that yet in America. We've got this barge-in mentality. You can't do that. God will decide who can approach and who can't, and how you approach, and how you don't approach.

God turned around and said...Okay Levi, you're him...these are the priests, okay let's go... Whoa! ...Nobody else come near, or I'll kill you.... Now *we're* priests, and bought by the blood and covered by the blanket of grace, and filled with the Holy Ghost. Now we're privileged to come near to Him. The people in the Old Testament would have given their right arm to have access like we have. Yet, sometimes our access is a pain in the neck to us, because we don't have the vision right. I didn't say "you," I said, "we" don't have the vision right.

IT'S THE ATTITUDE—NOT THE SACRIFICE—THAT'S POLLUTED

"... And ye say, Wherein have we despised thy name?" (still in Malachi)

Yeah, they asked questions; "What are you talking about?"

Verse 7, "...Ye offer polluted bread upon mine altar; and ye say, wherein have we polluted thee? In that ye say, the table of the Lord is contemptible."

Now notice, their sacrifice wasn't polluted—their attitude was polluted! You say ye offered polluted bread...where did we offer...? Because you *say*! So apparently, He reads thoughts and hears words. That's why He said in the New Testament, that...

"When you come to the altar and you remember that you have ought against your brother; leave your gift, go get reconciled, come back...."

"Why?"

"...Because your attitude is going to effect whether I accept this or not! ...Ain't no way you can offer Me something, and I look at your heart and you say, 'I hate that dirtbag'!"

God is going to say, "Well, then, I reject your offer." Why? Because in God's eyes, the offering and the offerer are one.

God accepted Abel's offering, because God accepted Abel as the offerer. It wasn't just that Cain's offering wasn't correct...Cain was incorrect! I can't find where God found any accusation against him, about offering the herbs of the field and the vegetables and the tomatoes and the fruit. I know we preach lots of sermons about it, but I can't find that. When God talked to Cain, God talked to Cain about Cain's *attitude*. And when He dealt with his attitude, then He said...If I can get your attitude straight now, I'm going to alter your offering...there is the sin offering over there...go buy your self an offering that I'll accept...but your attitude stinks, it's got nothing to do with tomatoes and vegetables and brussel sprouts...it's got to do with you.

GOD IS AFTER US—NOT OUR STUFF

See, Israel never learned it, and most of us have never learned it—God isn't after our money and our stuff and our things. He wants us! That's all He has ever wanted—Is us. Am I makin' sense here? Do you understand? Hold it, I'm not mad...I had a great day. I'm worth so much money, alive or dead. I have thousands that hate my guts...I have 10's of thousands that love me...I'm doin' good. I'm not ticked off. I feel like sometimes I come across..."boy he's had a bad day"...I've had a great day! I just believe this! This is the key to everything I've tried to teach for all these weeks. If our attitude is lousy, forget it!

ATTITUDE—ATTITUDE—ATTITUDE

Let's not build another church for a bigger box of nasty attitudes! I'll tell you, God can work with people who have a lousy aptitude and a great attitude! God doesn't need talent; He needs trusting people! He is still looking for a "Gideon" who is willing to lose more than he ended up with—If he can just get the attitude right. God would much rather deal with a prodigal son who runs away, and makes a mess out of his life, and loses his inheritance, and then comes back —than having to deal with that stupid elder brother who won't even go in to the party! Who is the worse of the two?

"Well I didn't leave the farm."

"Oh, yes you did...you just didn't leave it geographically! You left the farm when your attitude left!

Wait a minute; we leave this church every time our attitude is sour. "...Well, I'm here, bless God." I wish I wasn't afraid and intimidated by all you people...I would just politely ask you—Go home, go home...see if God can't do more with less...see if God still doesn't have a boy somewhere that can sling a stone in a giant's head and bring him down!

"...Well, I'm goin' through some stuff..."
"Well then, you need to worship."
"Will it pull me out?"
"No, it'll probably pull you in and pull Him in."

And if you, and He, are in the situation, who cares how big the situation is if God stays with me *in* the situation? He ain't got to take me *out* of the furnace...if He is willing to walk *with* me *in* the fire, fire can't hurt me! We're always wantin' God to pull us out of something. I'm startin' to learn...see, if I can pull Him down *into* my mess, I don't need to come *out* of my mess!

Verse 8, "...And if ye offer the blind for sacrifice, is it not evil? And if ye offer the lame and sick, is it not evil?"

WHAT WE OFFER IS A REFLECTION OF OUR ATTITUDE

They were offering God damaged animals. Now if you are not careful, you'll miss it and say, "Well, He was really bent out of shape, because they were givin' Him junk." No, no! The junk was a reflection of their attitude towards Him. God don't eat the hamburgers, He don't eat a rack of ribs, He don't drink blood, and

He's not interested in smelling smoke...that's not His bag...He wants us! So when they offered Him this junk, He just looked beyond the junk and looked at them and said, "Oh, you're giving Me the trash and the leftovers, and the junk in your life. That's your estimate of Me?" And He just was up to here, and said, "I've had enough with it. I'm sick of you. I'm sick of your oblations, I'm sick of your ceremonies."

Now He instituted the ceremonies, yet He says, "I'm sick of it." Why? Because it didn't work. It didn't accomplish in the people what He wanted to accomplish. That's why Romans 8 says, "the flesh was weak." It didn't do what God wanted it to do. God had to step in and do something else.

Verse 8, "...offer it now unto thy governor,"

Yeah, He said; Give it to the governor and see if he'll like it.
"...Will He be pleased with thee, or accept thy person?"

The governor will look at it...will he be pleased, not with your sacrifices, "with thee and with thy person?" Why? Because the person is a part of the gift! When I'm doing this, *(making an offering gesture with his hands)* this is a just an outward form of expression. God looks into my hands and my arms, way down into my spirit, and checks the attitude. Well...and sometimes He just looks and says, "Oh, Jeff, put your hands down, you're out of it." Wow! I wonder how many business deals are done during a praise service? How many bank accounts are balanced? How many cooking recipes are traded?

Verse 9-10, "And now, I pray you, beseech God that He will be gracious unto us: this hath been by your means: will He regard your persons? saith the Lord of hosts. Who is there even among you that would shut the doors for nought? neither do ye kindle fire on mine altar for nought."

OUR OFFERING IS AN EXPRESSION OF US

He said, "I have no pleasure in you, saith the Lord." Notice what He said. He didn't say, "I have no pleasure in your offering." He said, "I have no pleasure in you." Your offering is just an expression of you! When you give...we always think of offering as money...well, let's just use it...when you do this, *(offering up a closed fist)* "...Bet you can't get it out of my hand!" Do you understand that God is so awesome—He can make gold? The American government has never discovered how to make gold. Your Father can make gold! You think He needs your lousy "saw buck"? He makes diamonds, rubies, emeralds, and jewels. By the way, He is the one that has all the patents on Uranium! ...He's worried about your 10-spot? And then finally go, "Oh, I can't stand to hear Brother Arnold beg." ...You need to just go back and grab it and put it back in your pocket!

Verse 10, "...I have no pleasure in you, saith the Lord of hosts, neither will I accept an offering at your hand."

Notice how it goes. We got it reversed. We try to buy His favor. He said, "No, no...I won't accept you first; and then I won't accept your offering." So, apparently He is looking at me first; not the size of the bill.

OUR ATTITUDE WILL MAKE OUR OFFERING CONTEMPTIBLE

Verse 11-12, "For from the rising of the sun even unto the going down of the same my name shall be great among the Gentiles; and in every place incense shall be offered unto My name, and a pure offering: for my name shall be great among the heathen, saith the Lord of hosts. But ye have profaned it, in that ye say, The table of the Lord is polluted; and the fruit thereof, even His meat, is contemptible."

See, their attitude was doing all that. Now wait a minute, hold it just one second. We're under an indictment now, because God talked about us in Malachi. He said, "My name shall be great among the heathen." That's us! ...Going to be mighty among the Gentiles. That be us! I wonder how we make God look tonight? I'm so thrilled with God, I can hardly stand it!

Verse 13, "Ye said also, Behold, what a weariness is it!"

Well, let's be honest...I've said that. I was hopin' for an "Amen." You probably didn't hear me. I've said that! I've been weary, I've been discouraged, and I've been disgusted. I've been out of patience with people and myself. I usually manage to get out of patience with people long before I am out of patience with myself. That way I always feel better about myself. A few times in my life, I got out of patience with myself and I left the people alone.

GOD IS NOT DESPERATE TO ACCEPT ANY OLD THING

"...and ye have snuffed at it, saith the Lord of hosts; and ye brought that which was torn, and the lame, and the sick; thus ye brought an offering: should I accept this of your hand? saith the Lord"

..."Should I accept this? You think I am in desperate straits? Think I am in a jam? I've got a company of angels, innumerable, 24 hours a day, 7 days a week, blessing and exalting My name, filling the whole place full of glory and praise. Do you think I am in desperate straits to hear you say, 'thank you Jesus'?" He says, 'I don't think so. I let you play. I'm willing to create an atmosphere in your life that could help you."

GOING BEYOND COMMUNICATION TO COMMUNION

Various rituals and channels may aide us; such as singing, clapping, music, and prayer, to get to the place of worship, but only an acceptable attitude will allow us to step from ceremony to communion. Prayer is actually a communication between God's Spirit and man's. Worship is much more than that...I told you that. It is a communion between those spirits. There can never be any great communion until there has first been some preliminary communication. There has to be a warm up to worship. I'm going to try it again. A prayer-less person is never a good worshipper. I'll go a little further...a hit-and-miss praying person is a hit-and-miss worshipper. A person who doesn't pray often at home...their praising and singing will never become worship in public, for worship flows out of heart, of adoration, and love to communicate and express their feelings. But if you, and I, do not pray often, we have no feelings, only intellectual knowledge. There really is feeling in worship. There is feeling in salvation. I hope to God there is feeling in your marriages.

DON'T HAVE A 3:59 ATTITUDE

I never even liked working at Florida Power and Light and Western Electric when I worked in South Florida with guys who had no feeling about their job. I didn't like being with people like that. I hated working with people who got hired and said, "Where is the coffee pot?" I wanted to throw them slap out the door! All of a sudden, they've got themselves a job and all they want is a paycheck. I always kind of wanted to do the best I could, and learn, and be a better employee, and give the company 100%, and walk up and get my paycheck and say, "Well, I traded 'x' number of hours of sweat for 'x' number of dollars and I tried to make the company a better place." I wasn't a company man, and I wasn't trying to get promoted by snuggling up next to somebody. I just felt like…give 100%. You know what I'm talkin' about? Work with people who sluff off, always hiding in the bathroom somewhere reading a magazine, hanging around the coffee pot or somethin'…just all the time gettin' their benefits and never give anything back. I remember guys who used to almost get in a fist fight over punchin' out at almost 2 minutes after 4:00. We kicked off at 4:00, and man, 2 minutes after 4:00, they went ballistic. They were gettin' ready to leave at 3:45, walkin' around doin' an impersonation of a worker! Man, it got to be 3:59—they was like…I hate that kind of craziness. Wait a minute…let's turn it around. How about God waiting all day for us to get here and we come here with this 3:59 mentality. Oops!

A praise-less person is never a good worshipper, because praise is always prior to worship. A thankless person is never a good worshipper. A selfish, self-centered, stingy person is never a good worshipper. A fearful person, a bitter person, a jealous person, a resentful person, and the worst of all, a religious person, is never a good worshipper. They are too filled with the knowledge they think they have.

GREAT BLESSINGS SHOULD BRING GREAT WORSHIP

You can be so married to your interpretation of scripture and verse; you never take time to deal with the author. You got to watch out for "religious" people...ask Judas. Luke 12, the rich fool...stingy, selfish, has no room for God. Successful? Wealthy? Yes, and nothing wrong with success and wealth. Wealth should never stop worship. In fact, I personally think people who are blessed by God, and I'm not giving God all the credit, but the Lord said. "It is the Lord that giveth thee the *ability* to get wealth." That means it's a gift of God to work with your particular talents, and your uniqueness, and your dedication, and your commitment.

It wasn't just God that threw you a bone and all of a sudden it became a *T-bone*. No, that's not how it works. He touched you and gave you something, saw your potentials, knew that you would work hard, and sweat, and put 60 hours in instead of 35 ...and God blessed you. But I'll tell you; to me, a person who has wealth ought to be the best worshipper, because they look and realize and say, "This is God in my life!" Oh, it's true! It shouldn't always be poor people making the best worship. Poor people...

"...Well, they have to worship, because they have nothin' else."
What are you talking about? That's so silly!

PUBLIC WORSHIP IS BIRTHED IN PRIVATE

Notice very carefully; now there's a public worship service, and there is a private worship service. The private always gives birth to the public. The public cannot have the preeminence. The public worship is nothin' but an extension of the private worship. In every public worship service three attitudes will always be manifested, because three attitudes are always manifested in a private worship service. Notice carefully in Luke Chapter 7; there was a Pharisee that invited Jesus to dinner, and there was a woman who was a sinner in the city, which heard Jesus was there, and she came.

THREE ATTITUDES IN TRUE WORSHIP— THE WORSHIPPER, OBJECT OF WORSHIP & THE OBJECTOR

Now in a true worship service, the three attitudes that were involved will always be the worshipper, the object of worship, and the objector. Why? Because that flows out of private worship. And in private worship, three attitudes are also always declared. Three…always the same three: you're going to have the same three problems; except in private, you won't have a public critic. You will have the worshipper, you will have the attitude of the worshipped, and then you will have the attitude of the wicked one who watches. Thus, the wicked one finds its counter-part in the public critic.

It is so needful for you and I to have private worship. Here is why. Public worship will always be costly, criticized, and awkward, if we are not immunized by the private worship. The reason why lots of us do not praise and worship God any more expressively than we do is because our private worship is lagging. I didn't say we didn't love God, and that we're not saved and don't have the Holy Ghost. I'm just saying, it's lagging. And so what happens is, we have no corn in the crib, so we got to come to the public worship service, and being that we don't have any *real* move of God in our lives, and in our walk with God, we're waiting on everybody else to create an atmosphere. So we really can't contribute much to the public worship service, because there is nothing here.

"…It's just 5 years ago…Holy Ghost baptism experience."
"Man, you got a lot of miles off that tank!"

WE MUST BE BROKEN TO WORSHIP

Are you hearing me? One of the first attitudes of a worshipper will always be brokenness. That's why worship is far beyond praise, because thanks and praise are usually euphoric, excited, dancing with tambourines, dead Egyptians floating in the Red Sea…. But when you step past that praise service and get into the bold, beautiful presence…the raw presence of God, there will come immediately a sense of unworthiness and absolute worthiness. It will immediately...you don't have to have any music, it'll just go....

Has anybody, besides me, just got broken, and weren't thinkin' about anything? Didn't have no bad stories goin' on; just all of a sudden, the presence of the Holy Ghost stepped in, and all of sudden, there's just a calm and peace. You don't want to shout "Hallelujah" now, you just want to quietly bathe in His presence.

Luke 7, "...brokenness." It says they brought in a woman who had an alabaster ointment. She stood at His feet weeping. Weeping will usually accompany a worship service. Wild antics will not. Wild antics are praise and thanksgiving; they have their place.

A BROKEN SPIRIT—YOUR SACRIFICE

Psalm 51:17, "The sacrifices of God are a broken spirit."

A broken spirit. Now wait a minute; I want you to get this, because a broken spirit and a broken and contrite heart are *not* the same. You got to get this. A broken spirit..."broken"; the word translated in 51:17, in Hebrew, is *shabar*, meaning, "to shimmer." It means, "To break in pieces, to reduce." Tears are a good start. They help cleanse the soul. Tears are an expression of emotion that is erupting uncontrollably. Tears are not just sadness.

Have you never seen somebody win the World Series, or win a sports event, or win a miss America Pageant, or something, and they're standin' there with baited breath, and all of a sudden they say; "The winner is..." and, boom! They just break out in tears, because it's pent up emotion that just now expresses itself. Did you get it? Did you ever see airport, and train, and bus depots of people just absolutely uncontrollably crying? Have you never seen or heard...come on, you guys that watch TV all the time...have you never seen on the news...'cause that's all you have the TV for is the news!...when they found out that the people that were taken hostage, or POWs, or there was a flight accident and a plane crash, and you watched the terror, and fear, and the anxiety on the mothers and the fathers faces, and the husbands and the wives...when all of a sudden they announce they were saved? They absolutely erupt into tears and they just fall over in people's arms. That is not sadness, that is an expression of jubilee, and uncontrolled emotional high.

BROKENNESS BRINGS GOD CLOSE

That happens when you worship God. Just overwhelms you sometimes, just to have Him put His arms around you and say, "I love you in spite of everything you are, every mistake you've made, every vow, every promise you break. I will never leave you." And it's in those times of brokenness that you re-consecrate, re-commit; and you apologize and you repent in your deepest mode. It is in those moments, when your spirit is spilling out through your tear ducts, that you can be more transparent and more honest than ever before. That's why very seldom do you ever reach a high plateau of worship in a regular service. Now, you may reach it sittin' on a pew somewhere, and just..."away" with God.

IT'S DIFFICULT TO GET BROKEN & HONEST IN PUBLIC

A broken spirit in God's presence is called, by the scripture, an "acceptable sacrifice." A broken spirit can be caused by three things: situations, and setbacks, and life, but brokenness can also come from a worshipper's self-evaluation; "...I've failed...." That's why worship's got to be one-on-one, because you can't just stand up in public and say, "You know what I did last Saturday?" "You know how far I threw that hammer at that guy's windshield?" "Do you have any idea what I rented and watched and went crazy...wouldn't turn it off, but when it was over I said, 'I shouldn't have done that'." You might as well just be honest... we can't do that in public.

That's why brokenness is whimpering; it flashes in front of you and all of sudden you go, "Oh God." I don't know what they call this in the Bible...I don't know what the Hebrew and Greek word is, but the Brooklyn word you feel is "tingly." Do you ever get just kind of *tingly*? You feel about *that* small? Cuz, it's the same thing that you keep tripping over...I said situations...and setbacks...sometimes personal failure, self-evaluation...and there are other times when you are broken, and I am broken—by God's hand on us—either convicting us, or comforting us. What happens? We weep.

A BROKEN AND CONTRITE HEART

"...for the sacrifices of God are a broken spirit..."

Here it is now, watch; He goes a little further now.

"...a broken and a contrite heart, O God."

The second time He uses the word "broken", it's a different Hebrew word. It's *dakah*; not the same word. The first word is different. This word d-a-k-a-h means "to crush, to crumble, to bruise severely." Isaiah 66:1-2, tells us that God will stay with people who are of a broken and contrite spirit. He will make them His dwelling place. But this is interesting; David, writing this Psalm said, a "broken and contrite spirit." Anybody ever study the word, *contrite*? I got to lookin' up that word and studying it from the word where it came from—the original. The word that is translated *contrite* is the same word that we use for the process of making talcum powder! It appears on the bottle, or a can, of talcum powder and it will say, "a stone contrited." *Contrited* means a piece of a mountain, or a stone, that has been crushed and pulverized and pounded to such a fine form, it now is powder—easily pushed around. A wind can blow it. Water can mess it up. Ready for this? It's so fine it can get on everything! When I was reading this, I was writing these little notes and just before I came out, I wrote this in red ink. I was goin' over these notes and I said, "boy, a stone contrited so fine... in an entirely different form, it has the ability now to be blown around or float. Before, in the form of a stone, it would sink. Now it can ride *on top* of what used to drown it. Contrited. Losing all its boldness.

A LITTLE TALCUM FOR THE HIDDEN AREAS

Now, this is what I got. I was sitting at the desk, and Br. Hinote walked out and I just looked at him and said, "Contrite." It's like I had a flash in my mind...6 months old; watch...makes you smell good. You ready? Talcum powder is good for irritations of the flesh. My, my, my! It always has to be applied in places that you can't see. You missed what I was saying...you were thinking the wrong thing. You missed what I was just trying to say. What I'm tryin' to say is—the stuff that people see, and we're irritating and aggravating—It's the stuff they *don't* see that's irritating us, and God wants to go into the unseen areas and put some talcum powder there, so you won't be so irritated and be upset at everything else. Wow!!

BROKEN—LIKE THE ALABASTER BOX

One more thing; there are two more points I have to do in this. On the first point: Like an alabaster box, worship requires something to be broken. Our problem is we build up outer resistance and a protective wall around our emotions, so that we won't be hurt, or embarrassed. But when you build that wall up, you and I can never truly express tenderness, love, or honesty, because our society teaches against vulnerability, exposure, and transparency. And those are the very things that are at the core of the kingdom of God! That's why we are in a clash with this world. That's why most so-called "Christian worship", public or private, is just a club...gather around a few facts and a little intellectual bigotry, and lo— we have a church. Attitudes must be expressed. Must be expressed!

Luke 7:38 said she stood behind Him weeping and began to wash His feet with tears and did wipe them with the hairs of her head and kissed His feet and anointed them with the anointment. Thus, she broke the alabaster box. Notice this; she wept...emotion erupted, and now she did something, which was unprecedented: She let her hair down.

UNCUT HAIR—A SIGN OF SUBMISSION TO AUTHORITY

According to 1 Corinthians 11:15, you women...your hair is your glory. That's why we teach you not to cut it. It's your glory. It's a sign of your submission to authority. Hello?

I did a little study on this—letting down the hair thing—and found a very unique thing. Women only let their hair down in public if they were prostitutes. And women let their hair down in private only for their husbands, if they were married. It was a sign of total surrender and submission. Married women did not let their hair down in front of strangers in the public. It was only in the intimacy of their own parlor that she ever let her hair down. Watch; now stay with me.

WORSHIP MAKES A MESS BEFORE IT GETS BETTER

According to 7:39, Simon knew her reputation, therefore; he put her reputation into her worship. Peer pressure keeps too many of us from publicly releasing our affections for Jesus. It's not what others will think, it's what does He think? Notice, please, that her tears fell on His dusty feet, because He complains to them saying, "You gave me no water for my feet," therefore; His feet were still stinky and dirty. You know what she did? With her worship, she made a mess, because the water from her face touching the dust on His feet—made mud. Worship will usually make the situation worse before it gets better!

Now notice this, and I'm closing: She made the mess with her worship. Jesus didn't stop her; and then she took her "glory" and wiped up the muddy mess. This says to us, "Nothing is too good for Him in public worship!" Brokenness and humility, according to Isaiah 57:13, create a dwelling place for the presence of God; "...To this man..." and you ladies, too, "...will I look, he that has a broken heart and contrite spirit, who feareth my name I will look to that one. I, who inhabit eternity."

Isaiah 66:1-2, "I dwell also with him that's a humble and contrite spirit."

THE WHY & WONDER OF WORSHIP • BOOK TWO

Contrite. You won't forget that talcum powder, I promise you. Contrite. Pulverized to dust.

THE WHY & WONDER OF WORSHIP · BOOK TWO

THE WHY & WONDER OF WORSHIP

VOLUME FIVE · CHAPTER EIGHT

CHAPTER EIGHT

WORSHIP—THE OCCUPATION OF HEAVEN

I feel like I am stretching this worship subject, and it almost seems today, when I was studying, I said, "It's like an endless subject, maybe I just kind of need to bring the hammer down and say, 'okay, we've learned enough... now let's practice'." And I should finish these notes today, and, boom! ...3 more pages for an addendum! And it just seems like it gets bigger and bigger and bigger... It's the greatest thing that I think we could learn, and we need to learn the ability to worship. If we could grasp, in our minds and our hearts, the preeminence of worship, it will go on when prayer stops. It will be the theme of eternity. It is now the occupation of Heaven's occupants. Anytime we get into worship, we join with that crew.

THE PREEMINENCE OF WORSHIP

I don't know of anything any greater than to teach people the preeminence of worship, and what all is involved with it, and the awesome power that can be released from it. I have yet to teach the lesson on the effects of worship. We've built up to learning elementary things and preliminary things, but oh, the lesson that we need to hear on what happens when worship is real, and what is possible when worship takes place.

The devil is not dumb; he's a smart boy. Dumb for fighting God; but smart in the strategy against us. He gets us to trade worship for mechanics; to trade worship for preaching; to trade worship for a program—and we miss it. Worship has got to be a priority with us, and we have to learn how to be better worshippers. We do!

Luke 7:36, "One of the Pharisees desired him that he would eat with him..."

I wonder if we would have gone, considering our stand. One of the Pharisees desired that He would eat with him.

"...And He went into the Pharisees house, and sat down to meat. And, behold a woman in the city, which was a sinner, when she knew that Jesus sat at meat in the Pharisee's house, brought an alabaster box of ointment, And stood at his feet behind him weeping, and began to wash his feet with tears, and did wipe them with the hairs of her head, and kissed his feet, and anointed them with the ointment."

WE ARE THE REPLACEMENT WORSHIPPERS

Last week we were talking about the attitude of worship, and the three attitudes that usually will be involved in both public and private worship. It will be the attitude of the worshipper, the attitude of the worshipped, and the attitude of the non-worshipper. Those will always happen. Usually, in private, it will be the worshipper, the worshipped, and the wicked one—cuz the wicked one won't worship what you're worshipping. And because he won't worship what you're worshipping, he doesn't want you to worship, because you've replaced him.

Say what you want to about our adversary, but he does look at us as substandard replacements. I mean, he was in charge of worship. And when he sees our pathetic offering...now watch, it's not magic it's miraculous...God so loves it, that by the time it reaches Him, He puts it through a metamorphosis, and a transformation, and it becomes acceptable. And it just aggravates your adversary to death, because he knows how real worship should go. And when he sees us with our little bitty stuff, and it's so pathetic it drives him crazy, that God would reach down and say, "Oh that was just great, let Me fix it. Ah, that feels good...."

It's like God just looks at our adversary and says, "They've replaced you." Which then says to him that "you were easy to replace...look what I replaced you with." Always a bummer when somebody replaces you who is substandard. Work 20 years for a company and they bring in a machine! Been 18 years a secretary and they get a dial-a-page thing to take your place! It does have a real bad impact on you. It's even worse when you get fired, or you retire, and they do away with your job description. Boy, you really felt essential, didn't you?

One of the attitudes we studied was brokenness. Brokenness always ends up in a worship experience somewhere. She brought the alabaster jar; she has to break it...broken heart. David talked about it, and my last point last week about talcum powder. Remember that? Contrite. Remember what contrite is? Contrite is a part of a mountain or stone that has been so pulverized that it has changed form so that it becomes a powder. Powder so light that it can be blown by the wind and it can float on water. And David says, in Psalm 51, that "a broken and contrite spirit and contrite heart thou will not despise." So brokenness is always somewhere in a worship service and I think we need to go to my last point: humility. That always takes place in a worship service.

ANOTHER ATTITUDE OF WORSHIP—HUMILITY

Humility: That's why a lot of our camp meeting and conference praise services never even touch the top, or the bottom of a worship service. A lot of noise, a lot of activity—not much worship. Cuz humility gets involved with worship. Because humility is able to behold the object that is worshipped, and is humbled by it, overwhelmed by the awesomeness and the greatness.

Have you ever got into—Let me see if I can help you—A personal worship service? Not long, not super spiritual, just a time remembering the goodness of God and prayer answered; a time God came to your rescue; how good God has been; rehearsed sins in your life, failures, weak areas, weak points; and how the grace of God has covered it, and how the blood has bathed...all of sudden you're just humbled by the generosity of God. You're in a worship service! That's why, many times, it's very hard to be in a true worship service in a public service. It's hard. We call it a worship service, but really, it's just thanks and praise.

Now there are times, and thank God...there are times in our thanks and praise that we do step beyond the veil, and we step into brokenness and into an intimacy, and you'll notice that when you get into a real personal worship, the volume goes down. You don't mind saying, "Oh thank God for what You did for me, and how You healed and how You saved," but then when the Lord just kind of flashes in front of you this kind of secret area that you don't want anybody to hear about . . . "and we thank You for that one, too, we appreciate you, oh God, hallelujah."

Now I'm so glad the Lord is not hard of hearing, cuz I've had some of my greatest victories whispered; "Oh, remember this." "Oh, yes God, I thank you for that, I appreciate You very much." I've been in Alexandria every year they've had a conference. And year after year, when the Lord would mightily anoint Sr. Mangun, or one of the other speakers that would put us on our face, they would call us to prayer. "...Turn where you are and let's kneel and pray," and it's amazing how people would just, "oh, yeah, ooooo, yeah", and you just hear this big roar, and you're talkin' and you're just makin' small spiritual talk. And then, when you start gettin' down to the "nitty gritty" where you live, in areas that are junky and cruddy...slum areas of your soul...you get very quiet, and your face gets further down in the seat, and you're hearing them, and everybody is hearing you.

REAL WORSHIP IS INTIMATE

A real worship service is intimate and the only time you can really do a public worship service is when you go to total abandonment, and we have a hard time with that, because we are peer pressure people. Yeah, we are! This woman, as I remember, last time I had a few of you come to me about questions about her letting her hair down, and me giving you the illustration that usually a wife did that in the privacy of a home, or a prostitute did it in that day to enhance her chance of turning a trick.... Those of you ladies who wear your hair down, that's not the insinuation. You didn't hear what I was saying. She let her hair down, and her hair was her glory, and she was willing to have scrutiny and transparency and exposure, okay?

So now I'm going to go to the next little area...everybody understand where we were? Just a quick rehearse from last week; the last thing we did, she poured her tears out on His dirty feet and made little muddy mess, and then took her glory and let it down, and used her glory to wipe away the mess that her worship had created.

PRIDE—A HINDRANCE TO WORSHIP

Now we're going to find you tonight; I'm going to find exactly where you're sittin'. One of the problems that we need to overcome, in trying to be worshippers, is pride. 1 Peter 5:5 says, "God resisteth the proud." You don't ever have to worry about the devil fighting any of us. All we have to do is be proud, and God will fight us for him! "God resisteth the proud." Why? Because He knows that the best of us have nothing to be proud of! Cuz' everything we got was given, and everything we got can be taken away. In one sunset, you can go from a Prime Minister to a prisoner, or a prisoner to a Prime Minister. So we can't boast of anything. And Paul says; why do you people boast? Everything you got was given...everything you're using was lent.... Say; oh no, I earned this...! No, you didn't earn anything; the earth was the Lord's before you got here! So I don't care how much gold you got stuck away in a sock somewhere, when it's all said and done, God said; I'll take all my gold back, please.... Because all the oil is His, All the precious reserves and resources...all His. We're just allowed to use it passing through time.

"God resisteth the proud, He giveth grace to the humble." According to Luke 18:9-14, it's the story of the publican and the Pharisee that prays. We know the story, but do we understand the gist of the story that the guy smote himself on his chest and he said, "God be merciful to a sinner." Worship always involves honest humility. "...I am not a good man; I am not what I ought to be; I'm not going to live under guilt, but I'm not going to live under false pretenses either. Help me."

Has anybody in this church, besides the gentlemen that happens to be speaking right now, ever been bragged on, and boasted on, or credited with something? No? Yes? Well, you didn't understand the question. Has anybody in the house, besides the speaker, ever been bragged on, or boasted on, or given credit for something that, while they spoke, you knew it wasn't so? And you wished in your heart that it was? And said, "I really wish I was the great man you think I am." You have no idea how humbling it is to preach a service, preach a sermon, 5000-8000 people there, people wanting to take pictures, "...would you sign my Bible?

...would you sign my cast? ...would you sign my daughter's little note ...you're the greatest thing that's ever walked in a pair shoes."

And you're sittin' there all the while and sayin', "Oh lady, if you only knew the guy that I know!" "You're in love with a sermon; I'm having to live with the slob that preached it!" Now that doesn't give you a license to snoop around my life, saying, "He's a hypocrite!" No! It's just that I'm not where I'm wanting to be, and I'm not what they really think I am, because they think I'm a good man, or a godly man, or a voice from God—And I am really a man with many fractures in my spiritual cast. I am 20 years behind my time; I'm not what I want to be, and what they think is a "good man," to me, is disdainful. I have my eyes set much higher than that, you know.

PRIDE PUSHES GOD AWAY

Isaiah 57:15, "Thus saith the high and lofty One Who inhabiteth eternity, whose name is Holy; I dwell in the high and holy place...."

Now notice; "...with him also that is of a ...."
There it is again; "...contrite and humble spirit, to revive the spirit of the humble, and revive the heart of the contrite ones."

He said that I dwell in eternity, I dwell in the light that no man can approach unless I let him come. And yet I say to you I also dwell with those who are humble. Those who are not haughty, but humble; those who are broken and contrite and crushed and honest and transparent. Pride is something that pushes God away from us.

WORSHIP WITHOUT LOVE—SHALLOW AND PRETENTIOUS

Okay, 3rd point: When you are going to have a real worship service, there will always be love involved. Worship that lacks love is like a commitment without love—shallow and pretentious. Remember, worship is always love responding to love. Thus this woman, by her actions, expressed physically and emotionally what she felt inside. Therefore, worship has to have some way of expressing a feeling.

You say, "Well, I don't feel." You're going to have a hard time worshipping. Well, let me try it again. There is something drastically wrong with a silent, secret believer. Our mouths and our bodies were meant to express what we feel within. It is amazing that Romans 10:10-13 says that they have to call on the name of the Lord to be saved. So, if I understand what He said, to receive or experience salvation, one must open one's mouth! Strange that the doctrine now introduced after getting saved now shuts one's mouth...and sit in silence and stare now that you are saved.

YOU CAN'T REMAIN SILENT

Well, let me try it and see if I got it in the Bible: Romans 10:10, "For with the heart man believeth unto righteousness; and with the mouth confession is made unto salvation. (11) For the Scripture saith, "Whosoever believeth on Him shall not be ashamed."

What does He mean: ashamed? Silent.

Verse 12, "For there is no difference between the Jew and the Greek: for the same Lord over all is rich unto all that THINK upon him." NO!

Wish upon a star; rub your rabbit's foot... "for whosoever shall CALL upon the name of the Lord shall be saved." So apparently you have to get involved! You have to express something if you want something to happen. You couldn't ever convince me that a man, or a woman, who was dying would sit there silently. "House on fire...going to get me pretty soon!" I think they'd be screaming their lungs out, "...Get me out of here!" But when a person realizes they're lost and doomed to a devil's Hell, they can't just sit there and wait for something to fall on 'em, they got to say, "Hey! Help! I repent! Forgive me!" God says, "Sure," and He forgives us, fills us with the Holy Ghost, and then all of a sudden we go...comb my hair...get our clothes right....

"Who are you?"
"I'm incognito Christianito. I'm secret agent man."

Am I right? See, if we can't find some crazy concepts...you ever heard this one? "I don't talk about my religion, I live it." Now wait a minute! Would you run that by me again? "...I don't talk about my religion, I live it?" How is it possible that the thing closest and dearest to your heart causes you to be quiet? Whoops! Seems to me that anything that is very dear and precious and wonderful to any of us, in any category of our life...we can't get 'em to shut up! "Have I shown you my grandkids?" And a guy whips out an album that would give a gorilla a hernia to pick up! "Yeah, I just happen to have 1200 pictures!" "Seen the deer I got?" You never have to beg parents or grandparents to talk about their young ones.

Now watch how stupid that is; "I don't talk about my kids, I just produce 'em and watch 'em." Give me a break! Funny, you talk about the stock market; talk about the Gators; talk about the New York Yankees; talk about interest rates; talk about a sale at K-Mart; talk about a garage sale; talk about an old car; talk about a sale at Maas Brothers; Talk about the game; talk about your hobby...I see some people in this church talk about their garden more than they do about God! "Have I showed you my daffodils; you know I've got this rose bush....I live my religion."

There's other people that have another dumb statement; "I don't talk about my beliefs, they're too sacred, they're too personal." It's funny; then it must mean that you waste all your time talkin' about the fodder of the unsacred, and the temporal, and the unworthy. So you spend the breath that God gave you to talk about stuff that doesn't last. Apparently, you waste your verbiage on that which is not sacred.

IT'S NOT ABOUT NOISE—IT'S ABOUT EXPRESSION

Here is the one I like; "Well, I'm just not an outward person, I, ummm, I worship God in my heart." Is that right? Seems to me that angels, that live in the presence of God, spend their time saying, "holy, holy, holy," and you seem to spend your time goin', "Ummmmmmmm," And they're just servants, and we're sons and daughters! And they're watchin', and we're redeemed; and they're wonderin' about the mystery, and we're enjoying the miracle of the mystery and we're sittin' here goin' "Ummmmmmmmm,"

Seems to me, every time a scripture that beholds Him, they start blessing Him, that there's something inside that wants to be expressed. I'm not just talking about emotion; I'm talking about expression. You can worship God and have your lips shut and have tears flowing down your face; you're worshipping! You say, "Well, I'm not making noise." This isn't about noise; this is about expressing the attitude of worship. One fella gave a good illustration about the problem some people have in worship. He said, "It's like a tea kettle. A tea kettle never makes any noise until it gets enough heat downstairs." Maybe the reason why some of us don't make any noise is, there is nothing burning!

WHERE ARE THE WEEPERS?

Scripture says that she loved so much that she was unashamed to weep publicly. I've wondered what's happened to us where we've lost the weepers. There was a time when Pentecostals were known for as much slobbern' as they were for shoutin'. We'd get broken so easy, and just sob and weep, and fall over a pew. Man, we'd stop a whole service and just weep a half hour...40 minutes, and pray and cry. Have we gotten that polished? Have we got that professional? What's happened to the weepers?

This woman stood behind Jesus and just started weeping—just sobbing. I mean, sobbing to the point that tears washed His feet. Now something tells me she had to be close to the feet, and she had to kinda take.... See, there is always a lot of room at His feet. His hands are always crowded cuz that's where He is givin' out gifts, but there is never a crowd at His feet. Now there are miracles that can take place at His feet, but most people don't want to go there. There's no waiting line at His feet.

WORSHIP IS ATTITUDE EXPRESSED

She expressed what she felt unashamedly, because worship is an attitude that is expressed. The leper in Matthew 8, ran before the Lord and worshipped Him saying, "...If you will I know you can make me whole." He fell down prostrate, worshipped Him, told Him what he believed, showed it to Him..."I know You can." Worship is an attitude expressed, because he took his life in his hands going public with his disease. It was kind of like his worship act was now or never. "...If you don't heal me, I'm going to be stoned before I leave the hill."

Nothing is any colder than unloving expression. For I told you, love has got to be involved in worship. Have you ever been hugged or embraced by someone that didn't like you? Get one of those artificial pecks on the cheek, or a hug, as if to say, "I hope you don't have cancer 'til the morning...The Lord bless you...Later...."

How do you handle a worship act when Judas gives you a kiss? A kiss? Ever receive a gift from somebody that you knew that you only got it because it was an obligation? "Well, it's Aunt Theresa's birthday, give the old bag something and keep peace in the family." Am I right?

A LOVE FEAST VERSUS OBLIGATION

I remember as a little kid, my grandma used to live with us, she was the embodiment of the entire "Luftwaffe." Sprechen ze deutch? You know, sauerbraten, and kenduffelballs, and spare ribs and sour kraut, Heil Hitler! And every time she'd come in, we had to go through a riggamorole at Christmas and birthday; we had to go in front of mom and dad...and mom usually took time with Bruce and myself so that we would present the gift to grandma in front of everybody. You could never just give her the gift...you had to wait 'til all the relatives were there and then act like you were happy. "...Here grandma, you dirty ol'...don't worry about the ticking... just ignore it." And it was so miserable, because, on the other side of the family...my father's mother...she wasn't grandma, she was "nanny." And she was different. Nanny was fun to be with.

She never wanted you to give her a gift. She didn't want you to spend no money; she just wanted a hug and kiss, and sit down and, "...come on, I'll get you something to eat". Nannies always fed you. It was so much fun being with nanny. She loved you. Yeah, really! Kids aren't stupid, they can feel that. You make your kids go to some of your relatives..."do I got to'?" Whoops! I'm strikin' fire here. And there's other ones...if you didn't send for 'em, they'd live there! They enjoy being there; there is somethin' goin' on there. There's an interaction there, there is a love feast going on.

Fourth aspect that I want to talk about: worship's attitude. Remember; brokenness, humility, love, and the fourth one is, and this is one part of four...every worship service will involve giving. Giving! She broke the box; she poured out; she gave Him her best. Some commentators say it was a year's salary. Now, notice carefully: the Jew's worship was always a joyful, jubilant experience. It was loud, it was physical, but it always had this aspect to it—no Jewish person was permitted to worship without giving.

I'll prove it to you. Exodus 34:20, "...But the firstling of an ass thou shalt redeem with a lamb: and if thou redeem him not, then shalt thou break his neck. All the firstborn of thy sons thou shalt redeem. And none shall appear before Me empty." Wait, wait, wait—what? None shall appear what? "...before me empty."

Now notice what God says, now God set the criteria for worship. See, most of us have never understood that worship is laid out explicitly in this scripture. But most of the teaching comes from the Old Testament, and we just study the New. But He said; I don't want anybody that I've been good enough to redeem...I don't want you coming up empty-handed. It ain't because Heaven's in trouble; it ain't because heaven can't make another world if He needs one. God wants a spirit of brokenness and sacrifice and humility to accompany worship.

DON'T APPEAR BEFORE GOD EMPTY

Deuteronomy 16:16, "Three times in a year shall all thy males appear before the Lord thy God in the place which He shall choose...."

Now wait a minute...worship...see I got another lesson...I got to show you that worship is so ordained by God, He'll even tell you where to go! Join the church of your choice? Not so. God told the Jews where to worship, "...in the feast of unleavened bread, and in the feast of weeks, and in the feast of tabernacles: and they shall not appear before the Lord empty." He's got this thing—When you worship, bring something. But it doesn't always mean money—thanksgiving, adoration, praise, commitment, dedication, sacrifice, appreciation—don't appear empty.

It doesn't just mean to bring gold and silver; it talks about don't let your worship be empty. Don't let it be a ritual. Don't let it be void of life. "Don't appear before Me empty." Don't make the service leader to be a cheerleader to finally whip you up into something. According to the scripture, the Bible is teaching us that without giving, there can be no worship. All worship involved sacrifice, gifts, and offerings. Notice carefully; God made no provision in the economy of Israel for floaters—freeloaders.

WORSHIP REQUIRES SACRIFICE AND GIVING

I'm goin' slow. Psalm 96:7-8, the scripture says, Bring an offering, and appear before the Lord, and worship the Lord in the beauty of holiness, but bring an offering. And David, in 2 Sam. 24:24, said, "I'll not offer anything to the Lord, anything that doesn't cost me something." "...I appreciate the offer, Araunah, on your threshingfloor, but I'm not going to offer somethin' to God that you paid for...." That's why it's a strange thing, in Christianity, that we have worship leaders, or praise singers, that are supposed to do our praising and our worshipping for us. That's not supposed to be that way! They are to inspire us, and lead us into a worship atmosphere. But we have to do something.

According to a very strange scripture, 1st Corinthians 16:1 & 2, Paul has just finished some of the greatest teaching in the Bible, from 11 of Corinthians to 15 of Corinthians. He has taught on women's subjection, authority, hair shorn, cut, uncut...all the big argument all the time in Pentecost. He has gone to Chapter 12, gifts; Chapter 13, love; Chapter 14, gifts and spiritual authority. Chapter 15, the resurrection—the gospel, the death, burial, and resurrection. Then, all about the translation of the saints, the new body, the resurrection of the dead.... Man, he is moving and grooving in a dimension of authority and power, and all of a sudden he hits Chapter 16, and he says, "Now concerning the collection for the saints...." It's almost like... man, he was talking about resurrection body, glory, and victory, and submission, and sacrifice, and humility, and power of God; and gifts, and love and.... Collection? He said; Yeah, you can't really have any worship without sacrifice and giving. And so, on the heels of this, he says; Let me tell you something, boys and girls...you can do all you want to about learning about love, and about the gifts of the Spirit, and about submission and subjection, and about authority in the body. You can know all about the resurrection, but I'm going to tell you something: if it doesn't funnel down to your giving in worship, you didn't hear what I just taught!

Notice, he didn't bring the giving sacrifice out before the resurrection...he just kind of really stuck it to 'em with the resurrection. And the body you're going to get, and the glory you're going to get, and the majesty, and the treasure, and the rewards of the kingdom, and the judgment seat of Christ, and the glory that's comin,' and said; ...So what's a few pennies to you? Send 'em a check!

You didn't get it. He got 'em up here...other world minded; "Hoooooooo, I'm going to have a new body, and going to reign with Him, going to be Lords, princes and..." and he says, "Send 'em a check!"

"Ha! Oh, sure, how much you need, $5,000?"

He said, in the midst of teaching on authority in worship, he says, "Don't forget your giving." Why? Because our worship needs an attitude of sacrifice and surrender in giving.

Luke 7:38, "And stood at his feet behind him weeping, and began to wash his feet with tears, and did wipe them with the hairs of her head, and kissed His feet, and anointed them with the ointment...."

Yeah, she poured it all out....

"...Now when the Pharisee which bid Him saw it he spake within himself, saying, This man, if he were a prophet, would have known who and what manner of woman this is that toucheth him: for she is a sinner."

THERE'S ALWAYS SOME TO CRITICIZE

Now, here's what you need to understand. Anytime you're going to have a worship experience, and you express an attitude of love and sacrifice of commitment to the object of adoration, you will always have a non-worshipper close who will criticize you. Simon criticized! Simon criticized Jesus for accepting the worship, and this lady for giving it. He didn't say nothing about his non-involvement.

You didn't hear me! Isn't it funny that when you and I begin to truly worship God, there's usually a Simon around, or a Judas, who, according to John 12 ...Mary of Bethany pours out the spikenard upon Him. Judas, who said, "What was this waste for?" "...Could have sold this for 300 pence and give it to the poor," Judas says, (not that he cared for the poor), but he was a thief, because he was in charge of the church treasury. Boy! Jesus has got a different attitude towards things than we do; Jesus knew he was a thief. You can be understaffed...you can need a treasurer...the Lord looks at Judas and says, "I see you have a problem with avarice, thievery, and dishonesty. You're the kind of man I need for a treasurer. Okay? Right here."

GOD EXPOSES FOR US TO CONQUER

Now you're looking at me like I've lost my mind. I have not lost my mind. We just don't understand the way the Lord works. You see, God knows our weaknesses. We Pentecostals keep trying to insulate and isolate ourselves from everything that could cause us to fall—we've missed it friend. The Lord looks at every one of us and says, "You know I know every aspect of your life, and every failure and every kink in your armor. Here is what I'm going to do for you. I'm going to expose that area until you either conquer it, or it kills you."

Keep trying to hide behind something, and the Lord says, "'No, no, get it out here in the open and see if you can handle it, 'cause I ain't taking nobody with me to the City that doesn't overcome everything. I stood up for one insurrection with Lucifer; I won't put up with another one from the Church."

IS IT GOD'S CHURCH OR OUR CLUB

Oh, I'm making you nervous. You're still hopin' I'm not going to put a thief in charge. See, we don't even understand Paul's admonition to the church that when you had church problems and church discipline...you know what Paul said? He said; take the weakest and the least esteemed among you, and send them up there in front of everybody and let 'em judge the cases. We wouldn't trust those people with our decisions; this is our club! Whoops!

Isn't it funny that, if the Lord doesn't let you be slapped in the face with a critic like Judas or Simon, He'll give you one even closer. He'll let your family deal with you. Isn't it tough to worship with your husband or your wife next to you? Or your kids? Or your in-laws? You get up here huckin' and buckin' and smokin', and they're sayin', "Ohhhhhhhhh, I wish they could have seen you an hour ago. My, you have metamorphosed on the way to church."

REPENT AND GET ON WITH IT

You got to understand something; you can't let the devil, or your own personality, or other people, lock you into your past. Because you lost your cool, and had a bad day, and put both your feet in your mouth, or mishandled the situation with your husband, your wife, your kids, or at work, you cannot let that now, all of a sudden, set the temperature for this. It was bad enough that we made a mistake...We ought to' be able to have the tolerance and the liberty in the church of Jesus Christ to walk in here and say, "Well, I've been a jerk there, but I'm not going to be a jerk here; I'm going to ask God to help me, and I'm going to try to praise God."

And I'm going to tell you somethin' else; if you've been a nincompoop before you got here, and then you was a worshipper while you were here...if you were really a worshipper, and you offended that husband or wife—you'll take care of it when you finish your worship service. You'll tell them, "I'm sorry, I was less than I ought to be and I'm very sorry."

Well, you want me to take a quiz and we'll see how we're doin'? Anybody had a bad day? Anybody ever have a bad day, and you come to church hopin' you can shake loose of the bad day, but you got some of the craziness on your mind, and when you would have worshipped, or praised God, or thanked God, you just didn't do it, because certain people were near you, or because it was on your mind.... Maybe those certain people weren't ever here, but the thing was your mind. "...I told her off, I cut her off, I said something unkind to her, I didn't do...."

DON'T LET THE CRITICAL SPIRIT DEFEAT YOU

See; for every time you have a David dancing in the street, you're going to have an ignorant Michal hanging out the window sayin', "Oh, how glorious the king was today." You ever wonder why she said, "Oh how glorious the king was today"? Because she was with the king last night! She was with the king the last three weeks. She watched him in his daily routine. Let's give it another twist. He may not have been boogalooin' in the house. He may have just told the kids to go to bed without supper. He might have had an argument with her. He might have ignored her, but all of a sudden, the object of his affection came close. He divorced himself from "that" and said "this" takes priority. "This" is the Lord, and he just begins to dance before the Lord. See, when you're a real worshipper, you got to divorce yourself from things where you fail. And you can't let the critical spirit get on you.

I've preached conferences, and preached better than I could; just preached in the Holy Ghost; it just was awesome...it just came out great, blessed a lot of people, and then have my adversary attack me on the way back to the hotel, and all the way back on the plane sayin', "Weren't you somethin', those boys don't know what you and me know." And I literally let that dirtbag suck me dry, and drain everything out of my soul, not realizing that God knew when I was okay and God knew when I wasn't okay, and apparently the anointing wasn't stopped because I failed; because I did repent, and I did apologize, and I did ask God for mercy to help other people.

Some people think it's wasteful, other people think it's terrible, that Jesus ever allowed this woman to touch Him. Family, friends, church folks...I want you to turn to people next to you on the left and on the right, just look at 'em—don't smirk—just look at 'em. Now look back at me, and just in your heart say, "I'm not going to let them stop me, that's for sure!"

LIFE HAPPENS!—HOW DO YOU REACT?

I was in a restaurant yesterday, and sat down. I was the only person in the restaurant, and these two ladies come in with this animal-savage of a child, and there's 200 feet in that restaurant, and 12 or 15 empty tables, and the Lord had them sit next to me! I don't mind them sittin' next to me, but I'm there to eat a bagel and to study for an hour, okay? But "Throckmorten" here, is in a debate with the mother. The mother is only 35 and she is trying to talk to this child, and the kid is throwing milk up against the window and jelly on the floor, and she's just talking to her friend. "...Oh, oh; don't do that, Rodney, don't do that," and the silverware is comin' past your head, and I'm lookin', and I'm trying to read and sayin', "Lord? Help 'em, you know, and just...." And that lasted about 15 seconds, and I said, "Well," I said, "Lord, help me," and I just turned and looked a couple of times and I just was hopin' the mother would just kind of turn and I'd go, "Thank you Jesus."

And the kid would sit there, and be fine, and fall asleep and they'd think the child had fallen asleep...an early nap...and they wouldn't notice the swelling 'til they got home, and it would just be okay.... But I'm sittin' there, and I'm a man of God, and I'm full of the love, and mercy, and compassion of Jesus, and to save my soul from being lost in a devil's hell, I just picked up my Bible, picked up my books…couldn't make it—had to make two trips. It was very obvious I was going elsewhere, cuz they watched me as I went by. I walked over there, and just sat down, and I got all the way to the other side of the restaurant, and sat there and just cuz I don't want to be irritated, and I don't want to get annoyed with that, you know, they got upset and left! I could have saved the trip!

Now you're sayin, "What does that have to do with this little Bible study?" Plenty! Cuz I'm talkin' about worshipping God! And so when I go to worship God, and go home to start worshipping and praising the Lord, this video tape plays: …"showed 'em a mighty nice spirit there…couldn't take the little kid just throwin' a fit…of course, my time is precious…I don't have time for this foolishness…I'm studying Your word…that justifies me being a jerk! Now I wasn't unkind…I just saved myself from being ticked off." You don't believe it either, do you? That's just what the Lord said, "I don't buy it!"

NON-WORSHIPPERS ARE NON-GIVERS & SELF-RIGHTEOUS

Okay, I'm almost finished. In more ways than one, I'm almost finished. Please notice; this is very important; this is the best part of my whole Bible study. I have to tell you this, because you wouldn't be able to know it. Most non-worshippers…Simon in the story…are always non-givers. Let me tell you something; when you have people in a church family that have problems with giving and finance, they always have problems with worship. You show me anybody who can worship God, I'll show you somebody who can let go of their guilt. But Simon's not a worshipper, and Simon is measuring this as a waste, just like Judas isn't a worshipper, and he's measuring stuff by dollars and cents. Please notice, there's a great revelation in this little story. This man, Simon, said to himself, "If this man were a prophet; if He were a prophet, He would have known who and what manner of woman this is that toucheth Him, for she is a sinner."

THE WHY & WONDER OF WORSHIP • BOOK TWO

NON-WORSHIPPERS HAVE THEIR OWN REVELATION

Please notice carefully; people who are non-worshippers are usually non-givers and always self-righteous. Last point. Non-worshippers, or non-givers, self-righteous, and here it is—they always feel like they have a revelation that you don't have. That's why they quit churches. That's why they start cults, because they have an insight that you don't have. But you watch people who quit, people who start trouble, people who start other churches, people who start cults—they're not good at worship. Simon's not a worshipper, he's not a giver, he's self righteous, and worst of all, he thinks he has a revelation that's missed Jesus. I've been in this game a long time, people, and I've had to deal with all kinds of crazy stuff. "Well, the Lord showed me...." I don't want to call you a liar sir; I just think you're mistaken. The Lord gets blamed for a lot of craziness. "...Well, I feel like the Lord is telling me to...." Naah...I don't buy it.

The Lord never sows discord. The Lord never brings division. I'm going to tell you something; if the Lord leads you to leave...if it is the Lord...you will leave: and leave all this alone! You will not leave and then perpetrate craziness. You will not leave and use people that you've known as a platform to proclaim your new revelation. I've seen people all over this movement create all kinds of hell and chaos in people's churches. I think a lot of them were very honest and sincere, "...Well, I felt like the Lord...." Fine. I'm going to tell you somethin'; if the Lord tells you to go, you don't need anything you left to go with you!

CONCERN YOURSELF WITH THE OBJECT—NOT THE CRITIC

Though a worshipper may be attacked and criticized by a critic, the worshipper is kind of immune, because the worshipper is always concerned with its object, not its critics. I think that the biggest battle we fight is "what will somebody else think." You need to answer that. What does it matter? What does it matter?

Last point: Attitudes that are expressed during worship:

"And Jesus answering said unto him, Simon, I have somewhat to say unto thee. And he saith, Master, say on. There was a certain creditor, which had two debtors: the one owed five hundred pence, and the other fifty. And when they had nothing to pay, he frankly forgave them both."

Frankly forgave them both. "Which of the two will love him the most?" "Well, I suppose the one that he forgave the most." "Thou hast rightly judged Simon."

Verse 44, "Seest thou this woman? I entered into thine house, thou gavest me no water for My feet." 'You extended no courtesy to Me there is some water to wash My dirty feet, but this woman has washed My feet with her tears, and when I came in, you extended no courtesy to Me.

See, I'm paraphrasing; you gave Me no courtesy. Normally, you would give a guest a kiss. But this woman has not ceased to kiss My feet. And there was a common courtesy that you would anoint My head with oil, a little sweet smelling, but you ah…didn't do that. But this woman has poured out this alabaster and has anointed Me. So I say unto you now, notice that He is not talking to the woman. He says, "But I say unto you, her sins, which are many, are forgiven her." Oh, I like that. It's almost like God says; You will not provoke Me to get angry with you, Simon, because I am in a worship situation right now, and when I'm in a worship situation, I will just override your foolishness, and I will bless this worship. Because a person is worshipping does not mean the worshipper is worthy.
A worshipper knows they have a need and the object is worthy, and that's what makes worship so precious to God, because the worshipper knows we have no right to worship Him, but He has a need to be worshipped, because He is holy and great and glorious. And He wants my worship. So He accepts it when I offer it freely, and I don't have to have a good day; I can have a lousy day, but if I have an open, repented heart. And I can weep and say, "I need You and I'm not worthy of You, but You are worthy of worship, and while my worship is not pure and clean and holy, it's honest and sincere…would You transfigure it, would you transform it, would you turn it into something acceptable?" And God says, "I'll take that kind of worship, and I'll override your critic, and I'll override your bad day."

ATTITUDES EXPRESSED BRING ATTITUDES OF RESPONSE

Bear with me just a minute now. Verse 47, "Wherefore I say unto thee, her sins which are many, are forgiven..." Hold it right there! Attitudes expressed during worship usually involve attitudes of response. Get it in your notes. Attitudes expressed receive attitudes of response. Love generally receives love; anger receives anger. Hatred receives hate. Her love and worship released to her Jesus' responsive attitude of mercy. Not worthy—mercy—because worship blesses the object and presents the need secondary. Watch carefully...she loved much; she's forgiven much. Expression flowed from her emancipation. Her release showed in His response. If you are forgiven little, it's because you love little. Verse 48, "And he said unto her, Thy sins are forgiven."

"Thy sins are forgiven." That is the greatest aspect of a worship service. Now you thought I was crazy 15 minutes ago, when I told you you could have a lousy day and the devil, or your family, your friends, or your own flesh can drive you crazy and not let you get into a worship thing because of your failure. Don't let it happen! Here's your example; she is a sinner woman, she is not a godly precious woman. She is a sinner woman, but she has come and entered into a worship service, and out of the worship service she got the most wonderful experience—forgiveness. You can't get anything greater than that, than to have your sins, your mistakes, and your errors forgiven—from a worship service. Didn't happen from preaching, or good teaching, or Bible class, or Bible quiz. It happened from a lady who worshipped in the face of critics, overriding her own feelings of condemnation.

REAL HOLINESS—FORSAKE ALL THAT DISPLEASES GOD

You know, sometimes we're our own worst enemy. At least I am. Salvation is far beyond sinners just forsaking sins and being forgiven of sins. Salvation is really the sinner responding to God's love, and thus wanting to forsake any and all that displeases the object that we worship. That's what real Bible holiness is; out of a love and thankfulness and appreciation for the goodness and mercy and grace of

God, we would be willing to surrender and sacrifice and forsake anything and everything that would displease the object of our worship.

I think, sometimes, if we had better worship, we'd have to be less ritualistic, saying, "don't go here and don't wear that, don't do this and don't smoke that and don't drink that." Man, if you were really worshippers—"what does the lover of my soul want?"

DON'T CRITICIZE—BLESS 'EM

Verse 49-50, "And they that sat at meat with Him began to say within themselves..."

Now notice, again, the minute there is a worship service, and the worshipper gets from the object of worship what they needed, there will be the second set of critics.

"...Who is This That forgiveth sins also?"

There will be critics in the service who will criticize God for blessing something they know something about. Did I get that out of the bible? They said, "Who is this that responds to her worship, forgiving her?" "Why nobody can forgive sins but God?" "What's the big idea?"

And I've done it in this church, sitting on this platform, on that little pew. That's why the Bible says, "He that increases knowledge, increases sorrow." Sometimes you're just better off goin', "I don't know nothin'!" That way, if he or she comes boogalooin' down the isle you just say, "Bless em' Lord" instead of sayin', "Let em' break a leg on the next lap, would you?" It is so easy not to allow somebody to worship God, because "I know something." You mean, I'm the only guy in the whole place that's ever got a little annoyed with God, sayin';

"Why'd You do that?"

"Now You know, like I know, what she just said, and You know, like I know, what he just did. What is the deal? Here I am, trying to keep myself clean, and pure and moral—What are You doing? It's, it's, it's me..."

And God is saying, "Yeah, but she and him don't deserve it, but they need it."

Ooooh, you're playing church with me; you're staring a hole right in my shirt. You're staring a hole right in my shirt sayin', "I don't know what this man is talkin' about." "I've never had no bad feeling toward the Lord blessin' nobody."

Come on, look around and say, "I wonder who he's talkin' to?"

I've lost some of the greatest blessings I could have ever gotten from God just being' a jerk. Just sayin', "What in the name of good sense...carryin' on and acting like your talkin' in tongues and shoutin' and boogalooin' and doin' the watusi—couldn't tell the truth standin' on the Bible. Got the morals of a roach. In the name of Jesus, what's goin' on here?"

Did you get saved in the last 46 minutes that I don't know something about? See how easy it is to develop a mentality of earning and performance; and we violate all the stuff we talk about—"grace"? You know what we ought to do? When the Lord starts blessing people; "...Bless 'em, shake 'em good, fill 'em up 'til they leak, patch the holes, put some water in there...let's go. Hallelujah. God I want you to bless 'em." Now you're laughing at me like I'm crazy, but I'll tell you, if we would do that, God would be so pleased with us. The Lord would be so happy if we, out of an honest heart, would say, "Bless 'em Lord."

See, we only know the trouble that they failed in. We don't know how many times they've whipped that thing, and we just know about the one time they stubbed their toe, and broke their nose, and fell down. They might have whipped that thing 46 times, and we don't know how desperate and how hungry their personal prayer life has been, and they want victory over that, and God gives them a chance! Oh, I feel the Holy Ghost! God gives them a chance to get refreshed and renewed, and it ain't no time for me, or thee, to say, "Hey, what's goin' on?" It's time for us to create an atmosphere and say, "Awh, give 'em a blessing Lord."

RECEIVE FAITH, DELIVERANCE & PEACE THROUGH WORSHIP

None of us deserve to be blessed anyway. If the Lord would mark iniquity which one of us could stand. Hey! Say, Go thy way woman, thy faith has saved thee. Man, I'm just gettin' to my next to the best point. Say go thy way, thy faith has saved thee. Apparently, in the presence of Jesus, through worship, all three aspects can be experienced and received; faith, deliverance, and peace.

No better way...no better place to receive faith, deliverance, and peace than at the feet of Jesus. Never crowded worshipping' the Lord. True worship has got to flow from proper attitude. That's why Simon could never accept her worship, nor could he ever worship Jesus; he had a poor attitude towards Jesus. Just think how much worship we cheat God out of when we have a poor attitude towards each other.

THE WHY & WONDER OF WORSHIP • BOOK TWO

THE WHY & WONDER OF WORSHIP

VOLUME SIX • CHAPTER NINE

THE WHY & WONDER OF WORSHIP • BOOK TWO

CHAPTER NINE

The gospel of Matthew Chapter 4:1, "Then was Jesus led up of the Spirit into the wilderness to be tempted of the devil."

GOD CAN LEAD YOU INTO TROUBLE—FOR A PURPOSE

You need to understand something. It is possible to be full of God and for God to lead you into trouble, unless I'm in a comic book. The Bible says He was led of the Spirit to be tempted. It's not always your flesh that gets you in a face-to-face confrontation with your adversary. You can be a godly, righteous, Holy Ghost filled child of God and God just select you and say, "Okay, take 'em on."

THE TROUBLE WON'T DESTROY YOU

If you are led by the Spirit of God into a confrontation, ain't no way you can lose. God will never lead you into something to destroy you. He will lead you into something to magnify Him, expose yourself, develop yourself, learn your weaknesses, learn your mistake—but He will not throw you away if you stumble. That's an awful lot in one verse. Okay...and we go through the three temptations, and I won't read 'em, I just want to get down to the last one.

Verse 8-11, "Again, the devil taketh him up into an exceeding high mountain, and showeth him all the kingdoms of the world, and the glory of them; And saith unto him, All these things will I give thee, if thou wilt fall down and worship me. Then saith Jesus unto him, Get thee hence, Satan: for it is written, Thou shalt worship the Lord thy God, and him only shalt thou serve. Then the devil leaveth him, and, behold, angels came and ministered unto him." Notice—devils don't leave and angels don't show up until you talk. You got to take your stand in what you believe and you know to be true. Then, when you do, he'll leave and they'll come.

THE WHY & WONDER OF WORSHIP • BOOK TWO

THE IMPORTANCE OF WORSHIP

I want to talk on the importance of worship. The necessity of worship. I've touched all kinds of areas, but this I feel just kind of a desperate need in my spirit to share with you how important worship is.

Now according to this statement that Jesus made in verse 10, that thou shalt worship the Lord thy God, that service flows out of worship. Now you got to get this. He said, "Get thee hence Satan for it is written thou shalt worship the Lord thy God and Him only shalt thou serve." Service comes out of worship. If you are a lousy worshipper, you're just a mechanical servant. If worship is a pain in the neck, you and I are lousy servants, because service flows out of worship and worship flows out of revelation. You can't have proper worship if you have an improper object. You can't properly worship if you have a proper object but your focus is obscured. You have to be clear on who, or what, you are worshipping.

DON'T PUT TRADITIONS OVER GOD'S WORD

Paul charged them on Mars Hill that the god that you worship ignorantly...you built this altar to the unknown god...I'm going to declare Him to you. So it is possible to be sincere and be ignorant about what you're doing. In fact, in Matthew 15, verses 8 and 9; Jesus testified against the nation of Israel, His own nation, and said, "In vain they do worship Me, teaching for commandments the doctrines of men." They were using their own traditions over the word of God.

Now here's what you got to understand...most of our traditions come to us from a study, or an experience with the word of God that gave us an experience from the word of God. But what happens is we start to magnify what we heard, or what happened, to the point that we build a box around it; and the tradition now supplants, substitutes for the living, ongoing progressive word of God. So we get locked into tradition thinking that it is the truth; when it is the truth that always gives birth to tradition.

See; if you and I don't have a current word from God, if we don't have a worshipful spirit, we will eventually be locked into tradition and truth will just march on and leave us. But we'll keep saying, "But this is the truth!" Yeah, but the truth was a personality, was a being before it was a precept. God was and is the Truth long before He said He was the Truth. And God is Spirit and God is alive and God is constantly moving—He's progressive. See; the reason you have so many denominations is, that every denomination...I believe this...every denomination, every move, every something, had some type of illumination, revelation, or experience from or with God or the spirit world that gave birth to their concept, and they built their little troop. And then what happens is, we focus in on that and we learn certain truths that came out of that original revelation and illumination, which is fine. And we want to decipher from this and get away from this and we want to decipher that and we want to dissect this one and we want to make sure this is false and this is true and this is light and that's darkness and this is life and this is death and this is right and that's wrong and...; there's nothing wrong with that—providing that our ears consistently tune to what the Spirit is saying, so that the Spirit can take us from truth to truth and from glory to glory.

THREE WANT YOUR WORSHIP—GOD, THE DEVIL AND SELF

If you have a biblical revelatory experience and truth foundation, you will not lose it, you will take it with you as you progress in God. So Jesus tells the devil..... Now you got to understand something. Worship is so important because worship is something that both God and the devil want. Now that ought to tell you the supremacy of worship. Hell wants your worship! Heaven wants your worship. You're going to give it to somebody. You ready for this? ...And you got one that's even closer than them—*self* wants your worship. And if you worship and I worship self, we serve self, because you serve what you worship!

The reason there's a vast difference between the sinner and the saint is simply this; the sinner worships self's opinion, the saint worships God's opinion. That's all it is. And in every area of my life, and your life, where there is a conflict—it's *self* trying to keep its opinion strong. It's Satan trying to weasel in. And then there's God, boy you got a battlefield here. You got three major forces in the universe working on you. And the biggest problem is the one the does the most work goes to bed with you. You brush his and her teeth. You comb his and her hair. Self fusses and argues all the time…"I don't see the reason why…."

IT'S NOT 'MOVE ME'—IT'S 'MOVE GOD'

You'll never see *self* just jump up and say, "Let's praise God!" It won't happen! Self will say, "Let's hire somebody to do it." Whoops! That's why the concept of church is like a movie theater, it's an entertainment stage. Everybody up here performs for the spectators…"Hope they move me, I'm tired." Who ever told you that the service was supposed to move us? I thought we came here to move God! I didn't know we were supposed to sit here on our backside until God all of a sudden decided to move us. I thought we're supposed to move Him with our praise, we're supposed to move Him with our contrition, we're supposed to move Him with our confession, we're supposed to move Him with our faith. I don't think we're supposed to sit here and wait for Him to move us.

You remember now, the whole issue is worship. It's not a matter of whether you will worship—you and I will worship. It's a matter of *who* we worship. It's a matter of *what* we worship, and that is the saddest state of worship—to worship a *what* rather than a *who*, because a *what* has no life. Worship your job, worship your reputation, worship your money, worship pleasure, worship things, trinkets, toys, material; my Lord, those things don't even live! To think that millions of people are training their God given instinct to worship, and they worship an *it*.

TRUST HIM WHEN YOU CAN'T FEEL HIM

Well, Pentecostals have a problem; we worship a feeling.
'Oh my God, he's against feeling!"

Oh no, I'm the best *feeling* guy in the whole place. I like to feel the presence of the Holy Spirit, I really do. But I'll tell you what; I won't backslide tonight if I don't feel Him before I go to bed. I take Him at His word. He said He moved in, He's

THE WHY & WONDER OF WORSHIP • BOOK TWO

staying here. Hello? You might as well just say Amen, 'cuz there's lots of times you don't feel the presence of God 24 hours a day, 7 days a week. You just trust Him when you can't trace Him, you lean on Him when you can't feel Him, you believe Him when you can't see Him. Why? Cuz He's not a liar, He's the Truth itself. He can't lie. I never did like it, but as I'm getting older I thank God for the seasons when I haven't been able to feel the Holy Ghost...that I trusted the Holy Ghost.

See, when you first get saved, you're in the *feeling* realm. After a while, you know what God does? He just kind of divorces Himself from the emotional strata of your being. He says; okay, got to wean you off this now, now you got to go with the Word and not with the goose bumps. What I get afraid of is people who are so mature that they're all word and no bumps. "...I'm so deep in the word...." You're so deep, you're stuck in the river. Your anchor is stuck you ain't sailed nowhere in the last 20 years. The wind blows, the Bible says it moves where it listeth. If you read in the Greek, it says it moves where it is least resisted. ...Stand there like a thing, you're just a wall in the way.... Why don't you trade in your wall for a sail and let's blow up the river a while?

GOD WANTS TO TAKE US BEYOND WHERE WE ARE

There are places in God, ladies and gentlemen, you and I have not discovered yet. There are mysteries and secrets in God that God would like to show us and teach us. Oh yes, I'm not talking about some mystical ooogie-booogie stuff...that's not what I'm talking about. I'm talking about heights and depths and the majesty of God that lots of us have never touched. I know I ain't! What a tragedy that the only thing you remember about Christopher Columbus is, 1) he discovered America, and 2) he went to jail. He didn't discover much after America...one shot deal. That's like us holy rollers. One shot...I got the Holy Ghost...here's my dollar.

WORSHIP WILL CAUSE THE GREATEST CHANGE IN US

I'm talking about the importance of worship. Service flows from worship. From worship! Heaven and Hell both want man's worship, thus; it must be extremely important. Worship is resisted more than any other spiritual practice. It is resisted more than prayer. It is resisted more than praise, because it's tougher. It's resisted more than study. Why is worship the focal point of most of our battles? Because worship, and worship alone, has its own ability to cause the greatest effectual change within us. It can cause us to become what He wants us to be. It can deliver us from dishonesty and duplicity and playing games and being plastic and being shallow. You cannot get in the raw presence of God and play a church game, but you can sit in a church and circle your Bible and just smirk and go, "Praise the Lord," and it will never change you one bit. You get in the raw power of God and see if you're cocky and arrogant and foolish and…hold bitter attitudes towards somebody and won't forgive somebody. You get naked before God—you ain't looking to cover up! You finally give up after the first 5 seconds to cover up; you finally just say, "Lord fill me up—never mind trying to cover me up—I want to be like You!"

EVERY THING IS OPEN BEFORE GOD

Sometimes I don't think we believe the Bible when it says, "All things are naked and opened unto the eye of Him with whom we have to do." Naked and open; transparent. He looks at you…x-ray. He's got it all. It's scary. Get in the raw presence of God, He ain't playing games. He knows every thought, every intent, every past. He knows the future. He knows the present. Who you going to snooker, who you going to fool? Worship, real worship, will cause you to absolutely leave your safe zone. You will act so crazy, I don't mean just gymnastics for Jesus, I mean just start confessing stuff and talking to God and pouring your heart out to Him and asking for help in areas.

If you get into a real worship experience, you may not even care who's next to you. You'd be surprised, worship will set you free from peer fear. See, Bible study and praise won't do that. Real worship will set all of us free from hypocrisy and shallow pretence. Can you imagine getting in the raw presence of God and saying, "Ahh, how's the weather?" "How's the speckled perch in lake Okeechobee?" "How's the...how's things in Milwaukee?" ...Don't know where to put your hands. The stillness of God makes you nervous. Rather than have a blast from Him and just knock you over—for Him to just stand there and look at you.

MANY TIMES WORSHIP REQUIRES SILENCE

You ever walk into somebody who was in high authority in an office, or front of a judge, or a president of a bank, or anything like that and just stand there and they just kind of look at you? You're standing there and you feel like you got one of those stupid hospital gowns that don't close. You're just kinda standing there and he's looking at your paper, and they never look at you. They never have the courtesy to look at you. They just kind of say, "Ahh, JW Arnold, come up here." And they never look at you and go, "Ahhh hmmmm, ahhh ammmmm," and you're dyin'...you know you'd rather have the guy say, "Sixty days in jail—bread and water" than for him to keep going, "Aahh hmmm." And then finally looks up at you. Then you really feel like sayin'..."Speak, will you?" Sometimes that's, why we're bothered so much in a worship service, because many times worship requires silence from within, and you're wanting God to just shout and speak and He just kind of...silently musing.

WORSHIP FIRST—AND FOREMOST

You see, real worship will cause us to expand our adoration level towards God. The reason why worship is resisted, is because in worship, desires are birthed. In Hebrews chapter 11; it is extremely significant in the chronological order of the listing. In Verse 4 it says, "By faith Abel..." In Verse 5 it says, "By faith Enoch..." In Verse 7 it says, "By faith Noah..." I don't think that's a fluke! I think it was divinely intended to come listed that way. I think there is a procedural shine right here. It's just shining right through these pages. It is unique that the Holy Spirit, who inspires the authorship of this Bible, has the first guy listed as, "By faith Abel..." Now why Abel? Because Abel is noted for his worship. By faith, Abel offered a more excellent sacrifice to God, and by it received testimony from the

Lord. And even he being dead his gift yet spoke. Doesn't say anything else about Abel except his worship. Get it now. Worship first.

Then you come up to the next guy, Enoch. "By faith Enoch..." What did Enoch do? There's no listing of him being a worshipper. He's noted for his walk with God. You're not hearing me! This is progressive. You won't walk if you don't start out worshipping. Who comes after Enoch? Noah. What's he noted for? He built a boat. By faith, works, service. Worship, walk, work. Did you get it? It all starts with worship. We've raised a generation that's bypassing worship and working. Bypass worship and are told they can walk with God just by believing on Jesus. Taint so! God still chooses the mode of approach.

SEPARATE YOURSELF FROM NON-WORSHIPPERS

It was God who told and warned Pharaoh; ...you better let my people go, because they are worshippers and they're getting messed up with your stupid idols and I want them to come out in the wilderness and the dessert and hold unto me a feast. Read it in the original—a worship festival. I want them to come out and worship me. Watch what happens. You can't always worship surrounded with a bunch of do-dos that don't know how to worship. That's why He said, "Let them separate three days journey." Sometimes it would behoove you to just kinda put your hand up and say, "I think I'm going to change pews." "Crazy people sitting here." You can get in an atmosphere of people who are full of foolishness, and the day's activities and worrywarts—no faith. And you try to rise above all that craziness in an act of worship, it's tough. That's why you got to sometimes separate yourself.

IT'S PROGRESSIVE

Worship, as I taught you before, usually occurs within the veil. Remember the three sequences of that lesson I taught you? The outer court, the Holy Place, and the Most Holy Place. The biggest—natural light. The smaller—not natural light. A place of service; this light came from oil, came from the altar of the fire. Then, finally, no fixed light, no service light. Now it's the absolute raw light of God's presence Himself. You step inside the veil, it's just one-on-one, there's where worship takes place. It's always a progressive separation.

YOU CAN'T JUST BARGE IN ON GOD

Wait a minute. You can't get into the worship sequence like those nincompoops on TV and radio who tell everybody, "Just believe in Jesus." No! You can't barge in on God. Nobody gets into the Holiest Place without going to the altar, without dealing with the laver, without going into the Holy Place for bread, for incense offering, for the candlestick—you can't just go in! God went on record and said, "I'll choose who I'll approve to approach Me and I'll show by what method they can approach Me." Nobody barges in on God.

YOU CAN'T JUST 'BELIEVE IN JESUS'

I have a major problem with "I believe in Jesus." I really do! Cuz I think it's such a tragic insult to the majesty of Calvary and the new birth message and the resurrection and the ascension of Jesus...that a bunch of people on their way to Hell...unregenerated God haters...anti-Christ...you know what anti-Christ means? It means non-anointed. Christ is *Christos*; the anointed. Anti Christ means anti-anointed. They have no anointing..."I believe in Jesus." "You can't believe in Jesus, stupid. You're dead in sin!" "The only way you can believe is for the Holy Spirit to quicken you and liven you and help you to have faith to believe."

"I believe in Jesus." "I accept Jesus."

The issue's never been whether you accept Jesus, the issue's always been whether Jesus accepts you. He said, "We are accepted in the beloved." But you got to find a way to get in the beloved. How you going to get in Christ? You can believe into Christ. "Oh no you can't!" You have to be born into Christ. Just as Christ has to be born into you.

THE WHY & WONDER OF WORSHIP • BOOK TWO

NO WORSHIP TAKES PLACE IN OUTER COURT OR HOLY PLACE

There isn't any worship that takes place in the outer area of the place of meeting or the place of sacrifice. That's not worship, that's a place of sacrifice. Worship does not take place in the second sequence, which is the Holy Place. That's the place of service, there's no worship there, that's the place of service. They changed the bread, they dressed the lamps, they offered the incense—that's service. You cannot worship and work. Pharaoh...listen to Pharaoh's argument, "What's going on with you Moses and Aaron? You're trying to get the people to stop work." Right! You can't do both. This must stop; that this might begin. If this begins then that'll have eternity in it.
If it doesn't it's just wood, hay, and stubble. Work has got to flow out of worship. Worship has got to be birthed by revelation. You can't worship without revelation.

PRAYER AND PRAISE IS NOT WORSHIP

"...You know not what to worship." If you don't have a revelation, and all you have is human people giving you human interpretation and information, all you are is an intellectual worshipper, you're not in Spirit. "Prayer is not worship." Prayer is preeminently involved with one thing: My needs. "Praise is not worship." Praise is thanksgiving for the blessings to answered prayer. "...I thank You for what You've done, thank You for healing, thank You for saving, thank You for sparing, thank You for having mercy, thank You for being good to me, thank You for keeping me in a sound mind, thank You, thank You, thank You, thank You, thank You." That's not worship. Worship...worship is with God Himself. Worship is an exchange of worthiness of God by your spirit. It's love—making love to love. It's an appreciation and adoration for who and what God is.

BUT—WE DO NEED TO PRAY BETTER

Now, prayer, as it matures, will incorporate true praise and full worship. But not very many of us that I know, not saying you're not here, but I don't know...that we are probably better prayers than we are worshippers. And come to think of it, our praying ain't so hot. Anybody besides me like to be a better prayer? Anybody besides me like to be able to just pray and in about five minutes get in the Spirit and come back in an hour or two? Don't I wish I owned that button? Wish I could send that device to Pentecost. I'd be in Guatemala somewhere on a sunny beach, tanning, and spending my money. If I could just sell you this little device, you just say these twelve words...these equations...buy these three tapes, look at my picture and "poof" you'd be right in there and come back in an hour...sell billions of 'em!

PRAYER IS A WARFARE

But see, what we don't understand is that prayer is a warfare, and the warfare involves the presenting of needs, presenting of thanksgiving, intimacy, and exchange of love. And we're giving it to the One that our adversary hates; he ain't putting his weapons down and sayin', "Oh, you *need* to pray, oh, you need to get a prayer through, let me open the door here, will you be long praying? Got some relatives you praying over? I'll wait." Don't you get it? The minute you get ready to say, "Time to pray," your adversary is going to say, "You want to bet?"

You can be suffering from amnesia and the first five minutes of prayer you remember things you've lost, things you forgot to do, things you did...it's amazing how your mind will have a resurrection. Phone will ring, baby will cry, dog will bark, bell rings. I know I've said it, but it's worth repeating. You want to just try to remember what you forgot to do during the day? Stop for 10 minutes and start to pray, it'll come right to you. He'll tell you all the places you need to go and what you need to do, and if you've felt bad today, just pray! You just start praying, you'll remember all the junk that you said and you felt and you thought and you didn't do and you did do. It'll all come up and say, "Hi ol' friend!"

I'm going to tell you something. I've done a lot of reading. I know I look stupid, but I can read, and I listen to a lot of tapes, and I listen to a lot of preachers, and in a multitude of counsel there is safety, and also in a multitude of counsel there is confusion and an Excedrin headache. You can hear so many voices telling you how to pray and what to do..."Well, you start with this and you start with that, get seven steps, do...well don't start with this..." Start with praising and worshipping God, that's the Lord's Prayer; "Our Father which art in Heaven..." ought to be starting with Him.

START PRAYER WITH THANKSGIVING

Sometimes it's not as easy as starting with Him, because *I* need. I realize how terrible I am and a great need that I have and it's almost like I have to start with Calvary and I have to thank God for Calvary. And so mine almost starts out like, "I couldn't write a good tape series, or a book, because all these other guys have all the answers. They've written these books and who am I?" I mean they wrote books! I'm going to tell you, it's tough sometimes to start out in worship being that worship is the third sequence. So I kinda just start out giving God thanks, I thank...well...just look into my closet for a minute; I give Him thanks for His kindness and His goodness. I thank Him everyday for Calvary and the blood of the Lamb, and the keeping power of the Holy Ghost and the written Word of God.

And I'll take a journey for a while down the road and...don't bother me...doesn't seem to bother Him—that I remind Him of stuff that I reminded Him two days ago about thanking Him for this and thanking Him for that, because I'm trying to create an atmosphere of gratefulness and gratitude and thankfulness in my heart before I say, "Oh, by the way, I need twenty bucks." And the scripture says, "He already knows you have need, but He would appreciate it if you would thank Him for what He already did."

WAIT ON GOD

I mean, how many dads and moms here like it when your kids run in and say, "Slap me $5." "I'll give you $5 you can't spend." We have a "give me" generation. We have an instant gratification generation. Microwave, stir fry, instant mashed potatoes, instant everything. And, you say what you want to, it bleeds over in our own spirituality. We don't want it to, but it does..."You know, I'm in a hurry could you just lay it on me, I'll pray later." But, see, God...He's not going to get in a hurry, because He don't die. He don't get old, He's not afraid of cancer, so nothing bothers Him. So He just kinda says, "Well, wait on Me, or miss it." And most of us say, "I hate to miss it, but I've lived this long without it—I guess I can get by."

Let me tell you something that God is letting me know. I've been seeking God all these years, wanting the power of God and the glory of God; and God has made me to know, "Jeffrey, you lived all these years below and you seem to be functioning without it, I'll let you live the rest of your life without it if you won't break through and wait on me." See, we think there's some magic carpet going to bring it to us. Oh, no...it ain't coming.

IT'S YOUR ATTITUDE IN PRESENTING WORSHIP

Salvation is the blessing that we receive. Worship is the blessing that we give back to God for what He's done and who He is. Worship involves the presenting of our gifts to God. That's why the wise men came and presented their gifts, and worshipped.

Now, notice, the gift isn't the worship, it's in the presentation of the gift that your attitude and my attitude is revealed, you can't buy God off with twenty bucks. He don't need money. He would rather have my spirit, my heart, my attitude, my mind, my drive. He wants me. That's why He griped and complained...and I say that in honor and respect to God when I say...gripe. His complaint to Israel was that—

"Your heart is far from me. I never wanted all these rams and lambs murdered and slaughtered and millions and tons of liquid blood everywhere. I was trying to teach you a lesson of my holiness and your unholiness and your inability to approach me. Unless I show you, you can only approach through a sacrifice and a substitute and atonement, but this is not the issue, I didn't want this, I've always wanted you."

And He says, "…and so you've gone, and now you've traded the truth for tradition. Tradition's become a ritual, ritual has become lifeless and you're empty and I'm unhappy." So it shows me all over that after all is said and done, God says, "…it didn't work, I'm still unhappy and you're still lost. And you've got all this stuff I told you to do, but you're heart's not in it. You traded a quest for Me, for a formula." He says, "…your heart is far from Me. That's all I ever wanted was your heart."

Now, you might say, "Well, God, if you just wanted my heart, why all this other junk, why didn't you just say, 'give Me your heart'." "Because you don't understand how unholy you are and you don't understand how holy I am."

IT'S THE *LONG* REACH OF GOD

And I need to show this to you, ladies and gentlemen, when Adam fell from this high place of being in the likeness and imagery of God, he didn't fall three feet; he fell a couple hundred billion miles. See, you think he just kinda fell in the mud, like these little Baptist guys say, "He fell in the mud." Oh no, he didn't fall in the mud, he was on top of the Eiffel tower and he fell through the earth and come out on the other side and landed on another planet. That's how far down *we* went. And so when we look up, we can't see God, God's got to reach down for us. That's what condescending means—He steps down, waaaaayyyy down.

That's why Paul had such a magnificent understanding and illumination about what grace was. We are saved by grace. It's the long reach of the love of God—waaaayyyy down. But until we are made aware of how far we are and how far up He is, we'll treat our salvation like the Jews did…"it's just some sheep and ram and a couple turtle doves, what's the big deal? Business as usual." But if you're three minutes away from an electric chair and somebody walks in and hands you a pardon, you're not going to go grab a quick beer, eat a pretzel and laugh about it. Well, hello! Worship involves presenting our gifts to God. Ask Mary in John 12, ask the lady in Luke 7; in both stories it was Paul presenting his life for service; worshippers come to give not to get. I wish we could get that. I say it all the time, and I'm not saying that I'm there, I'm talking to myself, too.

OUR PRIORITY—TO BLESS GOD

I come to services and I want the Lord to bless, I ask God to bless me and bless the people. And yet, I know the deepest thing is that I might bless God. And yet, sometimes I feel like I can't bless God, unless I get blessed a little. It's like my well needs priming. Anybody remember the old wells? You used to prime 'em and you go, "You got to put a little water in to get the water that's in there—out." That's sometimes what I feel like; Lord if you just kind of...just give me just a little breeze, I'll be alright. You say, "Now Br. Arnold, you're contradicting what you said." No, I'm just trying to tell you I ain't got it altogether. See, I know what I 'posed to do, but I don't always do what I'm 'posed to do. See; my humanity keeps showing up. Sometimes I think that you folks look at me like Tarzan, that one night Jeffy *is* going to come swingin' in on the grape vine and just get this great move of God.

THANKSGIVING AND PRAISE IS A PRELUDE TO WORSHIP

A true worshipper comes to praise, not just to petition. We come not to be refreshed, but to refresh God, give God pleasure. Worship without cost is not worthy of the name. Consider Jesus Christ who the scripture says in Ephesians 5:25, loved the church and gave Himself for it. Let me ask us, what are we doing for the church? Jesus Christ loved it so much He gave Himself. So that means there's got to be a process, somehow. David said in Psalm 132:5...He said I want to built God a house cuz He's built me a house and built me a kingdom and kept me and been kind to me. I want to build something that can be a corporate worship place, not just a mobile tent. Worshippers will not withhold their best from their love object. They will never offer with reservation.

Critics and misunderstanding non-worshippers will never stop the worshipper from worshipping the one he or she loves. Now, that's easier said than done. "...I know I should, but sometimes I don't." "...I know He's worthy...." I know that. There's not anybody here that doesn't believe He's worthy, but yet, sometimes I'm almost unprovoked to perform. It's like every insurance company, every sales corporation wants 10,000 self-starters—there's usually three. That's why they bring all the self-help people in—to get them started again. And even that's only a jump-start, "…he won't go for four months."

We got the greatest message and the greatest product in the world and yet, for some reason, we also need jump-starting. That's why the beginning of the service is an imperative for the quality of the rest of the service. It is not something we do to get out of the way. It is not in the way, it is the way to the way. Thanksgiving and praise paves the way to a worship experience. Thanksgiving and praise creates an atmosphere where God can show His stuff. Thanksgiving and praise helps your faith stretch.

DON'T FOCUS ON THE JUDAS SPIRIT

Notice that when Mary, in Verse 12, broke the alabaster box and anointed Jesus, that her action really was a worship action—Impacted the whole house. Cuz the whole house was filled with the fragrance. 'Course everybody in the house was happy and nobody in the whole Pentecostal church will ever be happy. Even when Jesus is exalted, there'll be somebody there that's not happy. There's always a Judas spirit. And I'm going to tell you something; my battle is not to let the Judas spirit affect me. Because I pray and study and I seek God and I try to be sensitive to God and sometimes I find myself more sensitive to Judas. And I get up here in the pulpit and get ready to do something and my spirit just gets sidetracked to handle a Judas spirit and never magnify God while I deal with Bimbo…and finish…and finally say, "Bless God, I took care of that, but the sheep weren't fed—I killed a wolf, but the sheep are still hungry."

You say, "Well, what are you going to do about the wolf? I'll tell you what, if I feed the sheep and let the sheep exalt the shepherd, the shepherd will show up in a minute and take care of the wolf. That's what we're trying to do—get the shepherd to show up! We can't take care of the wolf; we're sheep, but if the shepherd will show up…!

THE WHY & WONDER OF WORSHIP • BOOK TWO

YOU MAY HAVE TO WORSHIP ALONE—IN A CROWD

You'll affect everything around you if you get into a worship situation. But you got to learn that you may have to worship alone. A-lone. A-lone. Not alone. A-lone. You may be the only one on the pew worshipping God. You may have to worship through stares. "...Oh what are you doing." "Why can't you be quiet?" "Must you always yell out." "I wish your hand would get arthritis." "I get so sick of watching you." Now there ain't no sense in being a fool and saying, "Ignore it." There ain't no way you can ignore it, override it, overcome it. You can't ignore it, it's there. It's like a barb, but you just say, "Well, you got a problem, I ain't got a problem. He's worthy, He's been good to me, He's been precious to me, I got more devils to fight than you, I've got more problems to deal with than you. I'm sorry that you're not excited about Him, but I'm soooo excited about Him, I'm going to wave my little fat hand around and say hallelujah Jesus!!" You got to do that!

YOUR FOCUS MUST BE ON HOW GREAT JESUS IS

I'm going to tell you something else; if I understand John 12, when the whole situation was over and Jesus rebuked Judas—I can't find out where the rebuke and the correction ever made Judas a worshipper. It just made him a scolded thief. You got to hear me now: if Jesus' presence, and Jesus being exalted in the middle of a grand worship service and Jesus rebuking Judas and correcting him and humbling him did not change him, don't be foolish enough that you're going to change somebody sitting on the pew with you just because you overrode their little obstacles. Judas didn't change, didn't change! He was in the greatest worship service there ever was...didn't change! He was there when Jesus come riding in on the donkey...didn't change him. He heard the multitudes' "Hosanna", he saw the miracles, signs and wonders...it never changed him. Why? Because until you get a focus of how great and grand He is, you'll never be a worshipper. You and I will just use Jesus for our selfish ends.

ALWAYS BLESS GOD IN SPITE OF........

Paul and Silas, in Acts 16, are in the prison. We know the story, I've preached lots of sermons on it, but they affected the whole prison, because they worshipped. They blessed God in spite of the experiences and the pain and the sorrow. That's not easy to do. Kind of tough sometimes, to say, "God, how come you didn't get me out of this?" I'm going to tell you the thing that'll give you an Excedrin headache. It's not what you don't know about God, it's what you know about God. The more you know about God, the easier it is to get frustrated when He don't show up. When He don't fix it. "...You could have healed this, you're going to save my marriage, you could have changed him, you could have gave me the money, you could have helped me with a job, you could have got me the education, you could have...." It's what you know about God that the devil fights in your mind about. Not the unknown. It's the known. When you know that He can fix it and He goes mute. When you know He can walk through your mess and just go –pppheewww-, and blow down every obstacle. You know right now God can walk into the judge's chambers and could fix that whole situation for your loved ones, your family, your friends, your neighbors—He could just whisper.

WORSHIP EVEN WHEN GOD STAYS SILENT

He could talk just like He did to Pharaoh and say, "Let the people go, or I'll kill you," and that guy'll wake up the next day and say. "I'll let you go and here— here's all my gold and silver...and take everything," and spoil Egypt. God can do that right now. And a lot of times it's very frustrating when you pray for people and you talk to people and you counsel with people and you worship with people and you praise with people and then God just somehow chooses to be aloof. And then your heart goes, "What do I believe?" "Where is God when I'm hurting?" Yeah! I'm not a virgin voice up here. I'm telling you the God's truth! It's been an agony in my life, for I've seen God do awesome stuff and then let somebody die when I've prayed for 'em. And I've seen Him let kids stay pukin' and throwin' their guts up for nights and I'm praying for 'em and He just goes...and so then you say, "Well, I must not have faith, it must not be the will of God, or...."

Now, you can't ever be stupid enough to say the devil is stronger. Now that ain't even in the picture. See, I can live with that if I felt that the devil was stronger than God and he slipped one over on Him, "...ha, ha...!" That ain't possible. That even frustrates me more when I know nothing can whip Him and nothing can fool Him and nothing can beat Him at His own game. It blows your mind sometimes why God chooses to do what He does, but you have to look and say, "He does all things well and my understanding does not reduce His majesty. He's still good, He's still great, He's still holy, He's still wonderful, He's still kind, and I'm going to serve Him like Job of old and if He slays me I'm going to believe Him and trust Him anyway."

WORSHIP IS ALWAYS PRIMARY

I'm talking about the importance of worship. I'm going to show to you by the scriptures the importance of worship. According to Exodus Chapter 20:1-5 and Exodus 34:14, God said that worship was the primary need for the nation of Israel. He said, "Thou shalt have no other gods before Me, for the Lord thy God is a jealous God and I do not want you to worship any images or any idols." So God goes on record; remember the law of first mention. Remember me teaching you about the law of first mention? When the law of first mention comes on, it gives you a foundation of which you can launch from.

You know the first mention of the word worship? Genesis 22: when Abraham offered Isaac. Worship that don't cost you nothing is not worth the name. Are you ready for this? The first time God deals in the principle of worship with the nation Israel is found in Exodus 20 when Moses is receiving the law and the injunctions from God. When God says, ...I want to be worshipped first and foremost, I don't want any idols, I don't want any images.... So what He said was; primary target boys—right here. I have the preeminence, and the absoluteness and priority in your life—we got together now.... He did that to 3 million people. So worship is extremely important to God.

A RELATIONSHIP WITH GOD ABOVE ALL

Our problem is, idols come in strange forms. Not too many of us still carry rabbits foots, or Ouija boards, or crazy little idols. But how about business, how about wealth. Now I'm going to violate some of you people's concept on things, cuz I know we're in a big thing about families and relationships, and I know some other teachings are phenomenal, much better than mine. I know that. But I'm going to tell you something. Contrary to what some people are teaching and telling you, don't ever think that your family takes priority over your relationship with God. Now I know I'm going to violate a lot of stuff here and there's going to be repercussions all over this place. I've heard this until I'm about ready to throw up. You say, "Well, God made the family." I'm going to tell you what, before God ever made the family, He had Adam who was doing just fine. It wasn't because God needed Eve; Adam needed Eve. Hello! I'm going to go a little further. And if Adam had walked with God and loved God like he should have, he'd a let Eve go. Now I know my wife is sittn' here and I love my wife, but "...bye...." You think I'm kiddin' you? My wife wants to start honkey tonkin' and drinkin' and being immoral and runnin' around and livin' like a fool? I ain't going to Hell for her! I'm not going to do that. You say, "Well, the family....? No! God's got His own family! As much as I love Patricia, there ain't going to be none of that.

I hear these nincompoops: "Well, I'd go to Hell for my husband." "Well, you *need* to go, you dope; I'm not goin'! You don't understand Hell to begin with." Nobody wants to go there. ...My wife doesn't want to serve God? Tough break! I'm coming to church! I'm going to *be* the church! I'm going to live in the Holy Ghost! If I have to live with a bunch of hell at home...? Fine! But I ain't going to stay home and live with a bunch of hell *and* go to hell with it!

Well, you just do all you want to about your classes on relationships, I'm going to tell you; I got my theory on it, too. My wife is the biggest fool walking in a pair of shoes if I start runnin' around with women and taking drugs and livin' like a fool and cheating and lying and stealing and beating her brains in and runnin' around on her...that she just says, "Well, I just...to save my marriage, I love him so, I just had to save my marriage, I just can't go to church no more." Now I'm going to tell you, I've been married to her for over 30 years; you'll never hear that song. She'd say, "I knew him well. Don't let the door hit you on the backside on the way out!" Well hello?

DON'T BE LOST BECAUSE OF SOMEONE ELSE

You got to make up your mind my friend that your going to live for God. If momma don't go, if daddy don't go, if children don't do right, aunts and uncles don't do right—you got to just walk with God, friend. There's going to be a lot of people who had families that are going to be raptured without their families They love their families, fast and pray for their families, but their families don't want to go. Don't stay in this world because your family doesn't want to serve God. God's worthy! That's my opinion you can just write it off. Take it to your relationship class, do what you want. I just don't buy into it, I didn't buy into it years ago.

My dad didn't want to serve God. You think I'm going to go to Hell because my dad didn't want to serve God? He had his own dumb concoction of what he thought religion was and what salvation was and he had this big thing about the American Indian...nobody witnessed to them...oh bologna, I ain't going to buy into all that crud and garbage. My other brother doesn't want to serve God, "...Well I'm, you know...." I hate it, you don't want to go—I'm sorry. Now it's not that they don't want to go to Heaven, they just don't want to serve God. "...Well, I like to serve God my way...." There ain't room in this for your way and His way. This is a one way street. Jesus said, "I am the way."

I don't want to be misread here. I can feel the vibes coming up here, "anti-family man...." No I'm not. My God man, we're the family of God. Come on, we're the family of God. What am I going to do with some of you people actin' like fools and living crazy and don't want to go to Heaven? You mean you want me to join you? You must be out of your mind! "...Well they're doing it...." Well, that's their problem, let's pray for them and help them to get through this trial and back on track. You don't go join somebody that's robbing a bank because he's broke. "...Well, Joe needed the money...." He may need three bullets! That is so dumb. "...Well, my husband doesn't want to pray...." Well, pray for him!

"...Well, my kids don't want to serve God...." Well, live the best you can and ask God for grace in your home, ask for grace in your life.

BEWARE OF IDOLS IN YOUR LIFE

I'm going to tell you something folks. I don't want to mess with your little golden idol theory and all. I'm just wondering, okay? I'm just wondering if God doesn't have various levels of standards for people in various situations that God would expect a lot more out of a couple full of the Holy Ghost than a woman who lives with a devil? That's not a license to live loose. It's grace. I wonder what kind of hell and sorrow and pain it must be to go home after a church service, after feeling the presence of God and be challenged by the convicting touch of God, and have nobody to share it with but some character who's always fussing and cussing and watching TV and smoking cigarettes and living like a fool and never wants.... My wife and I, we talk, we go to the restaurant, we go home, we share the things of God, we talk about stuff. What a rich marriage to have someone that you're married to that loves God. Just be aware of the idols—business, wealth, home, family, possessions, talents, popularity, power, prestige, pleasure, self-life idols. The Lord says; I want to be worshipped, I need the preeminence, I don't have an ego problem, I'm just so great, I deserve it.

LET'S PARTY!

To prove the importance of worship: it was God who gave Israel the 7 feasts; three major feasts, 7 total feasts—for one purpose. The purpose of the 7 feasts was so that they might come together in one holy conclave and they might exalt, worship, and bless God and rejoice in His presence. That was the purpose of the seven feasts. So God's into the party scene. God's not into church services that are like a funeral. God enjoys a good party. All you sour pusses that never smile in a service; you ought to hit yourself in the mouth just so you have to bleed or something. You just sit there and you just...I'm going to tell you...sternness and being stoic is not spirituality, it's kinda...it's another "s", *stupid*, you know, *stupid*. It's not spiritual maturity that you can stare down a service for an hour. What is that supposed to mean? That is so dumb. Never smile, never laugh, never cry, just... "...so happy to be here I can hardly stand it." Nobody else can stand you, either!

YOU ARE THE CHURCH

In the Old Testament with 7 feasts, they had one purpose; to worship God. In the New Testament they were given scripture for weekly gathering to worship. Acts 20:7, "gathering together for prayer, for the breaking of bread and fellowship." Matthew 18:20, "they come together two or three in My name there I am in the midst." Hebrews 10:25, "forsake not the assembling of yourselves together as the manner of some is. So much more as you see the day approaching." What day? The day of the Lord. What's it saying: You don't need less church. You got to hear me; this building, this denomination, is not the church. The church is you. The baptized, Holy Ghost filled believer—you are the church.

Now, you can have church where 2 or 3 are gathered together in Jesus name. Wait a minute, some of you loose cannons. Let me nail you down with a chain, 'cause you like to say, "Oh yes, we can have church anywhere we want to." But it seems strange to me that you say, "Oh yes, we can have church anywhere we want to, but we don't want to be with the corporate body." "We don't want to add nothing to it and we're so spiritual it can't add nothing to us." But I thought we we're lively stones—Ephesians 2—built up a holy habitation of God through the Spirit that we might edify one another and magnify the Lord and evangelize the lost. I being with you brethren and sisters, but I enjoy corporate getting together.

FORSAKE NOT ASSEMBLING TOGETHER

I think it's a wonderful something when the body can get together. I'm leery of people who just say;
"Well, I don't need to get together."
"Why? That's what...why?"
"Well, because you have nothing you can add to me."
"Well, I have nothing I can add to you."

Well, then, there's a problem. Then, if that is the case, you need to get together with me and help me. And how in the world are you going to obey them that have rule over you, being that you ain't got no one that's got rule over you? And who's going to give an answer for your soul, being that you've appointed yourself the bishop and pastor of your own soul? Don't you understand, that God loves you so much that He'll usually put someone over you that's inferior. To first, grate on you, and then grace you. See, you thought I was going to say superior. Oh no! I know I'm inferior, that's why I work at it. I know I ain't got no business teaching nobody, I need to be taught, I don't need to be in charge of nothing. I need for people to help me. This is no game with me.

IMPORTANCE OF WORSHIP IS PROVEN BY SCRIPTURE

The importance of worship is proven by Exodus 25:18 and Exodus 25:22. God gave them the tabernacle plan and said, "let them make a sanctuary for Me, for a place for them to worship Me, for Me to communicate with them, and for a place for their learning. This is neat: The tabernacle plan engulfs and encloses and includes 7 full chapters, 243 verses, detailing and describing the tabernacle, its furniture—and the purpose was worship. You ready for this? There's 1 chapter and 31 verses declaring all of creation, because the purpose of creation is not as high as worship! It's historic and learning only. You ready for this? And there's only one verse in the entire Bible for the entire cosmos and He made the stars, also. Apparently, unimportant to God.

People trade in their lives trying to find comets, trying to find the Milky Way, studying what's going on out there and God just said, "I made the stars, also." Boom! Trillions of 'em, light-years away, "...no big deal." "...You're a big deal to Me—that other stuff's nothin', I just make stars." Boom! 1 chapter for the whole creation, the whole universe—no big deal. "...7 chapters for your worship! 243 verses to teach you how much I love to be worshipped, and how much I deserve to be worshipped, and how much I delight to be worshipped, and what a blessing it will be if you will worship Me."

THE WHY & WONDER OF WORSHIP • BOOK TWO

IT'S PROGRESSIVE—WARRIOR, WORKER, WORSHIPPER

Consider the arrangement of the camp. Remember, God is a God of order; 1 Corinthians 14:33. He is not the God of confusion or disorder. When God set up the worship, He set up with a tabernacle which was in the center, because Jesus Christ was in the midst of the candlesticks. Tabernacle's in the center; now this is neat. He gave rules how everybody was supposed to line up. The nearest to the tabernacle were the priests. Aaron's sons camped closest to the tabernacle. Why? Because they were in charge of national worship. After them came the Levites; they were in charge of the service of the tabernacle. Important, but not as important as the worshippers. Watch this; after the Levites came the warriors, so notice how God holds things in priority. Worshippers, workers, warriors. People who do all the fighting are the furthest away.

Note also, when God gave 'em the picture of worship...the ages.... See, everything with God is order. When God got ready to give Himself priests, according to Numbers 4:3, the priests had to be 30 years old before he could be a priest. Now this is neat; the Levites had to be 25 years old, according to Numbers 8:25. The warriors, according to Numbers 1:3, had to be 20 years old. So, warfare was associated with youth, inexperience, and immaturity. Work and service was a little better—they had a little more responsibility—they were 5 years older. But the worshipper was to have relationship *and* maturity, they had the greatest experiences and the most spiritual knowledge—they had to be at least 30. Now I'm going to hurt you...that's why those of you who have been in the church a long time...you are indicted by the Word of God to teach new converts how to worship. You that claim to have the Holy Ghost 10 years, 20 years, and sit like a Mt. Rushmore, sit empty and void like Grand Canyon, still as a cemetery, cold as a funeral, God won't put up with it.

WORSHIP TAKES PRIORITY OVER WORK

According to Job 32:6-7 and Titus Chapter 2:1-6, said let the aged teach the younger. Job 32 said, let years speak and show us the way. In Isaiah Chapter 6, if you'll just go home and read the first 12 verses, I think you'll get a great blessing out of it, but I found something I've never found and I've preached Isaiah 6 for 20 years. "In the year king Uziah died I saw also the Lord high and lifted up and His train filled the temple." And the Seraphims were there, flying angel creatures of God, the host of Heaven, God's worshipping crew. The Bible said, "they cried one to another, and said, Holy, holy, holy is the Lord God Almighty, the whole earth is full of His glory, and the posts moved at the voice of them that spoke," and there was holy smoke in the place, it filled with holy smoke. But I found something today I'd never seen before. These Seraphims are described as having 6 wings, said, "with twain they covered their face, and with twain they covered their feet, and with twain did they fly." Listen to this—God let me see it today; He said…look at it…wow; Those that are involved in My worship, more than the Earthlings, they use four of their wings in reverence and worship—only two of their wings for service.

Two wings covered their face in reverence—two wings covered their feet in reverence and worship and adoration; only the other two wings do service. Twice as much is given to worship and reverence in the heavens than what is given in service.

Now, if heaven gives us a picture that worship takes priority over work, have we got the cart before the horse?

THE WHY & WONDER OF WORSHIP • BOOK TWO

THE WHY & WONDER OF WORSHIP

VOLUME SIX · CHAPTER TEN

CHAPTER TEN

2 Samuel Chapter 7:22-23, "Wherefore thou art great, O Lord God: for there is none like thee, neither is there any god beside thee, according to all that we have heard with our ears. (23) And what one nation in the earth is like thy people, even like Israel, whom God went to redeem for a people to himself, and to make him a name, and to do for you great things and terrible, for thy land, before thy people, which thou redeemest to thee from Egypt, from the nations and their god"

Psalm 86:5-10, "For thou, Lord, art good, and ready to forgive; and plenteous in mercy unto all them that call upon thee. Give ear, O Lord, unto my prayer; and attend to the voice of my supplications. (7) In the day of my trouble I will call upon thee: for thou wilt answer me." That's faith talking! (8) Among the gods there is none like unto thee, O Lord; neither are there any works like unto thy works. (9) All nations whom thou hast made shall come and worship before thee, O Lord; and shall glorify thy name." Worship glorifies God's name. It's not something that we need to get out of the way. (10) "For thou art great, and doest wondrous things: thou art God alone."

THE CAUSE OF WORSHIP—GOD

Worship is no more or less than the celebration of God. Celebrate means to commemorate with a festivity, such as an anniversary, or a holiday, to honor or praise publicly, to mark a happy occasion by engaging in a pleasurable activity, to perform a religious ceremony joyfully, to observe a holiday or a special occasion with a festivity, to have a good time. Worship flows from wonder. Unless you and I are filled with the wonder of something, or the awe, or the astonishment of the adoration, we will not be very good worshippers. We cannot just worship from memory. We must recall, we must force our minds into a meditation on a picture and a focusing of how great God is.

If we could somehow grasp, constantly, consistently, always, the greatness and magnitude of God, it would be easy to serve Him. It would be a pleasure to bless Him and exalt Him, but we flow up, and we falter back. We arise, and we descend. We have problems, because life blurs the focus. Life knocks the lens out of kilter, so that life sometimes has a way of drowning out what we know is right.

When I read these scriptures I am sure most of us, unintentionally, when it said, "for thou Lord art great," we just kind of went, "Yeah, yeah, yeah, yeah!" But when you talk about God being great, you are talking about some stuff!

WE MUST BE EXPOSED TO GOD

The only way you can truly worship God is to be exposed to Him. The exposure that causes an astonishment. A meditation that moves you. Sometimes you can step into a realm of worship without any music, without any preaching, without a church service; just by meditating, and thinking, and recalling, and remembering how great God has been to you in the past and the fact that He is changeless. That is why it behooves us to do everything we can to create an atmosphere that is conducive to the presence of God manifesting itself. The scripture is true; "Where two or three are gathered together in my name there I am in the midst." But there is a difference between Jesus being in the midst and Jesus manifesting Himself.

GOD MANIFESTED—NOT JUST 'IN THE MIDST'

The minute you come together with two or three people with the purpose of magnifying God, receiving the word, or praying, or extolling the virtues of Jesus Christ, God says, "I am right in your midst." But we go through many, many services where we do not sense God, because *midst* and *manifest* are not the same, which tells me we are every time "this" close to the miraculous manifesting Himself. You won't have to reach up to bring Him down, He is here. It is just that sometimes when we walk in we just go, "Woo!" "Boy, I felt the power of God." Well, the two nights that you didn't feel it…"Just as much God."

See, sometimes God sovereignly chooses to manifest Himself, because maybe He thinks that they ain't going to make it tonight, I better help him. It has been a mystery to me over the years of serving God that I've not prayed any more, I've not fasted any more, I haven't done anything better or worse, but just walk in and POW! God makes your hair stand up and your skin move everywhere and tears run down your face...you feel fire shut up in your soul, and you are goin', "Woo!" And you haven't done anything, the music hasn't been any better, the preaching hasn't been any better, or any worse. God just somehow sat down on the pew next to you and said, "How you doin' bub?"

OUR COMFORT ZONE—WHERE WE SIT IN CHURCH

That's even why, sometimes, we choose certain seats in the church, because they are safe. Nothing happens in that area. We have certain places that are safety zones..."no wackos sit here, the noise makers are over there." That doesn't mean that everybody has to manifest their joy, or their rejoicing in the same way, but if you have a propensity towards quietness and stillness you don't sit next to a voice box.

If you like to just kind of sit there and ingest it and take it in, you are not going to sit next to someone who goes "Youhhh!!" Because the first time they knock your wig off you are going to be ticked off. The first time they dance on your pocket book comin' out the aisle you are going to be mad about it. The first time they reach over and say, "Oh, come on, let's run together," you're going to slap 'em and say, "Shut up and you sit on down here."

Now, for those of you that somehow have a gift from God that you are allowed to run all the time, why don't you check the course out for yourself before you start dragging people all over the place. I know you mean well, but some people don't want to go with you. Some people are blessed by participating in the race; other people get a kick out of watching the race.

YOU CANNOT HAVE A HIGH VISION OF GOD AND LIVE LOW

A low view of God has always birthed lesser evils in our lives. You cannot maintain a high vision of God and live low. You cannot have a fine focus of your Father and then walk in slavish, foolish sin. The world of so-called Christianity tolerates all kinds of ungodly practices for one reason only: They have no real vision of the majesty of God. Anytime you get a *real* vision of how great God is, you and I will not practice evil.

Israel had power with God as long as Israel had a great vision of God. When Israel got sidetracked with false deities, false religions, false cults and false gods, they lost their true vision of the majesty of God. They began to get involved with craziness.

LESSER EVILS OCCUR WHEN GOD'S MAJESTY IS DIMINISHED IN OUR EYES

Let's be honest. A lot of the lesser evils in our lives, whether we want to call them sin, or weights, or distractions, or unsanctified practices; they come because we lose the majesty of God's portrait. You couldn't be possibly staring in your spirit at that bloody hill of Calvary, and the brutalized body of Jesus Christ and then go have an affair with somebody. It won't fly. Something's got to be blocked out, something's got to be locked out.

The human mind and the human spirit has a unique, uncanny ability to just shut 'er down. I know what I am talking about. I found myself just doin' some of the dumbest things, allowing some of the dumbest things, and I am an encyclopedia, if you please, of biblical knowledge, but when your flesh wants to do something you lock this door, you pull the wires out of the speakers and you go, "Alright, here we go…." When you are finished, it talks to you and the vision returns and you feel embarrassed and ashamed and a jerk and you say, "I know better than this, what in the world…?"

WE NEED A VISION OF GOD'S GREATNESS

The catalyst to a real worshipper is a vision of the greatness of God. Not God, but the greatness of God. One of the things that made David a tremendous worshipper was that he was awed by God's greatness in comparison to the world's deities, which were jokes. And he constantly married himself to the greatness of God, so that it provoked him and motivated him and moved him to write, to whirl, to dance, to bless, to praise, to magnify, to do war, to do battle. The only time he fell into sexual misconduct and sin and murder is when he lost his vision of the greatness of God. His repentance, which is recorded in Psalm 51, takes him back and says, "I've done this great sin against thee O Lord, You are so holy and righteous and magnificent and great. How could I have ever done something like this?" "…Because for a moment you lost the vision of His greatness."

We live in a world that is baptized with limitation, and it is such a precious gift to us that God would allow us to turn to a living God who has none. None what? No limitations. He is not locked in to time and space and matter. He can manifest, He can move, He can be in one hundred million places at the same time. He can never diminish, never have a bad day. He is great! People talk about people being great who hit homeruns and throw footballs and slam hockey pucks across ice, or run a four-minute mile, or a bikeathon, or they go to Boston and run some 26 miles and they say, "Oh, they are great." …And the guy falls over! But now, when you say God is great, He don't fall over, He finishes the race and says, "Anybody want to run again?"

See, if I didn't believe in the greatness of God, I'd go crazy. If I didn't believe in God's greatness compared to what this church is, or what I am, I'd lose my mind. If I didn't believe that God was greater than the organization that I run with, the preachers that I know, fellow Christians that I am aware of, other organizations, other religiosity, I'd go loony tunes. I'd hate to believe that the height of my religion and my enterprise in the Spirit had to do with just the greatness of mankind. It far transcends mankind. I am dealing with a God that is so great…"that eyes not seen and ears not heard neither has it entered into the heart of man the things which God has prepared for them that love Him but God has revealed them unto us by His Spirit." He has not revealed to us in the fullness of what they are. He reveals it to us in the embryo stage of what they are; the harvest is in the acorn.

GOD IS A 'SEED' GOD

God is a seed God. He deals with us always on the level of seed only. When God gives you a promise of a harvest, then He rolls you out an acorn. It can be frustrating: "You told me a forest!" He says, "You're right, it is in the seed." "Bury the seed, water the seed, fast and pray over the seed, believe Me for the seed, I am telling you that the whole forest is in that seed."

That is why, if you can get one word from the King, you got all the King's stuff, because the King and His word can't be separated, it can't be dissected. Him and His word are one. When you get the promise, you have to trust God for the fulfillment, because God always speaks from the end vantage point. He speaks from the end of the thing, declaring the things that are not yet manifested. Yet, they do exist, because if God says anything—it exists!

WHEN GOD SPEAKS IT—IT EXISTS

When God says, "I will do this for you, and I will give you this and I will bless...." and then nothing changes in your life, that's the trial of your faith. You have to believe that when God speaks something...remember God doesn't create anything unless He speaks it; He created the Universe by the verbiage of His mouth, He released divine energy through the words of His mouth. He is the one that tells us that life and death is in the power of the tongue. He is the one that says that the promises of God are "yea and amen."

When God speaks something, it is now existing. It may not have manifested yet in time, it may not have come in manner, it may not have reached the block that you are living on, but it exists. If you can water it, then you can believe God for it and you can hold on and let your faith birth it. God will manifest what He has spoken into existence.

I have promises that God has given me 20 years ago. As far as I know they have yet to come, but they exist somewhere. They exist more than in the mind of God; I got it out of the mouth of God. I'm not too hot about the ones in the mind of

God, but if I get one from the mouth of God...! You've heard of the 3M company? That's God...Mind, Mouth, Manifest!

OUR FAITH MANIFESTS THE PROMISE 'IN TIME'

But see, you can't tell when it's going to manifest. That's why you have to hold on in the trial of your faith and keep trusting God and believing God. You have got to be willing to look bad. Some of us want to keep looking good. We want to have all these tremendous promises, prophetic promises of God and rich things that God has promised to us and still look good. You can't do it, because you live in a world that says, "Show me!"

"What do you mean—healed? You look sick to me."

"What do you mean God is going to bless you, your check just bounced!"

"My God shall supply all your need according to His riches in glory by Christ Jesus." He is the resource; He has the revenue. It is our faith that manifests that *thing* in time. When God tells you something, He just steps back from telling you and says, "Well, let's see what your faith will do with that."

Hebrews 11:17, "By faith Abraham, when he was tried, offered up Isaac: and he that had received the promises offered up his only begotten son, (18) Of whom it was said, That in Isaac shall thy seed be called..." here's the key... (19) "Accounting that God was able to raise him up, even from the dead; from whence also he received him in a figure."

BOOST YOUR FAITH—ADD UP WHAT GOD HAS DONE FOR YOU

I got to looking up that word, "accounting." It is a Greek term used for mathematical equation. It means "to add up previous things." He is going up the mountain...Abraham has a promise that the promise is going to come through Isaac. God has just told him something that contradicts, seemingly, everything He had promised him. So what does he do?

If you are facing a dilemma from a declaration from God that seems to contradict what He has told you before; it is time to get out your adding machine and your computer and start adding and "accounting." It is a mathematical term, Abraham "accounted." He counted up previous episodes in his life and he finally realized that God couldn't lie and God hadn't contradicted Himself. There is just something God is going to do and the Bible said that when He went up on Moriah, He *accounted* that God was going to raise Him from the dead. When you start adding up what God did for you in the past, it gives you faith to believe that God can do something brand new that He has never done before.

THE TRIAL OF OUR FAITH—BELIEVE FOR WHAT HE'S NEVER DONE BEFORE

See, the trial of our faith isn't just to believe God, it's to believe God to do something He has never done before. That's where the Pentecostal rank is tied, that's where we are trapped, that's where we are locked in. We are locked into yesterday. We need to let yesterday catapult us into a fresh faith for tomorrow. We need to let all the faithfulness and the goodness and the rich heritage that God has given us bring us to a reality that says, "Accounting—God did this, this, and this. He is going to do something new that is going to blow my socks off!"

He is saying, "Accounting Him able...." To do what? He wasn't told what He was going to do; it had never happened before, and the devil was telling him it was impossible. Sometimes you just have to sidestep the issue and just start counting and adding up all the stuff God has done, and when you finish adding it all up, here is what your conclusion will be: He can't lie, He can't fail, He can't change, and no word of the King is void of power, and what He has promised He is able and willing to do.

Abraham's thinking; There is only one thing left I can figure out the sum total of all that I have added up, is that I am going to experience a resurrection on that mountain—I'm comin' down with the boy. Abraham said in Genesis 22:5; ...You stay here, me and the lad go yonder to worship and we shall return. That is the voice of faith! That is not the voice of understanding. We can get mixed up, cuz faith and understanding fight each other. Understanding wants to know how. Faith says, "God told me." Understanding says, "Fool!" Faith says, "God ain't telling a lie!"

WATER YOUR SEED OF PROMISE

There are a bunch of promises given to us individually where a lot of us are waiting for God to do it and God is saying, "Why don't you water the promise a while?" Remember, you get the promise in seed form. No seed can grow that is not buried and watered. You got to water it with tears, you got to weep during the night, you got to trust God when your heart is breaking, you got to hold on to the things of God even though everything looks crazy and impossible and even your fellow believer says, "Ain't no way it's going to happen."

That's right, there ain't no way it's going to happen to the carnal mind and there ain't no way it's going to happen to my understanding, but this supercedes and surpasses my understanding. God is the Lord of the Spirit world and He can do anything He said He could!

I wonder if you could go home tonight and "account" God able to do what He promised. Could you just add it up? Well, He didn't fail me there...and by the way, "He did give me and Sarah that baby. Her womb was dead and my body was dead and He just kind of zapped us and we had a little bambino. Let me see if He gave me a life from a dead body and a dead womb, if He takes a life He sure can regenerate it." So Abraham walks up the mountain and says, "We're comin' back!"

ARE YOU WILLING TO LOOK BAD SO GOD CAN LOOK GOOD

When God gets ready to fulfill His promise to you, He most likely won't do it in public. The Bible says that he and the boy went together by themselves. God won't let the thing happen in public lest you want to get an 8" x 10" picture taken and start selling subscriptions. Here is what God will do: God will let you and I, who have the promise, look bad in the public.... "But you promised!" "That's right, I'm goin' to do it." "...But I'm lookin' bad...." "That's part of the promise." "No flesh is going to glory in My presence. I don't share the stage with nobody. If I step center stage everything gets off the stage. I am not going to give my glory to idols, I am not giving it to images and I am sure not giving it to a bunch of Pentecostals."

Now, are you willing to look bad so that God can look good? Most of us, and I am at the head of the class, don't want to look bad. I'll accept a little looking bad, but not long. The worst kind of bad looking is looking bad among church folk, because we have a baptism of critics.... "I know, the Spirit told you, yeah, sure." "I know, you had another one of them dreams...."

"You go to heaven by faith, you go for cash down here." But I got news for you, the cash down here comes from where you are going; "He giveth thee power to get wealth." He still knows where the fish is that has the coin in its mouth. The angel that strengthened Jesus is still alive right now. The angel that came to Elijah's rescue under a Juniper tree is here right now. The angel that showed up for Joshua getting ready to take Jericho is alive right now.

I'm telling you that every angel that we have need of is here right now. Every answer that we have need of is in the will and purpose and heart of God. We have to believe for the manifesting of what He told us. That's why it's called the *trial* of your faith. It's not the sea cruise. It's not the boat tour to Honolulu of your faith; it's the *trial*. In fact, one guy called it the fiery trial. In other words, when God gets ready to do it, He turns up the heat so that you are uncomfortable.

WE ALL NEED A 'MORIAH' MIRACLE

You have to understand that God calls you and I to a Moriah miracle. He is not only going to do what He said He is going to do, but He is going to give you a fresh revelation about Himself that you ain't never seen. Because it wasn't until he went to slay the boy that the angel said, "Hey, stop, now I know that you fear God seeing you have not kept back your only son." And then God begins to swearing, and God begins to promising, and God begins to prophesying about their future..."I'm going to bless them that bless you." "I'm going to curse them that curse you." "You are going to be the head and not the tail." "You are going to be above and not beneath." He says that He is going to make sure that you possess the gate of your enemy.

In other words, if you do something now, God will give you a fresh revelation for your tomorrow. He didn't go up there wanting to hear from God about tomorrow. He went up there to do a sacrifice unto God by faith. He believed God was going to make him kill Isaac. He didn't know anything about a resurrection—had never seen one—but he believed God was able to resurrect the boy, he didn't know the ram was up there. It was a trial of faith. He had no idea what God was going to do, but because he did it, he not only got his boy back, but then he got God to take center stage and start promising stuff that blew his sandals off.

YOU HAVE TO GO UP YOUR MOUNTAIN BEFORE YOU CAN COME DOWN WITH A MIRACLE

When Abraham walked down, remember; he walked up the hill with a heavy burden, he came trottin' down with a real heavy blessing. He is walking up with his head down; he came walking down with his head up. He said, "I am going to be the head and not the tail, I'm going to be above only and not beneath, my enemies are going to be underneath my feet, I'm going to possess the gate of my enemy." That means the place of rulership, the place of leadership, the place of government, the place of decision. "I'm going to be over them." What enemies? The ones that you don't even know about yet. You've got enemies that you don't even know about, but God knows about them and I'm glad that God can give you a promise about stuff you haven't even faced yet.

You and I climb up a mountain to give God a sacrifice and God, who made the mountain, is looking down through time and He wants to share with somebody what He is going to do, but He can find so few who will go up the mountain...because you got to look bad to go up the mountain.

YOU DON'T LOOK GOOD GOING UP THE MOUNTAIN

Even Moses didn't look good going up the mountain. They thought he got killed up there.

Something else happens: The longer you stay up in the mountain for God to do His stuff, the worse it gets for you in the valley. When he left they were saying, "Hey, go Mo', go!" When he came back they were half-naked and having sex orgies, dancing naked around a calf and the whole place had gone nuts. "...I was only gone 40 days, what in the world happened to you people?"

But, see, they weren't worshippers, they were only people who wanted to get out of sin. They were only people who wanted God to fix their mess and then leave them alone. God don't fix our messes so we can go orchestrate our life and write our own agendas. He has an agenda for every life.

OUR LEVEL OF WORSHIP DEPENDS ON OUR CONCEPT OF GOD

Worship rises and falls with our concepts of the King. If you and I are not good worshippers, it's because our vision of God is small. You can't worship big if you got a small deity. You can't worship to get something from Him; that's not worship that is sneaky praise. He is too smart for us; He knows the end from the beginning. You can't snooker Him. You can butter up people, but you can't butter up Him. He made the butter!

When you get a real vision of God, you get a picture that is full of glory. The glory astounds us, and the more we learn of God and the more we experience God, the easier it is to worship. Our vision of God is what determines the level of our worship. So if God is not great, then your worship can't be great, because one is born from the other.

PRAISE IS A MUST!

Now, it's a shame if you are not a good praiser. You know what that means if you are not a good praiser? Praise has got to do with God's performance for you, so that means if you are not a good praiser, you are sitting in silence and hands folded and lips locked and knees crossed saying, "He ain't never done nothing for me, and my silence is a protest that He ain't never done nothing."

Now, if He has performed for you...ain't got nothing to do with you being emotional...did He wake you up this morning? Did He start you on your way? Did He get your heart pumping? You didn't have an aneurysm, did you? You weren't cursed with some kind of crippling disease? You put a day's work in today? You will have a paycheck this week? You do have a home; a vehicle? You may not have everything you want, but considering the other 50 countries of the world you could live in—your doing okay! You could live in Bosnia, or the south part of Russia...you could live in south Turkey.

HOW MUCH DO YOU PRAY FOR OTHERS

You could live in Manitoba, Canada with a river comin' by...and there goes your house. I wonder how many of us have prayed for those poor people that have lost their homes and their vehicles and everything about their life...we just read about it in the paper, or watch it on TV and say, "Poor slobs." It ought to touch our hearts saying, "God, I don't understand why this is happening, but show mercy to these people and help them and touch the hearts of people to show compassion."

You can do a lot, my friend, if you take some time to pray. You probably didn't pray, because you don't think God is big enough. I'm telling you, you can pray here and God can show up there. God is so great He can take your prayer and mobilize and it and manifest mercy and grace in people's lives that we know nothing about.

Could it be, the reason that we don't pray for the president and his wife, besides the reason that we don't like them, is that we don't really believe that God is big enough to make the man's mind change. I'll tell you what; there was a mind a lot great than his; there was a fella named Pharaoh. He was a brilliant mind. He held three million worshippers captive and somebody got ahold of the heart of God and God got ahold of that man's mind and changed Pharaoh's mind.

We are instructed to pray for civil authorities and government authorities and federal authorities; people that are in charge are under the auspices of the canopy of God. We need to pray with God's greatness in our minds believing that they are able to make godly decisions, so we can live a life of peace. I don't pray much for the president…don't like him. I pray for him three four times a week, but I don't think I pray very sincerely, I don't like him. Now if God would kill him, or if God would just shake him and make him go on NBC and confess all the affairs he has had…I'd stand back and say, "Praise Jesus."

But God is probably not going to do that, because the problem with God is that He wants to be good to everybody. I want God to expose him and God is saying; "Naw, let me cover him."
"But he is guilty!"
"Yeah, just like you."
"Yeah, but if he got exposed and everything got honest…."

And God says, "Right, it would be a bigger disaster, more suspicion, more problems, more governmental chaos, why don't you just let me forgive the man and go on?"

I find myself just thumping my hand on the table and saying, "It ain't fair."

It's like God is saying, "Yeah, well, you pick somebody you want to go on the gallows with and I'll take care of you two at the same time." "Oh, but I'm Your child, I am forgiving, You are great, great is thy faithfulness, great is thy mercy."

THE MAGNITUDE OF GOD'S MERCY

It's like God says, "Right, you funnel mercy only to those you like, and you disqualify my mercy for homosexuals, for lesbians, for drug addicts, for degenerates, for honkey-tonkers, for people who practice things that you think are pathetic and poor, or, which you used to do all your life until I stopped you. It's amazing you can't show pity and mercy to people who are now trapped in the stuff that you used to enjoy. I could have let you stay in the bar and I could have called them, instead." We don't understand the magnitude of His greatness. His greatness is good towards me when I need His greatness.

I'm not so sure I want His greatness touching people that I don't like.... I heard the news coming to church tonight, that some animal-idiot took those two little girls off that school bus and took them away and molested them and murdered them and they found them under the bridge. My blood boiled! It could have been my daughter! It could have been one of our kids! Every day that my daughter had to go to school, or ride somewhere, I plead the blood every day that she wouldn't get molested, or raped, or picked by some wacko. Every day, pray for your kids that go to school that God would protect them from perverts and degenerates and witchcraft people and all kinds of craziness.

I'm praying tonight for that mother of those two dead babies. She has that void in her spirit and her heart. Maybe she's not Baptist, maybe she's not Presbyterian, maybe she is atheist for all we know, but I'll tell you what; she is hurting, she is in anguish. We need to pray that she doesn't get bitter and that she doesn't get baptized with hate.

Can I get into empathy and sympathy and compassion with her when I am far removed? Thousands of miles away? And I am so angry that I would like to put him in the electric chair myself? Why do I feel that way? Because at certain times when things violate my concept, God's greatness, to me, diminishes when it deals with others. When I am in desperate need, I need God's greatness. When you are in desperate need, you deserve what you got, because you are a trespasser....

God is so Great! So Great! So Great! I need to see Him as Great! "...Great for my family, great for my home, great for my problems, great for my sickness, my pain, great enough to save my husband, save my wife, turn my children around, great enough to make my nerves get calm, great enough to give me peace when I am in a storm...."

DON'T LET THE STORM DIM THE PROMISE

It is one thing for the greatness of God to speak to your storm and say, "Peace be still." It's a greater thing to step in the chaos of your storm and say, "Let's ride it out together." Anybody can escape from something, but you have to have ahold of something to ride it through. It was Apostle Paul that said in Acts 27, "There stood by me this night the angel of the Lord whom I serve and who's I am." He didn't tell Paul that He was going to end the storm, He just told Paul the end result of the storm was going to be that they would be spared and washed up on an island.

Don't let the promise of God be dimmed by the storm that you are in right now!

THE WHY & WONDER OF WORSHIP • BOOK TWO

THE
WHY & WONDER
OF WORSHIP

VOLUME SIX · CHAPTER ELEVEN

CHAPTER ELEVEN

Psalm 29:1-2, "Give unto the Lord, O ye mighty, give unto the Lord glory and strength. (2) Give unto the Lord the glory due unto his name;" then it tells you how to do that -- worship the Lord in the beauty of holiness. Holiness is beautiful.

Sometimes our perspective and concept of holiness, in our trying to make it practical in every day living, we sometimes have not made it very beautiful. Here is why: because the flesh does not want to beautify God. Holiness is of the Spirit. To get from my spirit to God I must pass through flesh. It is the barrier that says, "Don't do that," and it resents when I tell it what pleases Him. It does have a mind of its own. Romans says, "The carnal mind is enmity with God." That means enemy, adversary, resistant.

Psalm 95:1-5, "O Come, let us sing unto the Lord: let us make a joyful noise to the rock of our salvation. (2) Let us come before his presence with thanksgiving, and make a joyful noise unto him with psalms. (3) For the Lord is a great God, and a great King above all gods. (4) In his hand are the deep places of the earth: the strength of the hills is his also."

You know what that means? "...the strength of the hills?" It means all the resources; gold, silver, oil, jewels. It's all His!

(5) "The sea is his, and he made it: and his hands formed the dry land. (6) O come, let us worship and bow down; let us kneel before the Lord our maker."

Psalm 96:1-11, "O sing unto the Lord a new song: sing unto the Lord, all the earth. (2) Sing unto the Lord, bless his name; shew forth his salvation from day to day. (3) Declare his glory among the heathen, his wonders among all people."

WORSHIP—THEN WITNESS

Notice please: *witness* follows *worship*. See; it says sing, it says bless, it says worship; after you are finished with that then are you qualified to talk about Him.

It's kind of like God saying; I appreciate all your efforts, but I don't really want any shallow dingbat witnessing to anybody about Me.

We live in a generation that doesn't know beans about the deep things of God, but wants to tell everybody about God. I'll tell you something; God is not in a fix. He does not need a carnal-minded, worldly, pretentious wacko to witness about Him. The heavens and the earth witness enough about Him to blow everybody's socks off.

What God wants is a witness from somebody who has been a worshipper, because your witness will have worth and power and anointing in it—If it flows out of someone who has worshipped. You may not be able to explain your doctrine, you may not be able to explain the Godhead, the mysteries of the atonement, justification by faith. But you could say, "I was on my way to Damascus and a light knocked me down and a voice talked to me, rolled me in the dirt and when I got up I was blind—couldn't see. I had an experience, but it was preliminary. It sent me on to get another experience and I let a no-name talk to me and pray for me. He baptized me in Jesus name and God filled me with the Holy Ghost!" "I don't know much about some stuff, but what I do know is: 'Once I was lost and now I'm found, once I was blind and now I see, once I was mistaken and now I've got the truth'!"

ALL OTHER GODS ARE IDOLS

(4) "For the Lord is great, and greatly to be praised: he is to be feared above all gods. (5) For all the gods of the nations are idols; but the Lord made the heavens."

Now notice; you cannot be "Cafeteria Christians," ...pick and choose what you want. You cannot just take *some* scriptures, because you don't want to be offensive to your ding-a-ling neighbors who don't know anything. This guy writes for everybody, once and for all. All the gods of the world are bologna, they're idols, and nothing, and they are fake, and they don't have any power. And the Bible says, "The idols have a devil behind them."

Paul wrote to the church and said, "know ye not that those folks who worship idols are worshipping devils." It's not an innocent little thing…"Oh, they're mistaken." Oh no! It's not mistaken—they are manipulated. If the gospel is hidden, it is hidden to them who are lost and whom the god of this world has blinded their minds. Can I help you? You know how you get our mind blinded? It's not because you were raised wrong. Satan is permitted to blind the minds of anybody through unbelief.

WE ARE HIS SANCTUARY

(6) "Honour and majesty are before him: strength and beauty are in his sanctuary."

I am His sanctuary. Hebrews 3 says you are God's building; you are God's sanctuary; you are God's temple; you are God's house. Strength and beauty is in God's house. Beauty is what everybody sees. Strength is what you get when you need it. Strength is usually unseen until it is called for.

(7) "Give unto the Lord, O ye kindreds of the people, give unto the Lord glory and strength. (8) Give unto the Lord the glory due unto his name; bring an offering, and come into his courts. (9) O worship the Lord in the beauty of holiness: fear before him, all the earth. (10) Say among the heathen that the Lord reigneth: the world also shall be established that it shall not be moved: he shall judge the people righteously. (11) Let the heavens rejoice, and let the earth be glad; let the sea roar, and the fulness thereof."

CONCENTRATE ON 'HIM', NOT THE 'HOW'

We have studied worship for almost 24 weeks and I hope I am here when it finally hits. I am going to tell you something; it is one thing to ingest information, it is another thing to assimilate it into practice. I really think that 99.9% of people that are here week after week about worship, about grandness, and the greatness of worship…we really, deep in our heart, want to be better worshippers and know how to worship. But I'll tell you something; if we would not concentrate so much on the *how* and just on the *Him*, the *how* would be accepted.

GOD IS SEEKING WORSHIPPERS

You have to understand how important worship really is. According to the Bible, worship is revealed by God's word as something that God desires. John 4:22-24, "God is Spirit and they that worship him must worship him in spirit and in truth."

"But the hour cometh, and now is" (Jesus is talking to this lady) "when the true worshippers shall worship the Father in spirit and in truth." It's not in a mountain, it's not in a place—It's about a person! "for the Father seeketh such to worship him." I know we use that over and over, at least I do, but I can't get away from the impact of that it seems to be the only thing that God has ever gone looking for. God "seeketh" worshippers! We seek workers, we seek methods, we seek acceptability. We seek a ceremony, a ritual...a method by which 1—2—3...it'll work. A formula...exactly! But the Lord is just looking for a worshipper.

ANYBODY IS QUALIFIED TO WORSHIP

Notice the kind of worshipper that He wants: One that will worship in spirit. Small "s"—that means *human spirit*—and in truth. So worship has got to be in spirit, and it has to be sincere and honest! That means anybody is qualified to worship God, sinner or saint, because if a sinner goes to worship God, the first thing that comes out of their mouth is an apology. The hypocrite and the liar won't worship, because they won't get honest. Worship requires sincerity and honesty. It does <u>not</u> require perfection.

Worship is something God desires according the scripture; it is something God delights in; it is something that He deserves. He delights in it, because he designed it. Nothing, or nobody, can worship God that God does not allow them to. God has to create desire in something for it to happen.

NON-WORSHIPPERS ARE ON THE DEVIL'S TEAM

The devil doesn't worship God, because God took his desire away. So he hates you, because God works in you—and myself—to create in us a yearning to worship. So we are His replacement, and for that the devil hates us. Greatest joy you can give to the devil is to sit and do nothing and just stare, because then he says, "Hey! They are on my team, they are just as dumb I am." In fact, he says, "We are dumber. You've got the privilege. I don't have the privilege and you don't exercise yourself." The devil says, "I wish I had a chance to worship God again, but God just took that desire from me when I usurped my position and started submitting myself as an object instead of him, so God just stripped me."

I'm going to tell you something; you lose a lot when you stop being a worshipper. If you read your Bible, Isaiah 14 and Ezekiel 28, especially Ezekiel 28, when He talks about Lucifer, who walked up in the garden of God...walked among the stones of fire, and lists all the jewels that covered him. He was the anointed cherub that covereth. He had musical tabrets; he was a mobile music machine.

THE DEVIL'S POWER IS IN HIS VOICE

His greatness came from his voice. That is his power right now. He has lost his power to use his voice in worship, so he uses his voice in wickedness. But it is the weapon that he has—the ability of suggestion. He did not come to Eve as a terrible *something*; he came as an unbelievable charisma voice. His power is in his voice! Anybody besides me ever fought with what you think is the devil, or the forces of evil? Anybody besides me ever fought power of what you thought was the devil, or demons, or evil? You know how it came to you? Voice, image, picture, suggestion, feeling—Voice!

LEARN THE VOICE OF GOD

When Elijah was in the cave and he was running away from Jezebel, you notice that God puts more emphasis on a still, small voice than He does on signs and wonders. A mighty wind blew and wrecked the place. A fire came...earthquake...God wasn't *in* any of it. Now He did it, but He wasn't *in* any of it. A still, small voice got the guys attention. It is a good statement for Elijah though; he had been discouraged sucking his thumb and running away. He still was able to find a way in which God communicated with him.

You must learn to get the voice of God, so that God can communicate to you without having to give you an earthquake. God may choose not to bring an earthquake into your life; what will you do then? That's why he said, "Thy word have I hidden in my heart that I might not sin against you." "...I can't trust my emotions; and the wonders."

WORSHIP FLOWS FROM, AND BACK TO, GOD

Worship flows from deity. It's God's creation and God's design. He creates worship. He allows His creatures to experience it and feel it and sense it, and through that they worship back to God. The beautiful thing about worship is that in the wake of it the Lord is blessed and He leaves a blessing behind..."For the blessing of the Lord maketh rich and addeth no sorrow therewith." So, the object that the worshipper worships is magnified, but the worshipper is transformed.

The object of worship is two-fold: It is that the object be exalted, adored and magnified, and rightly enthroned, because He is altogether lovely. The other aspect of worship is so that through worship I am transformed into the image of the one that I worship. I become what I am looking at, I become what I am adoring, I become just like what I give my allegiance to. In other words, I say about Him what He says about Himself. That's why when Isaiah was in the court and had the dirty mouth, the angels didn't chase him out. If I'd of been an angel I'd 'of thrown the bum out... "Hey, that guy's got a dirty mouth, he is gripin' and complainin' and pointin' his finger at everybody...." But the angel was instructed to touch him and cleanse his mouth, so that he says the same thing about God that the angels are also.

A HOLY GHOST WORSHIP SERVICE—EVERYONE SAYING ABOUT GOD WHAT THOSE IN HIS PRESENCE ARE SAYING

See; that is the blessing of a real Holy Ghost worship service. It can spill over into people that are not thinking or singing the same thing, and eventually they join in and chant the same chorus—"Worthy!!!...Is the Lamb!!!" That's why I say I hope I'm here when this thing blows into one massive worship service. Woahh!! Brother, when everybody in the house starts saying the same thing about God that everybody in God's presence is saying, you ain't going to be able to hold the place!

That's what happened at Pentecost, they all got to sayin' the same thing that God was sayin', and the wind blew into the place and almost wrecked the place and 3000 people got the Holy Ghost in just a few minutes.

WORSHIP ENTHRONES GOD SO HE CAN LOOSE HIS POWER

I was talking to a fellow the other day that has many signs and wonders in his ministry, and of course I'm inquisitive. I'm trying to find step 1—2—3..."what am I doing wrong, what am I not doing right?" You know, he doesn't know anything about me, he doesn't know what I preach, he has heard me on tape sometimes, but he hasn't heard any of this. He said, "You know, Brother Arnold, we were thinking about that the other day when we got to talking about it. And the people who have blinded eyes opened...we've had a few people raised from the dead...we've had a lot of cripples come out of wheelchairs, we've had deaf ears unstopped..." he said, "about 90-plus% of all our miracles happened in a worship service when we didn't pray for anybody!"

You see, worship enthrones God in the atmosphere, and when God is enthroned and when God gets happy and you get to braggin' on God, He looses His power and it just flows. I wouldn't sit next to somebody that ain't serious about this. Worship is our response to God's greatness and God's goodness and God's grace.

GOD IS B-A-D—TERRIBLE

The greatness is the "Who." I read it to you Psalm 95 and 96, "He is great, He is awesome, He is above all gods," He is out-of-sight! Come on, remember that lesson I taught you, "God is b-a-d." That's a good bad. The Hebrews called God, "terrible." That was before they had us "jive" people from the 50's and 60's saying, 'that was c-o-o-l." Or someone who had a glass pack on his car and it went, "poppoppoppop...." We'd say, "that's bad, wheeewww, that's bad." Or, you just lower that 53 Chevy way down and have those little mud flaps sittin' there and those dice there on the gear shift and say, "Woooo! That's a bad machine, baby!"

Now, you didn't mean that car had to go to the junk shop. You just meant that that was fine and beyond average, above normal...and you needed one of them for your birthday. Well, that's what the Hebrews did when they walked around and said, "God is terrible." I know we look at the word *terrible* and say, "Oh, that's just terrible!" No, when the Hebrews look at that word *terrible* they mean, "He is Awesome." "He's b-a-d." "He has glasspacks." "It's Jimmy Dean in a 1950 Mercury, It's bad...." I don't mean evil, I mean when some kid would come over and get in a fist fight and knock somebody's brains out..."that dude is bad!" That doesn't mean he was bad bad; that means..."give the man room...that's one bad dude...he eats nails...that's a bad dude."

That's what you would call it when Samson carried off the gates..."That's some kind of bad dude." Anybody who can tie a hundred...two hundred fox tails together and burn down a few thousands acres of corn..."that's a bad dude." I mean if you can take a jawbone and kill a thousand people in an afternoons work..."that's a bad dude.

God is the original Terminator. He wiped out the whole nation of Egypt in one night. Oh yeah! You talk about a Terminator! You're a little late! I'm talkin' about the *original* Terminator. God built a boat and terminated the whole place. He did it with rain. God is b-a-d. I wish we believed that, because we're part of this!

GOD IS AWESOME

See, the reason why the angels keep going, "Holy, holy, holy is the Lord God almighty..." what they are really saying is, "He is bad." "He is some kind of awesome." You hang around Him enough you can't say anything bad about Him. You just have to brag on Him. The heavens are full of His glory...the earth showeth His handiwork...He is so awesome.

I wish something could happen to some of us that we could get overwhelmed with it. Just put our private little pity party and the hell in our life aside for a minute and just let Heaven shine in our souls and say that God is some kind of awesome. "He may not get me out of this, but I know He could get me out of this if He wanted to." "He's awesome."

I'm sorry to keep waking you up like this, but there ain't no sense in wasting some good stuff here. God is awesome. Every time I say that, He is happy. "You are awesome; You are mind-boggling to me. You are greater than my problems; You are bigger than my finances. You are more awesome than my fears, anxieties and worries. You are bigger than any trial that I could ever get put in; You fill the entire universe. You are so awesome You can fix anything You want to fix; and You are so awesome that if You choose not to fix it, I'll trust Your decision not to fix it—if I needed it fixed You would have fixed it."

PRAISE GLORIFIES GOD

Psalm 50:23, "Whoso offereth praise glorfieth me:" Now this writer said, "Offer God glory to His name." That's one of the ways to glorify Him is to offer Him praise. Praise is offered according to performance. Psalm 150:2, "Praise him for his mighty acts: praise him according to his excellent greatness."

The whole Pentecostal movement has learned; the whole Charismatic movement; the whole Assembly of God movement; Church of God movement; Spirit-filled movement...whatever you want to call it; the whole movement has learned how to praise God according to His mighty acts.

"Check's in the mail...healing is comin'...name it and claim it...blab it and grab it; it's all according to His mighty acts! Fine! What are you going to do when He don't *act*? I don't think I'm a jerk, I think that I've been chosen by God to teach this to you. I don't think I just came up with this! We could possibly be the only assembly around that is trying to worship God according to His excellent greatness!

GOD'S GREATNESS IS NEVER DIMINISHED

If He lets you go to a concentration camp, His greatness has not diminished. He could kill or capture you in a second. He could thump you on the head and give you an aneurysm, he could drop down and hand you his Lugar. He could do it! So God's greatness is never diminished because my situation is horrendous. But if all we learn to do is bless God because "the check is in the mail" and "the healing is coming" and "my husband to be is right around the corner" and "the church is going to grow" and "things are going to work out" and "my marriage is fixed up." What happens if God chooses to *strain* your faith and *try* your faith where your marriage isn't fixed up and you had to just walk into work and say; "Well, I'm not as happy as I'd like to be about this situation, but I am awed by that *other* situation—You are great and You are fabulous and You are wonderful and my business is with You!"

WE NEED PERPENDICULAR RELATIONSHIP TO DEAL WITH THE HELL OF THE HORIZONTAL

And that is the trial of our faith, because while our business is with Him, most of our living is here. That's why we need this perpendicular thing so that we can go through the hell of the horizontal. If we spent more time with this, this other stuff would be trivial. "...I can handle this junk...I wouldn't sit suicidal under a Juniper tree sucking my thumb thinking, 'Well, how come God didn't kill ol' Jezebel'?"

It wasn't in His plan to kill Jezebel at that time. "How do you like that Elijah?" "Now what are you going to do, suckin' your thumb?" "Goin' AWOL, because

God ain't workin' for you?" He just called fire down, ain't no one done that! He just ended a 3-1/2 year drought with a 63-word prayer meeting! Jesus, have mercy! You just outran a chariot for 19 miles. The hand of the Lord was on you! You are not a gymnast for Jesus! The hand of the Lord was on you! You girded up your loins and ran...outrun that dude 19 miles and wasn't even tired! That one old bag is unimpressed with his press release and he quits his job. Well, come on, paint yourself in the canvas. So easy to look at 1 Kings 19 and say, "What's the matter with Elijah, he acts like me." How many times have you ever looked at that and said, "Boy, if God used me like God used him I wouldn't suck my thumb and get discouraged." Ain't so. Ain't so.

Anybody besides me come out of a good Sunday night service boogalooin' and talkin' in tongues like a Chinese laundry, feeling like you can leap over a wall and run through a troop and before sunrise the next morning you get two phone calls and you are ready to kill yourself? Little clash with your husband or your wife— and Poof! Anybody ever lost the victory over how they smashed your garbage can when they went to empty it? Run the isles and talk in tongues...and the next morning the neighbors dog has kind of put your garbage all over the lawn. "Praise God!"

WORSHIP IS OUR RESPONSE TO GOD'S THREE G'S—GREATNESS-GOODNESS-GRACE

Remember what I said; worship is our response to God's greatness, God's goodness and God's grace. The three G's. The greatness is the *who*. The goodness is *what* He has done. The grace is the *method* of how He did it.

Psalm 50:23, "Whosoever offereth praise glorifieth me: and to him that ordereth his conversation aright to him will I show the salvation of the Lord."

WORSHIP IS THE PLATFORM FOR REVELATION

Now watch what He just said. Your mouth and my mouth, and my worship of God and my ascribing greatness and goodness is the platform for future revelation.

"To Him will I show the salvation of the Lord." Well, I thought the man's already saved! No, no, your level of salvation is just that—a level. I believe that. Saved, really saved, and good-God-Almighty saved, holy saved, way out there saved, and the man is so saved he hasn't been back.... You ain't never seen anybody saved like Enoch. That guy got so way-out-there-saved he didn't even come home.

Come on, you might as well know that in this church, right here, there are levels of people. I probably think most of us are saved—I hope. Some of us are hanging by the skin of our teeth. Some of us are saying, "I'm not quite sure." That's good, keep pressing on!

Have you ever looked at people in the sanctuary during a service and just, it's a good envy, and say, "Boy, those people walk with God." Well, what are you doing? Crawling? I know what you are saying, that some how they have reached a place in God that you haven't reached. Possibly because they either paid a price that you haven't paid, or, or, or—I know this will mess with your theology—or God somehow just took them.

Elisha's farming with 12 yoke of oxen; he's no spiritual dude. He's playing in dirt, manure and dung, and he is a farmer. In fact he is a rich kid. He has 12 yoke of oxen. He ain't on welfare. This kid has got some bread. Elijah walks by and goes, "Whoosh" ...runs after him..."let me go kiss my mom and dad goodbye and I'll be right with you." Watch what Elijah says, "Do what you want. What have I done to you? ...and moves on.

A SOVEREIGN CALL OF GOD REQUIRES SURRENDER AND COMMITMENT

You would think he would have encouraged him; he just sovereignly called him. No, the sovereign call will always be followed by a surrender and commitment to the call. I think God has tapped a lot of us on the shoulder at different times in our life and we missed it. I don't think we deliberately missed it; we just missed it!

Let me make it easy for you. I've missed it at times. I think there are a number of crisis times in our lives—pivotal places. There are crossroads when all of a sudden God...there was an impulse, there was a drive, there was a motivation. And the longer he did this the faster Elijah walked away: and the more faint the feeling was that took place...I started saying, "Was that God or was that not God?" See; the things in the Spirit have to be responded to instantly, because they fade, because God is always moving.

WORSHIP INCLUDES OBEDIENCE, SACRIFICE AND ASCENDING HIGHER

Genesis 22:5, "And Abraham said unto his young men, Abide ye here with the ass; and I and the lad will go yonder and worship, and come again to you."

Remember the law of first mention? Remember that one? This is the first mention of worship. Now let's go into a lesson of worship. Abraham ascends the mountain to worship God. Therefore; worship always includes obedience, sacrifice and ascending higher. To worship God is to do what Abraham did, which was to give God total preeminence to the exclusion of all other things. In real worship, self is totally denied, and the thing you love the most is surrendered.

WANT A DEEP MOVE OF FORGIVENESS—WORSHIP

That's the best way to get the deepest move of forgiveness in your spirit is to worship God. You didn't hear that, I said, the thing that we hold on to and love the most...it is possible for you to love the fact that you have an infraction against you and you are waiting for *them* to apologize. In my life I've held on to things where people have violated me and did me wrong; I was waiting for my turn at bat, and when I got into a worship thing the Lord said, "I'll take that!" You have no idea sometimes how hard it's been to relinquish it, because I want to prove to that person that I was right and they were wrong. ...I just struck fire!

You have no idea what it is like to pastor people and pour yourself into people and fast and pray for people and love their children and love their marriage and pray for their home and then they just kind of kick you in the shins and say bad things and walk away, or whatever they want to do. You step back and you turn around and you say, "I don't want any bad feelings," but all the time inside you saying, "Oh, but I've got some, and I'm just going to pray that God will humble them."

I've never had anybody do me bad and then ask the Lord to humble myself. I've never had one time in my life, until recently, where, when I've been hurt from someone in the our church and I said, "Lord, whatever you are trying to teach me in this, whatever you are trying to develop in my spirit and you want me to have a Christ like attitude, I want to bless them if this is of God. If it is not of God, deliver them from the spirit of deception and delusion. Help me to honestly and sincerely not hold an offended spirit and not enjoy watching them hurt." You can't do that if you don't worship!

WORSHIP WILL COST WHAT YOU ARE HOLDING ON TO

That's why a lot of people don't want to worship. It will cost you things that you are holding on to. Remember the time I told you about a couple in the church who wrote me that bad check and forged my name on it and I kept it on my sun visor? Remember that story? And I went in to pray in Mississippi? I was praying and the Lord gave me this beautiful message in my mind about Joseph and his brethren and how that church needs forgiveness, "...man these bunch of dingies...they won't forgive each other I will do what I can to help them...." This hand just came down and there was that check.... I still remember to this day just arguing with God saying, "Now wait a minute that's different!" "That dirtbag owes me that money." "That dirtbag's check bounced and my check bounced all over the U.S. and I had to pay $80-100 in fines for this bum."

And God listened while I presented my case Perry Mason style. He waited until I was finished. Then God said, "If you don't forgive every man his trespass against you, don't come asking me for none anymore."

See; forgiveness is costly. Especially when you've been wronged and it kills you when it looks like they're going to get by. You almost want to run after them and say, "Wait! Hey!" ...and God just wipes the slate clean and you are sittin' there with a muffled mouth while they walk around telling everybody...shaking their head, "Praise Jesus!"

WORSHIP MUST BE BASED ON REVELATION

Worship must always be based on revelation. I've told you that about 100 times, but you need to get this. Abraham goes up the mountain in 22:5 as a direct result of a revelation. Listen carefully to Genesis 22:1-2, "And it came to pass after these things, that God did tempt Abraham, and said unto him, Abraham: and he said, Behold, here I am. And he said, Take now thy son, thine only son Isaac, whom thou lovest, and get thee into the land of Moriah; and offer him there for a burnt offering upon one of the mountains which I will tell thee of." That's a bad translation—"tempt"—it really means "to try." He tested Abraham.

WORSHIP MUST BE GUIDED BY THE WORD

Worship must always be guided by the Word. The Word is a lamp unto your feet and light unto your pathway. It is an illuminating factor. So you worship by the Word; therefore you can overcome your circumstance. If you worship by your feeling, then when your kid is sick or dying you won't be a good worshipper. If you lose your job and you don't believe that God will supply all your needs according to His riches in glory by Christ Jesus, you're going to be preempted by the circumstances—that will preempt your worship.

"How can I worship God when all 'this' is going on?"
"Because, 'this' didn't do anything to Him." "'This' is just messing with *you*."
"Oh, but I just can't help myself."
"Why don't you finish the sentence. Oh, I can't help myself, because I am so...disobedient?"
Our worship is guided by the Word—our walk must be guided by the Word. Our warfare must be guided by the Word and even our work for God...ask Noah. Warfare...ask Joshua. Our walk...ask Enoch. Our worship...ask Abraham. ...Guided by the Word!

THE WORD HAS LIFE IN IT

That's why it is so important that you study the written word and you also have an active Rhema word—a living word—in you. God needs to impress. When you study this Bible, when you study one Psalm, or just study one Proverb, you need to ask God when you read, "Lord, anoint my mind, anoint my spirit, to grasp this precious truth." Don't just read it to be reading it; it's alive! It's got life in it.

There's lots of times that I read scripture and I don't understand beans of what I just read. And I just go back and say, "Now Lord, I'm sorry, I just assumed that I could read this and know this, please, open my eyes, cause me to grasp this." Let me tell you this; God is not subject to time. If you will pray that prayer many times...you study...you will get the answer later. Sometimes you read something and you say you prayed that the Lord would help me and... "I didn't get much out of it now." Kind of like the farmer that sowed the seed... "Well, I didn't get much corn right now."

The harvest is in the seed. Time will take care of it. How many people besides me; when you needed something, all of a sudden the Holy Ghost went "Phhewww" and a scripture came...and a thought came...and a word from a song came...and somebody praying for you...and a memory of what God has done for you..... That's how God works!!

PUT SOMETHING WORTHWHILE IN YOUR SPIRIT

Come on, it's the old thing; garbage in—garbage out. That's why TV is dangerous. That's why certain literature is dangerous. Certain music is dangerous. Hey, certain conversation with certain people is dangerous. Garbage in—garbage out. Well, wait a minute. God in—God out. Good news in—good news out. Faith in—faith out. Power in—power out. Trust in—trust out....

What did David kill Goliath with? What did David put in the bag? He didn't kill Goliath with hopes and dreams. He took time to stop by the brook and put 5 stones in the bag and said, "I'm going to kill this sucker." He was smart enough to not just grab one stone. Some of us only grab one promise and put it in and say, "Okay God." Man, I keep shoveling it in there. I'm putting 50 and 100 in there. I don't know when I'm going to need this one and need that one, I'm going to keep putting it in there...." It'd be embarrassing to run up to a 9-1/2 foot guy trying to kill me and reach in a bag that I didn't take time to put anything in!

BUT—PUT ENOUGH IN

There are some devils and demons that you fight that you better fight long distance. You don't want to step up in the face of some things. That's why he put five in the bag. I've heard all that stuff—J-e-s-u-s, and Goliath had 4 brothers—that's all phony. It preaches good and sells tapes, but it's a bunch of bologna. David didn't kill Goliath's other 4 brothers with the other 4 stones. What David was saying is, "I'm pretty good at this, but I'm not that good!"

Isn't it funny; David was willing to be in the service of the Lord and willing to miss? But we've let the devil tell us, "You better not miss, you better not say nothin' in the name of the Lord and it be wrong!" "You better not try to give a message in tongues and trip over your tongue." "You're only allowed one stone in this church." "If that's really your rock from God, it will do the job."

SERMON NOTES—JUST EXTRA STONES

One time in scripture it says that there were people who were left-handed who were so great with a sling shot that they could, within a hairs-breath, kill things. Never been recorded that David was that good...that's why he got five stones. You didn't hear me! That's why I write notes. I've had people condemn me and say, "You know, if you was really a preacher, you wouldn't need them notes, you'd just get that word of God in your heart and let it burn, boy!"

I went to a Bible school at this evangelism conference and I preached for 2000 people, the place went crazy for an hour and ten minutes. I could have gotten voted in as Pope! The next day I go to talk to these students and they ask me the dumbest questions:

THE WHY & WONDER OF WORSHIP • BOOK TWO

"Do you use notes?"

"What do you mean, do I use notes?"

"Well, we were taught that we need to pray and study and let God write it on your heart and just preach."

I said, "Who is the fool that told you that? Of course I write notes. I usually don't stick to them, but I write them."

My wife used to complain when I would evangelize, because when I would evangelize I would preach "out-there." She said, "Why do you write all them notes, you're 'out-there'?" I'd say, "Well, they don't know what my notes say." My notes might say, "Don't preach this." I had 30 or 40 students come and ask if they could look at my notes. I said, "Sure." "You preached from this?" ...Plus, notes give you something to look down to when it ain't going good.

WORSHIP WITHOUT REVELATION IS RITUAL

Worship is predicated on revelation. Worship flows out of a word from the Lord. If you take revelation away from worship, then all you have is ritual, dead form, bondage, lifeless religion. That's why you cannot just be an historical believer. You cannot just say, "Well, I live my life by the Bible." Now wait a minute, the Bible is the highest criteria; it is the highest judgment standard, but God breathes and talks to us and quickens this Bible. Remember, the letter killeth but the spirit maketh alive.

If Abraham did not have a word of revelation from God, his act of sacrifice becomes murder. And when we don't have a fresh word or direction from God, then what we think is ministering light, is ministering death to people. We are giving them church; and they need Christ. We are giving them UPC; and they need Jesus. We are giving them our concepts; and they need a converting Jesus that can transform their lives and take the junk out of their lives and give them something worth living for. This church needs to pulsate with revelation from God lest we just give people religion.

Without revelation—without quickened word—then acts of supposed praise and thanksgiving and worship, according to the scripture, do not bless the object being worshipped, nor do they enhance and bless the worshipper.

SINCERE BUT VAIN WORSHIP—RITUAL

Here is what God's complaint to Israel was; "I won't accept your worship because your heart is not in it. In vain do they worship me teaching for commandments the doctrines of men." So God says there is such a thing as sincere but vain worship. Ritual.

I was wondering tonight when we started this service...I know that Wednesday night is a tough night for us. People work hard; I know that. I know it is a sacrifice for you to be here. I do appreciate it and so does God, but I just wonder when...I'm thinkin'...what in the world are we up here on the platform doing all this for? Are we locked in to a form? "Okay, here comes...going to play a song...and the praise singers will sing and we'll pray a prayer and take up an offering and have a little Bible study and hopefully get out of here on time and.... What are we doing?" Don't you see how easy it is to just fall into that, even though God has repeatedly used this "format."

DON'T DEBATE—RESPOND

Worship is always conditioned by obedience to a revelation. Genesis 22:3, "And Abraham rose up early in the morning, and saddled his ass, and took two of his young men with him, and Isaac his son, and clave the wood for the burnt offering, and rose up, and went unto the place of which God had told him."

If you will get a fresh word from God you and I will do what Abraham did. He responded promptly. You can't debate the word. You must respond to it. Get it? Responding to a fresh direction from God transforms that act of obedience into an act of worship, but if you debate it, then you start to decline. Now you are a trespasser, because God has given you a fresh word and you are rationalizing it. "...What will they say?" He didn't talk to them, He gave it to you!

TRUE WORSHIP IS ALWAYS COSTLY

True worship is always costly, because it is a presentation to God of our Isaac. When the wise men came they did not come empty-handed. They worshipped with Gold, Frankincense, and Myrrh. But that wasn't the only thing they gave to Jesus. They gave their personal adoration; they gave their long trip to Him.

Mary, in John 12, with the Alabaster flask: it costs you something to worship God. Listen, that's why worship is the hardest thing. To repent, to step in the baptismal tank and be baptized in Jesus name, to throw your hands up and receive the Holy Ghost and speak in tongues is easy compared to being a consistent worshipper, because you can comply to that just out of a sense of duty, just out of scriptural proof. You can do that almost heartless.

But not this: 2 Samuel 24:24, David...we know the story. He is on the threshing floor. He says, "How much you want for this place." The angel's got his sword and is killing all kinds of people, because of a judgment. A judgment came on him because he did not take the shekel of the tabernacle. He didn't take the census money. The angel killed those tens of thousands of people because of David. David told them, "I want you to number Israel." Israel was given specific instructions that they could never take the census of the nation until you took the census tax. You had to give an offering. He didn't take the money. God took it as an affront.

So God sent the angel to kill thousands of people. David saw the angel with his sword drawn over the threshing floor and he fell down and worshipped saying, "Please don't kill the sheep, they didn't sin, I did!" He admitted it!

It was pride and arrogance of his own heart, but he didn't take the census money. If you read that scripture about the census money it says that there be no curse or plague on your people. So that angel turns around as instructed by God; "Put up your sword." He tells him, "Offer unto the Lord here a sacrifice." Now he has a fresh word from the Lord...a revelation.

Watch; revelation is always followed by obedience and cost: "I want a threshing floor, I want to erect an altar here to the Lord." Araunah says, "Look, here are the oxen, here are the animals, you can have..." He said, "No, no, no, you are not going to fool me."

DON'T LET FAMILY AND FRIENDS FOOL YOU

See; you have friends who will fool you. You got people who will help you worship. They will stop you from worshipping properly. He said, "I cannot offer anything unto the Lord that does not cost me something." I wonder how much of our worship doesn't cost us anything. If it doesn't cost you, it can't produce. I'm telling you the truth! God's complaint to Israel was that they were offering stuff that was junk and refuse. It didn't cost them anything.

That's why God has always commanded a tithe; not just of our money, of our time, of our talent, of our ability. God has always wanted the first fruits of everything. Why? Because, "All 10th's are mine." "Everything is mine." "The Earth, the field, the seas, the heavens are mine and I want you to have it." "So I want you to honor me and show your intelligence, give me the first fruits." What is He saying? "Give me the best!"

THE BEST BELONGS TO THE LORD

There was a message I preached? The fat is the Lord's? The fat was the best part. It's what they make candles out of, it's what they made stuff out of. The fat is what made the meat sizzle and gave it flavor and gave it aroma. They weren't supposed to burn the fat; the fat was unto the Lord. They weren't supposed to burn it for themselves and keep it for themselves. The fat was to be burned unto the Lord. "The first part is mine."

GOD FUNCTIONS ON PRINCIPLE—NOT EMOTION

But God doesn't eat fat, He doesn't eat hamburgers and pizza. He doesn't use money. It's a principle. Don't you get it? God is never moved by emotion. God never functions, or acts, because of emotion. God always functions on principle. And the more we learn how to live and legislate our lives by principle, the more god-like we are becoming.

ASK YOURSELF—IS TITHING A PROBLEM FOR ME?

Any tithers out there? Got my check, $78.00 bucks a week. I put $7.80 aside. I didn't touch it. I was taught that way. I'm not complaining about you that don't tithe. That's your problem. You've got bigger problems than dealing with me. That's your problem. It's an act of trust. It's saying, "You know, I really could use this and God doesn't need it, but this honors God and God will bless the 9/10's left." Don't you get it? You aren't the only person that ever paid tithes with money that you needed.

I made $3.50 an hour. Man; 7, 8, 10 bucks a week…that was like a half of million dollars. You could fill your car up in those days with $5 bucks worth of gas. 20 gallons - 5 bucks. Give this lady and this guy 5-10 dollars of my money every week? Ha, ha, ha! And the devil will magnify it…"they're driving a nice car and mine is draggin' in the street." "Two and half bucks would buy a muffler clamp." Whoa, I just struck fire again! That's what it's about. …Always amazes me, every time I touch money there is a certain segment of this assembly that goes silent.

I keep good notes. According to my notes I haven't taught a lesson on tithes in 10 years. I just kind of mention it in passing every once in a while. According to my notes I have not taught a standard Pentecost holiness series; hair, dress, make-up, jazz, junk, trinkets, jewels. I haven't taught one of them in almost 9 years.

I've taught a lot of grace. I've taught a lot of trying to fall in love with God. If I can get you to worship God, your heart would flow into such a river that would say, "Hey, whatever He is pleased with." Then I can just casually, occasionally, once in a while, just make mention about something where we need a little help in this, instead of having to blister somebody for two hours and feel like a fool when I'm finished. I'm going to tell you something; if I make you do something and you do it out of obedience...yes, you are blessed out of obedience, but you lose the richest blessing, because you are unhappy about it.

BEWARE OF STRANGE FIRE

Worship is not a cheap thing. It is not something you and I can offer carelessly without self-sacrifice, but worshipping is a dangerous area, because there is such a thing as offering strange fire. Because worship involves sacrifice and God killed those boys with their strange fire, because they didn't have the sacrifice and they didn't get the fire from the right place. So the sacrifice of worship and praise must be kindled by the sacrifice out by the brazen altar. Worship must be unto the Lord, realizing His greatness, His goodness and His grace.

Hebrews 13:15, "Let us therefore offer up the sacrifice of praise even the fruit of our lips giving thanks unto God by Him."

WE MUST NOT HIRE IT DONE

We must guard against hiring, or allowing, or expecting others to do my worshipping. We do an injustice to our praise singers, to our song leader, to our music directors, to our choir people...we do a disservice to them and a dishonor to God when we somehow sit back and say, "Okay, move me." "It's okay to hire me, there's no problem with hiring me." Fine, but you don't want to hire a worship leader that worships for you. You want worship leaders that will lead you into worship. It's kind of like the platform and the pew coming together under His canopy.

To just hire somebody, or for me to put someone here to take care of the praise, or the worship, as if it were an insignificant, something in my way...it's not. It's the way into the way. I've taught you that. Praise and Thanksgiving is a way into worship. It's the platform that let's everything get ready for the preaching of the

Word. To lean back in our chairs and just observe and have sealed lips and locked wallets and folded hands is horrible.

THE DEVIL KNOWS ABOUT WORSHIP—THAT'S WHY HE FIGHTS US

Let me say it again: It costs to be a worshipper. That's why the devil fights you. Let me tell you something I haven't told you according to my notes. ...1987 my notes said this, that's a 10 years ago. ...The devil knows more about worship than anybody. He got his training from God. He practiced in heavens amphitheater. He got so good at it that God let him be in charge of the entire heavenly host praise system. He knows the *wonder* of worship. He knows the why of worship. And he knows the results of worship. He knows that worship will move God. And so he comes among us to fight us with thoughts, aches, and pains, business distractions, side issues, feelings.... I know I'm telling you the truth.

The devil fights us, our flesh fights us. How does your flesh fight you? Ego, pride and image. Others fight us. Because if you start truly worshipping God you convict and embarrass them for them, staring as if to say, "Well, what do you know that I don't know, are you trying to be spiritual?"

"Yes, I tried being carnal—it ain't worked."

The cost to a worshipper is strong, because you must rise above weariness.

"Too pooped to participate. I'm weary."

"That's funny, you are weary sometimes when you go to work. You are weary when you take a vacation. You are weary when you work in the garden."

THE COST TO WORSHIP IS HIGH

The cost to a worshipper is very high, because we are at times forced to fight to bring our thoughts into captivity. You know I can sit sometimes on the back porch, or in a restaurant and I can just sit there and my mind can be so free and I get ready to pray and seek God and my mind becomes the Lincoln Tunnel...Causeway in Fresno.... I remember everything I needed to do; feelings and emotions erupt. I finally just say, "Oh man, let me sit down for a minute," and you say that and your mind goes...ah, tranquility. You start to force yourself into thinking about Him, and all of sudden...Lincoln Tunnel again.

Okay, the cost of worship is the forcing of us to resist peer pressure. Listen carefully. The cost of worship involves the separation unto God. Verse 5, "The lad and I go yonder to worship." That means worship involves a definite decision of the will, and an action followed. "We go yonder." So when I have to worship, I have to say good-bye to home cares, to business affairs, to hobbies...I have to say to these things, "You abide here, I am going yonder to worship God."

I've been in this a long time. I tell them dirtbags to stay but they drag along. Real worship requires concentration, commitment and the crucifying of the flesh. Hebrews 10:22, "Let us draw near." Worship requires action and faith.

ASCEND WITH A BURDEN—DESCEND WITH JOY

Genesis 22:6, "They ascended upward." What does that mean? When you worship you ascend upward. Thus leaving the average, normal, behind. Worship results in the blessing of the object and to the worshipper. Abraham ascended with a heavy burden—the potential death of Isaac. He descended with a blessed joy and a fresh revelation from God about his future.

You have no idea what God might tell you when you decide to sacrifice in worship. What He might give you is a clue about what is coming around the corner. You see, when you really worship, God reveals more of Himself to you and I, and in so doing we receive a greater appreciation for who and what God really is.

In Genesis 8:21 Noah offered a sacrifice and worshipped God and the smoke entered into the nostrils of God and it got God to swearing. Noah opened his heart to sacrifice and worship, God opened His nostrils in receiving that worship.

And when you fill God's nostrils with the aroma of worship it will open His mouth in giving back a blessing. "...I will bless you, I swear I will never do this to mankind again." You have no idea what God wants to say to you until you step into worship. Worship is responding to God's revelation.
John 9:35, "Jesus heard that they had cast him out."

WHAT IS WORSHIP—RESPONSE TO REVELATION

Now this is a blind guy that Jesus healed. A big argument whether he was blind; a big argument whether he was healed. "Go see your mother and father." That seems so funny to ask a man, "Where is your mother and father?" And they argued, because they didn't want to get kicked out of the synagogue, and so finally he starts talking to them and he says, "Well, I don't know. He just put mud on my eyes and sent me to the pool and I washed and I see." They said, "Well, this man is a sinner, give God the praise," and he said, "Well, whether the man is a sinner or not, I don't know, but what I do know is once I was blind and now I see."

Then he got really crazy and said that if that man was a sinner he couldn't do nothing. They ain't never heard of a sinner opened up a man's eyes. Then, see, religious people get real ticked off when you start instructing them with truth.

"...Are you trying to tell us something?" "We are the teachers around here, you're the dummy?"

You see, that's how religious people get when you show them anything they don't know. They threw him out of the temple. And Jesus heard that he got thrown out. Don't ever be afraid of being excommunicated by religion. Jesus will find you!

"And when He had found him He said unto him dost thou believe on the Son of God?"

Watch this… "Do you believe on the son of God?" …he answered and said,

"Who is he, Lord, that I might believe on him?"

He didn't' just say, "No." He said, "Who is he, that I might believe on him?" "...Jesus said unto him, thou hast both seen him and it is he that talketh with thee."

Watch; he found an honest man that said, "No, I don't know."

And God said; ...Oh, I love finding your kind of people, here is a revelation—poof! "I'm Him."

As soon as He gave him the revelation, watch what this guy does; "...And he said, Lord I believe. And he worshipped him."

What is worship? A response to a revelation! He didn't say the guy had everything right in his life. He was as lost as the White House is. He is as lost as Bangladesh. Ain't got nothing to do with lost and good and bad. It's got to do with responding to revelation.

"Who is He?"

"I'm Him."

"I believe." Hallelujah! And worshipped Him!

ORDERING INFORMATION

Please call us, fax us or see our web site at www.gainesvilleupc.net for the most current listing of all books in print and books in text on CD-Rom by Rev. Jeff Arnold.

and

CHECK WITH US FREQUENTLY FOR NEW TITLES

TRUTH PUBLICATIONS

8105 NW 23rd Avenue
Gainesville, FL 32606
PHONE: (352) 376-6320
FAX: (352) 376-7105
Internet: www.gainesvilleupc.net